THIS IS NOT FOR YOU

This
Is Not
For You

An Activist's
Journey of
Resistance
and Resilience

Richard Brown with Brian Benson

Oregon State University Press   Corvallis

Library of Congress Cataloging-in-Publication data is available
from the Library of Congress.

∞ This paper meets the requirements of ANSI/NISO Z39.48-1992
(Permanence of Paper).

ISBN 978-0-87071-302-6 (paperback)
ISBN 978-0-87071-305-7 (e-book)

Photographs by Richard Brown can be viewed online at
www.richardjbrown.me/photography

Oregon State University
OSU Press

Oregon State University Press
121 The Valley Library
Corvallis OR 97331-4501
541-737-3166 • fax 541-737-3170
www.osupress.oregonstate.edu

To my parents,
Agnes and Richard Brown,
who could see in the dark

Contents

*Galleries of photographs by the author appear
before Parts II, IV, V, and VI*

Foreword

It's hard to say exactly when this book began. But if I had to choose one moment, I think I'd point to the day, four or five years ago, when a teenager who'd just seen me give a speech to families of new police—a speech about cops' work, and their well-being, and their responsibility to take care of themselves so they can do right by us civilians—came up and asked me, "How do I do what you do?"

I don't remember what I said. All I know is, I didn't answer his question. I couldn't. And that bothered me. It bothered me because I loved that that boy had asked what he'd asked, and I wanted nothing more than to help him learn to walk the path I've walked. And I just didn't know how to.

My first thought, when I sat down to think about this, was that I should probably make a checklist. A how-to, I figured, thanks to twenty years of military training, that I ought to create some sort of structured learning. But when I tried to do that, I couldn't make it work. I couldn't fit my life into checkboxes. So before long, I scrapped the how-to. And I started thinking bigger.

For years people who knew me had been saying I ought to write a book. Whenever I told them stories about my life—and I did, often—they'd say, Richard, you *really* ought to write that down. Well, I'd always taken that as mere flattery. And anyway, I was no writer, never had been. But the more I thought about a book, the more I liked the idea. And so I decided I'd try and find a writer. Find someone who'd help me write whatever it was I needed to write.

I looked for a while, asked around, brought up my plans as often as I could. And finally, after about a year, a conversation I was having brought

Brian Benson into my life. At that point, all I knew about Brian was that he was a writer and he worked with other writers. I invited him to lunch. On a Friday in January, we met up at a Jordanian restaurant, and we talked. For three hours, we talked. I don't think either of us knew it yet, but on that day, at that table, a journey and a friendship began.

We met again the next Friday, and the next, and so on. I'd talk, and Brian would listen and ask questions. And though some of his questions felt like more—*way* more—than what was needed for the thing I thought I wanted to write, I liked answering them. In doing so, I got to sort of relive my life. The more I did this, the more I came to see how my past shaped what I'd done and who I'd become—and at some point, it became clear to me that I couldn't just write a how-to or a checklist, because that wasn't how I'd learned. I'd learned from listening to others, from seeing what they'd done and making my own meaning. And I wanted to give other people—people like that teenager—the chance to do the same. So I wrote this book. This memoir.

I wrote this memoir because I want to answer that teenager's question. I wrote it because I want to show him, and anyone else who cares to listen, what it looks like when a person decides something is important, then decides to do something about it, and keep on doing something. I wrote it because activism—especially activism around police, and extra-especially activism around the rift between police and Black people—is slow, painful, mostly thankless work, and it's difficult to get folks to want to sign up, and the only way I've ever succeeded in doing so is by telling stories about the work I do, stories about the things I've learned and gained from it, stories like the one you're about to read.

I wasn't born an activist. Not even close. I was a loudmouthed kid, then a loudmouthed adult, and I never wanted to get too involved in much besides my own life until, one day, a switch just flipped. From then on, what I tried to do was listen. I listened to the activists before me, the community around me. In time, I even learned to listen to some police, and they to me. We grew together, all of us who stuck with it, though way too few of us did. Nowadays when I run into a community member or cop and I tell them what I'm up to, they'll say, "You're *still* doing this?" And I'll say, "If I don't, who will?"

It's not a rhetorical question.

As I write this, we're in the midst of a mass uprising against police brutality and in support of Black lives. Thousands are out in the streets. Young Black leaders are getting long-overdue attention. White folks are suddenly talking about race, police, and power. On the one hand, I'm so energized by all of this. But I'm wary, too. Because I have seen this before. I mean, maybe not *this*, exactly, but I've seen so many mushroom clouds of popular energy bloom over the land, and I've seen *every* one of them dissipate, slowly, until the skies are so blue and clear you'd never know something had exploded.

I don't know how the world will look when you finish this book. What I do know is, someday, if not now then soon, the streets will go quiet, and the headlines will change, and most people will step away from the work and back into their day-to-day. And I really hope that you, reader, will not do that. I hope you won't step away. If we want lasting change for Black folks, we need legions of us doing the work, day after day after day, even—especially—when that work isn't making headlines.

I won't lie, either: sticking with the work isn't easy. It is life-and-death crucial, but it is *not* easy. It can often feel overwhelming. And lonely. Can feel like walking through a dark tunnel with no light in sight. I'll tell you this, though, you can make your own light. And you'll need to.

I've made my own light, mostly, by finding all sorts of things to be passionate about. I've made light by taking pictures, a few dozen of which you'll find scattered throughout this book. I've made it by building relationships with young people, and helping them, and hoping through them. I've made it by turning my life into a story I enjoy telling, and then telling it, and telling it, and telling.

No matter who you are, I ask you this: please *hear* my story. Please try to suspend your judgment and let go of whatever you think you know and come in ready to listen and grow. Please read this book and take all you can from it. Please use it to make your own how-to.

And please know that I told this truthfully, as best I could. I've got a good memory, but I'm eighty-one, and I'm told that's pretty old, so I bet I've forgotten things, or misremembered them. I've compressed time in a few places, and I've renamed some characters and omitted others entirely, for the sake of brevity and clarity. But I haven't lied. I have tried hard to tell my story right. And to anyone who disagrees with my recollections or opinions, anyone who thinks this ought to be told differently, or lived differently, I implore you to tell it better. Live it better. When it comes to stories like this one, we will always need more.

Richard J. Brown
Portland, Oregon
June 2020

The Presentation

October 2016

How it begins, today and yesterday and probably tomorrow: I'm standing alone in a ballroom miles from home, getting ready to talk to a white cop who won't want to listen.

This cop, he's over by some coffee urns, holding court with two other white men in shirtsleeves. They're looking at him like he just walked on water. Probably saying how much they liked his speech, the one he gave a few days ago, to kick off this conference, a national conference on community policing. That's why I want to talk to him, too. Because I saw that speech, and I didn't love it. And because this man is not your average cop. He's also a scholar, and a lawyer, and director of the organization putting this conference on. He's a leader of cops. A cop other cops learn from. And I need him to learn from me.

I check my wristwatch. It's barely noon. There are more talks today, and seeing them is the whole reason I came all the way to Tempe, but after three days of sitting and standing, standing and sitting, walking from panels to trainings to luncheons to more panels, I'm tired. I'd like to go to my room, just sit at the window and enjoy the fleeting feeling of looking at something new. But I can't do that. Because what this man said—and what he *didn't* say—bothered me. And a thing I've learned is: if I don't bring up what bothers me, who will?

My name's Richard Brown, by the way. I'm retired. I've been thinking, lately, of making cards that just say that: *Richard Brown, Retired.* Some folks think my cards should say, *Activist,* but I don't know. I've never felt a need to advertise that. And anyway, *Activist,* it feels too broad, or maybe not broad enough. My friend Ronnie once said I'm like a geodesic dome: at any one time, you can only see a few panels, but if you move around me, you'll find more and more and more. So maybe what I really need is a whole deck of cards: *Richard Brown, Photographer; Richard Brown, Walking News Quote; Richard Brown, Grandpa to All; Richard Brown, Black Man in a White Room.*

That last card, it's the one I need today.

Today I'm at Mission Palms Hotel, in Tempe, for the Problem-Oriented Policing Conference, an annual affair for the few who care or profess to care about community policing. Probably, if you've ever even heard of community policing, you think it's an add-on, an à la carte item—just a few officers shaking hands and petting kitties while the rest do the "real" work. But community policing is a philosophy. A religion. It is the ethos of a police force that partners, top to bottom, with civilians on the problems that *lead* to crime. I know this because, for a while, police in my city actually adopted this philosophy. Those were good years. They were hopeful years. They are long, long gone.

I'm thirsty. I head to the cooler and fill a paper cup. As I drink, I scan. There are a few hundred people here, but I'm one of a dozen civilians and maybe the only Black one. By now, I'm pretty much used to this. I've spent a lot of time with cops. I've ridden along with them, walked crime scenes with them, trained their trainers, gone to their retirement ceremonies. For a time, I was a regular at these conferences, too, but lately I've been out of the loop. I guess that's why I came: to see what I've missed, what's changed.

I wish I was more surprised to say that not much has changed.

These last few days, I've sat through dozens of presentations by police about their successes in community policing. A trio from Washington explained how they'd tidied up a cluster of motels at the center of a prostitution ring. A group from England told us about cleaning up a neighborhood plagued by drunken brawls. And a few officers from my home of Portland, Oregon, spoke about "engaging the community" in an effort to deal with drug dealing and violence on a corner near a college campus.

That bugged me.

It bugged me because I *live* in that community. For years I've lived there, blocks from campus. And I'm telling you: Portland police didn't engage anyone. No regular people, at least. This project wasn't about regular people. If it had been, they'd have helped us with that corner decades ago, when crack was flooding the streets, when kids were killing kids, when we were telling police exactly how we wanted to be engaged. They didn't listen, though, not until last year, when the college president, keen to clean things up in advance of a campus expansion, began talking about stopping the violence. Then, the cops *engaged*. They sat down with that president and some business owners, and they made a plan, then got up in front of the cameras and told the rest of us about it. That's what gets at me. Police know how to do community policing. They just mostly do it with people who already have power.

This cop is still over there, talking with his fans. I can't tell if he's noticed me noticing him. Probably. I'm kind of hard to miss. Today I'm wearing a tan suit and hat, purple shirt, tan bow tie, and a sterling tube on my lapel—a tussie-mussie, it's called—that holds a purple silk flower. I got the tussie-mussie from a TV show based on some Agatha Christie detective story. But the bow tie? That's all me. I've worn one most days for as long as I can recall. It gets some attention. And it makes it easier for white folks, who can describe me as the guy with the bow tie instead of just the Black guy.

Off to the left, something flashes. The skin behind my ears goes tight, and I spin left, reach down for my camera. And now here it comes, the double disappointment. Because that flash? I think it was just overhead light strobing off a mic stand. And I'm not even carrying my camera.

Used to be, I didn't miss a picture. Not a one. My feeling was, any change around me, it could be something, and good or bad, I wasn't going to miss it. Honestly, that's still my feeling. But lately I'm missing a lot. Take yesterday: I walked around Tempe for three hours, on streets full of people, in softening light, but I didn't take a single photo. And that hurts. Because for years, taking pictures was all I did. I photographed thousands of Black faces and a lot of white ones, too. For a time, I couldn't go outside without someone asking, hey, wasn't I the picture man? And I was, until one day, I stopped. Just like that, I did. Stepped away from my camera and into the frame. I've stayed there for decades. And though I have no regrets about that—no regrets about where I've gone, what I've done, or why—I do miss taking pictures. Every morning, I tell myself I'll start again. And every evening, I tell myself again.

Finally, this cop is on the move. He's walking like he's being watched: chin up, shoulders back. I *really* don't want to talk to him. Just thinking about it makes me tired. After years of making people listen to what I have to say—about respecting us, about treating Black boys like boys— I'm wearing down. And the best way I can explain it is, this thing has been happening. The thing is, I start crying. I start, and I can't stop. I'm not one of those men who's got a thing about men who cry. I have nothing against criers. I just never was one, not until lately. But lately, whenever I flick on the TV, I end up on one of those dramas where someone's struggling to make a difference, struggling hard until, near the end, with everything against them, they break through and make it. Or hell, maybe they don't. I couldn't tell you. Usually, by that point, I can barely even see the screen.

And now here comes this cop. About to stride right past me. If I'm going to talk to him, it's got to happen now, so I muster a smile and extend a hand.

"Hey there!" I say. "Glad to see you."

He stops, and he gives my hand a shake, still holding that half smile, looking me over, probably wondering how he knows me, if he knows me, if he's confusing mine with another Black face.

I let him wonder.

"I'm Richard Brown," I say eventually. "From Portland. Thanks for your speech."

He relaxes and releases my hand, thanks me for being here and compliments my bow tie. But already his eyes are moving toward the door, toward whatever's more important.

I jump right in. I begin, as always, by complimenting what I can of his speech. I let him know who I am: a civilian who's spent years working with cops, many of whom who eat, breathe, and sleep community policing. Once he's smiling, I switch gears. I tell him that *none* of what I've heard today feels like real community policing. I tell him about the Portland cops and what their talk left out. And then I tell him what I'm here to tell him: I tell him there was this *other* meeting, of the International Association of Chiefs of Police, like a week ago. And he sighs, like he knows what I'm going to say. And what I say is: their president? He apologized for police's "historical mistreatment of racial minorities." It didn't go far enough, at all, but it was a big deal. It was rare. Papers ran headlines about it for a day, but since then it's been crickets. I haven't heard a word about it here. So I ask, "Why?"

"That man," he says, his smile now gone, "got a lot of flak for that statement."

I drop my eyes. I've heard white folks say words like these way too many times, so I'm feeling a lot. But I know how white folks feel about my feelings, and I can't have this guy running off, so I gather myself and say, "I bet he did. But I'm glad he said it. And I hope someone here will, too."

I see it in his face: he doesn't have time for this. For some cranky old Black man who just wants to criticize. But I stay where I am. I wait. Because if he asks me a question—any question—I can begin to tell him what he doesn't know. I can tell him that I've ridden along in squad cars hundreds of times; that I've been on more search warrants than most active officers; that for a few years—a few *decades*—cops would page me pretty much whenever there was a shooting, a bust, a whatever involving Black people; that I led a citizen foot patrol every night for a year-plus in a gang-addled area the police were barely policing; that, for a decade-and-a-half, I ran a weekly meeting that brought civilians and city officials into one room to solve real human problems; that I've felt, for years, that a city is a yardstick, with police at zero inches and Black folks at thirty-six and everyone just yelling; and that I've been standing strong at eighteen inches, and I'm still standing, but I'm getting tired.

This guy isn't asking me anything, though. Of course he's not. He sees no reason to. He's just shaking my hand again and saying, "It's nice to meet you," then heading on his way.

I watch him walk off. I try to swallow my feelings, just move on. But it's hard. Harder than ever. Because every day I get older. And lately it seems that's the only thing that's changing.

Two months later, early morning in early December, I'm making the hour-and-a-half drive to Salem to visit to the Oregon Department of Public Safety Standards and Training, aka the Academy. The Academy is the place that trains and certifies every law enforcement officer in Oregon. Every last one. And I come down here, week after week after week, to try to help them do it right.

I started here a decade ago as a governor-appointed board member, and when I termed out three years back, the director asked me to keep coming, so I did. I don't have a title anymore. Now I'm just a civilian who keeps showing up. Mostly I sit in on trainings. My presence, it makes white folks—and it's mostly white folks—think harder about what they do and don't say, and if someone says something incomplete, or ignorant, I address it. I'm forever pushing the people in charge, too, to overhaul the curriculum, make it so that race is woven in everywhere, not balled up in a corner to be picked up for an hour, then set down and forgotten. It's slow work. Slow doesn't begin to describe it. But what we do here touches all cops. It catches them when they're young, before their habits harden, before they're on the street with a gun in my neighborhood. So I keep coming.

Most Wednesdays, I'd be parking my coupe in the back lot and walking through the courtyard and over to the classroom where MacLellan—a good teacher, if a bit too fond of sports metaphors—teaches his use-of-force class. But this week's special. This week, right here at the Academy, there's yet another conference on community policing, this one specific to Oregon. There are a whole bunch of guest speakers, one of whom happens to be that cop from Tempe. So today I'm heading over to the Hall of Heroes to catch his speech, and then catch him, continue that conversation we started.

I walk into the hall and say my hellos—to some instructors, some recruits, a custodian—and then I take a seat. I sit through the guy's talk, during which he again attaboys cops for some half-assed community policing. When he's done, I clap, I stand, and I wait. I watch him smile and shake hands until, finally, he's free. And then I walk up and say, "Hey there! I've been thinking about our talk."

I'm not wearing my bow tie. Rarely do at the Academy. And I'll admit: it feels good, standing here, watching this guy's cheeks flare as he wonders how he knows me, if he knows me. After a moment, I take mercy and remind him. His eyes flash from confusion to relief and right on to impatience, and I ignore that, just smile and say, "We're happy you're here."

Maybe it's because of that *we*. Maybe it's because, as I talk to him, a few people—an instructor, a recruit in her fifth week of training, a receptionist—walk by and say, "Hello, Mr. Brown." Maybe it's because I'm now mentioning Hope and Hard Work, that meeting I led, the one that brought cops and the community together to solve problems, week after week. Whatever it is, this guy's nodding. Seems like he's really hearing me. I'm getting ready to transition back to his speech in Arizona, to the things he and the rest did and did not say, when he cuts in. "You know there's a city in Florida that's thinking of trying the sort of meeting you're talking about? I just spoke to their chief. Maybe you should, too."

All I can do is drop my eyes. Stare hard at speckled floor tile. I'm thinking of that saying about how you can see a person's soul through their eyes. I'm thinking I don't want this man seeing mine. I take a breath and look back up. I tell this man he's misunderstood me. I tell him that I'm not asking for advice. That I *did* this thing he's only considered. That I'm not proposing anything new at all. That I brought police and Black people into the same room, every week, for sixteen years.

Somewhere behind his eyes, a light switches on.

"Sixteen *years?*" he asks.

Suddenly, he's interested. He's animated. He's asking me all sorts of questions. At least I think he is. But at the moment, I can't hear him. Can't hear much at all. I'm sinking way down into myself, sinking deep, and all I can make out is a low, watery drone.

I'm tired.

I'm tired of having to work so hard to be heard. Tired of having to explain why I belong where I am. Tired of being ignored because I don't have a badge, a bunch of abba dabbas after my name, a fancy title, a white face. I'm tired of saying the same things to people who aren't listening, who don't have enough urgency, who aren't tired enough of watching Black boys die.

I raise my eyes. Seems like this cop has stopped talking. He's looking at me. Maybe he's finally decided he's ready to hear what I think, what I can teach him. Good for him.

I glance over his shoulder into the cafeteria. Across the way, three white recruits, who look not a day over twenty, and who I know just finished a training about firing weapons, are laughing, laughing so hard they're almost crying. Beside them are a couple of instructors, old guard cops, the sort of cops I could reason with for five centuries and still they'd never change their minds about anything.

I look back at this cop standing before me. There's a large part of me that doesn't want to open up to him, to this man who deserves none of what I have—a part of me that's feeling too tired, and too proud, to say what I've been saying for so long to men who are terrible listeners and expert forgetters.

And yet.

I can already feel them, these old words, swimming up out of my chest.

PART I

EXCUSE YOURSELF

Harlem, New York

1939–1956

1

A Boy in a Room

My earliest memory: it's late summer, Harlem, nineteen forty-three or four. I'm in the candy shop below my family's first apartment, leaning against a case of caramels and looking at my mother. She works here. She's wearing a pretty dress and sitting, legs crossed, on a stool behind the counter. There are a bunch of other adults, too, all clustered around the cash register, rustling papers and smoking cigarettes and speaking a language I can't understand, but only because they won't let me. Whenever I wander over and wedge my head in between knees and hips, the talk flickers out, and someone —my mother, usually —looks down and says, "Excuse yourself." So I do. I excuse myself, and I lean against that case, and I look out at the passing people and passing cars, feeling bored, nothing more, because I'm still so young, too young to know I'll be hearing these words for the rest of my life.

Home was a Harlem brownstone. We had a small apartment. Just my folks' room, a tiny kitchen, and a parlor where my sister and brothers and I slept. The only bathroom was a shared one down the hall, so we washed in the sink and peed in night pots my mother emptied each morning. When I was five, we moved up the street to a tenement at 128th near Madison. That place had its own bath and a second bedroom—which I shared with two, then three, and finally four siblings—and from one level to the next it was twenty-four steps, so you had that times six, and we always ran the whole way.

We weren't rich, but I don't recall ever falling asleep hungry; my mother was always cooking vegetables and beans, and sometimes she'd make fungi and fish, a stew from her childhood home of St. Croix. My dad cooked, too—usually barbecue, which I loved, though I'd have to spend hours afterward scrubbing fat-charred dishes—but mainly what he did was work, fixing stoves in restaurants, a job he learned from cousins who'd left Carolina for Harlem well before he did. It was filthy, back-busting labor, and he did it five days a week, at least, from the day I was born until the day I left, and though there was a long time when I couldn't appreciate that or much else about him, looking back now, I do.

When my mother wasn't at the candy store or dealing with us, she was at the kitchen table, drawing. She'd gone to school for fashion design and was always drawing models in fancy clothes. Sometimes at night she'd have visitors, and she'd draw for them. My best guess is they were clients, but I can't say; she never told us much about her life, and if I asked, her response was usually along the lines of, "Excuse yourself." Whenever those folks came over, we kids got sent to our room. So I'd stand, ear to the wall, listening, wondering how those visitors looked and how she looked to them. I wanted them to see what I saw, which was: I was in awe of my mother. She was just so, so graceful. Everything she did and said and wore was pure class. Whether those visitors saw it I don't know. I just know she never made much money from her art. And that I, as a boy in a room, couldn't fathom why.

I was amazed at how she made people on a page come to life. She'd done these drawings of skiers carving powdery slopes in bright clothes, and I'd pull them out and stare at the skiers' misty breath and parkas and bobble-top hats. I checked out every skiing book from the library, too. Part of that was, I thought I wanted to be a skier (years later I'd try it and hate it), but mostly, I just loved how I felt when I looked at those drawings. Even at that age, I just *knew* I'd be an artist. Already had opinions about it. When one of my grade-school teachers had us make a Santa, with instructions to trace the face, then attach a cotton beard, my thought was, *artists* don't trace. So I drew my face freehand. And my teacher got mad. I don't quite know why. Don't know if I ended up cowing to her, either. What I do know is, I never stopped feeling that, if you were an artist, you should make something unique, something yours.

If I were a shrink, I'd probably say that impulse comes partly from the fact that, in my youth, nothing was mine. Everything was shared. Meals and chores. Space and time. Everything. My world was small. My world was seven people in a sixth-floor apartment. Sure, we went out plenty—we'd go to the Y and to the movies and to church with my grandparents, and my father would take us down to the barbershop or out on Sunday drives, and my mother would bring us on errands, always keeping us close, away from the dope addicts on stoops and the corner preachers who whipped up wild crowds with words I wouldn't have understood even if I'd been able to hear—but mostly, we kids were in the apartment. We had no choice. If our folks were at work, and we weren't in school or on the way to or from, we were home, period. They didn't want us in the streets, they'd say. Wasn't safe, they'd say. Sometimes, if I was feeling especially brave or foolish, I'd say that *other* kids played in the street all day, and I'd ask why we couldn't, too. And to this, they'd each answer, invariably, "Because I said so."

Thing was, they had a point. It wasn't safe. This was Harlem, post-Renaissance, postwar. Guys were coming home from Korea stuck on dope, shooting up in alleys. We had gangs, and they fought in the streets with fists, bricks, and sticks. There were so many people and not much work, so robbery was common; once, the liquor store on our block got held up, and the guy at the counter tried to shoot it out and got killed. But really, that's maybe the only not-so-safe incident I was aware of. Well, that, and once a guy got stabbed in the head with a screwdriver. I heard it, and then, through a window, I saw him lying on the ground, moaning. Later that night, I saw somebody pull the blade out of his head.

And then there were the cops. The thing with cops was: you avoided them. "You stay out of their way," the adults always said. "If you must talk to them, don't argue, just do what they tell you." So mostly, I did. I avoided them. I don't recall many—maybe not any—run-ins with cops as a young-ster. There was one night, though, when we were living above the candy store, when I heard something. Loud voices, scuffling feet. I went to our patio, my siblings behind me, and though it was dark, I could see people fighting. I heard shattering glass. And then hands were on my shoulders, yanking me inside. The next morning at school, I heard that some of the people in that tussle were cops, and one had shot somebody. For a long time after that, I thought the sound of a gun was glass, breaking.

As a youngster, though, I didn't see danger. As a youngster, I just wanted to be out with all the others, with Johnny Campbell and Carlton Smith and little Melvin—only boy I knew who was as short as me—and with Larry, my goody-two-shoes, straight-A-plus cousin. "Why can't you be like Larry?" my folks would ask. And I'd wonder that, too. I'd wonder why *I* couldn't play whenever I wanted, like Larry. Because understand: in our street, something was always going on. So many children, every day, out spinning tops and shooting lodies and playing marbles and hide-and-seek and every type of ball you could imagine. Bethlehem Steel owned a building on the corner, and we'd divide the street into squares and slam handballs against its brick wall. On that same wall, we tacked up a peach basket, shot horse and three-on-three. We'd play stoopball, too—like baseball, but the stoop was home, and you'd bounce the ball off it rather than hit a pitch—and on weekends, older guys would play football or stickball and we little ones would watch. And all the while, the Goodes, a family who lived on the first floor, would be playing all sorts of music on all sorts of instruments; I once found a mandolin with only two strings, and I gave it to the youngest, Sonny, and you never heard anyone pick a mandolin like that.

I did get to be a part of all that, sometimes. When my dad got home from work, he'd often sit on the stoop telling lies with the other men, and if that happened, we children got to come down, too. But if we got home early or he worked late, we'd be stuck inside for hours. Sometimes we'd sneak out. As we played, we'd keep an eye on the corner, looking for his car, and if we saw it we'd run upstairs. We didn't do that often, though. When we disobeyed my father, he got mad, and when he got mad, it was never a whole lot of talking. So, usually, while the Goodes were playing music, and the other kids were playing stoopball, I was up on the sixth floor, forehead on the window grates, watching life happen without me.

It wasn't like I was bound and shackled, though. Just cooped. So I'd mope for a while, but inevitably, Rodney and Pamela and I—Gary and

Jeffrey weren't born yet—we'd make our own fun. We'd play Super Circus with the dog. We'd draw out lodie squares on the floor. We'd play basketball on an over-the-door hoop until Ms. Arrendell downstairs started yelling about the thumps and squeaks. During all of this, supposedly, *I* was responsible. That's how my folks saw it: I was the oldest, so I was the one who had to account for the broken lamps, the dings in the plaster, the elbow scabs. But my siblings never treated me like an older brother. Rodney, Pamela, and I were within four years, and I was smaller than them, so there wasn't a whole lot of *I'm in charge*. At least not until my father would come home and survey the damage and tell me, with a belt or bare hand, that, yes, I sure was.

Over the years, he gave me *so* many ass-lickings. The first one I can recall was when I was real little, in the candy shop with Mom. She was on her stool, and she'd told me not to do something, and I got sad, so I laid my hands in her lap and put my head there, too. Well, she felt I'd hit her. That night, she told my father. I tried to argue my case, but he shook his head and told me to go get a belt. All I had were my cloth belts, from school. I got the blue one. When my father saw it, he laughed and told me to try again, and I came back with another cloth belt, a brown one. "Forget it," he said, and just pulled off his plastic belt. He wore my little butt *out*. The way I like to tell it, the welts all said: *Made in USA*.

From then on, spankings were routine. I was a chronic bed wetter, and my dad thought it was because I was too lazy to get up (it wasn't), so he'd spank me. And if I mouthed off, or didn't get the floors clean enough, or looked at him wrong? Spanking. Often, spankings would come with lectures, which I hated, my thought being: look, you just beat me, you don't have to tell me nothing. But looking back, the worst beatings were maybe the ones that went unexplained. Like the day I peeked in my dad's dresser and found a gun. I didn't touch it. But somehow he realized somebody'd been in the drawer, and he decided it was me, so he made me lay my hands on that dresser and he pulled out a wood ruler and *pow!* My hands looked like catcher's mitts for a while after that. He didn't give a lecture that time. Didn't say a word. So I didn't understand why I'd gotten such strong discipline just for rooting around. Years later, though, I'd find myself at Lackland Air Force Base in basic training, cleaning my rifle for the first of too many times, and when I smelled the oil, I'd realize for the first time that gun in the drawer was real.

It wasn't all bad in that apartment. Every night we'd eat supper as a family, and after we'd cleaned up—my dad had real high standards for how and how quickly that happened—we'd all gather around the radio. We had a fake fireplace—which my folks claimed Santa would come down, though it wasn't hooked up to a chimney—and we'd sit there and listen to the shows. We listened to everything. *True Detective* and *The Lone Ranger*, *Fred Allen* and *Straight Arrow*, *Amos 'n' Andy*, *Baby Snooks,* and *Fibber McGee and Molly*. When *Grand Central Station* came on, we'd wait and wait, and when the host called our stop, 125th and Park, we'd hoot along with the train whistle. And the fights—I loved the fights. The radio men made you feel like you were right there. "They're exchanging blows!" they'd say, and I'd be in the ring, too, popping and ducking. I wanted someday to be able to do that. To talk like that, tell stories like that.

We had a TV, too, which we watched a bunch, especially when Black folks were on. On the streets of Harlem, Black people were everywhere, but on the TV? White faces, all the time. I don't think that I, then, really got what that meant. All I knew was, when there was a Black face on the screen, we'd all be there, watching. Sid Caesar and Jackie Gleason often had Black performers, and the Bowery Boys and the Little Rascals both had a Black actor, too. For us children, it was just good entertainment. I'd guess it meant more, much more, for my parents. But we didn't ever really talk about those things.

Again, though: growing up, I was surrounded by Black people. You still had folks left over from the Harlem Renaissance just passing you on the street. Artists, athletes, intellectuals. Sugar Ray Robinson, the boxer, owned a block just west of us, and he'd drive by in his lavender convertible, top down, music up. Langston Hughes lived across from the school. Roy Campanella had a liquor store nearby, and Joe Lewis had a restaurant, and you'd see them on the block or at the YMCA, where all the athletes came to teach camps or just hang out. Sandy Sadler came. And Don Newcombe. Even Jackie Robinson. I met him three times, and I've got pictures of me and my friends beside him, our heads at his hips. Whenever I saw any of those guys, I'd get excited, maybe even gawk a bit, but I never asked for an autograph. Because the reverence for them wasn't about knockouts or RBIs. It was just that they'd *done* it. They'd risen above all the stuff Black people had to deal with. And though I didn't yet have a big understanding of what that meant, I was always hearing from adults that Jackie and Sugar Ray and Langston and the rest had to be twice as good as the best white guy to get where they'd gotten—and I just knew, when I was in their presence, that I felt something big and warm and rare.

It wasn't just celebrities, either. There were so many adults I gravitated toward and looked up to. Like Mr. Gill. He lived in our building and was refinement to the *n*th degree. He had this deep voice—was an opera singer—and his mustache was finely trimmed, and he always wore a tam and an ascot and used a dark, thick walking stick. When he talked, you listened. And if he asked what you wanted to do with your life—and he did, all the time—you'd maybe say, "I don't know," but later, you'd keep thinking about his question. And there were the rarer occurrences, too, like when the 369th Division—the Harlem Hellfighters—came marching through. I remember that day so well: standing at the window, looking down at Fifth Avenue at all those soldiers in their dazzling uniforms, thump-thump-thumping in perfect unison, their matching steps and stops like some sort of secret language.

All of that just made it harder to be stuck inside. When I'd hear at school that other kids had seen Sugar Ray rolling by, or run into Mr. Gill on the stairs, I'd get a twist in my gut, even if I'd seen them a day before. I hated missing out. And as time passed, I began to resent my folks for it. Now, years later, having seen what I've seen, having met so many kids with too much freedom and too few rules, I get it—I get that my folks were just trying to protect me from things I didn't know to be afraid of. But then, I could only see the walls around me. And I couldn't think of much besides getting out.

2

What I Saw When I Looked

In an old yearbook, under a picture of my wild-eyed, smiling face, there's a caption that reads, "Richard: always running, always laughing, never a worry, never a care." It was Eleo Pomare, this wiry Colombian who'd grow up to be a pretty famous dancer and choreographer, who wrote that about me. And man, he *got* it. He got how I was in school, and how I wasn't, and why, eventually, I'd drop out.

At home, I was stuck being Richard: eldest son, doer of dishes, receiver of spankings. But at school? At school, I got to be Richie. The transformation happened the second I left home. I'd say bye to my folks, and I'd step out the door in my shined shoes and pressed shirt and tie—every day we wore ties, no casual Fridays—and then I'd bound down the steps, from the sixth floor to the third, where I'd pick up my friend Carlton. As we walked, we'd use our voices to simulate instruments, and we'd play songs—the Inkspots, the Nutmegs, whatever was on the radio—and along the way we'd pick up other kids, all of them singing and trumpeting and drumming their thighs, and by the time we got to school, we'd be this little orchestra, laughing and tooting and singing, ready to do anything but learn.

Thing was, I had such good teachers, especially in grade school. Every one gave us a big dose of Black history, so there was no question about how much there was to appreciate about Black people. And they went way beyond what you'd expect. Like Ms. Davis from fourth grade, one of two Black teachers I ever had. She'd often bring us hellions to her home after a day of teaching to listen to *classical* music. When I think about that now—how tired she must have been, how much she must've cared—I find it amazing. But at the time, I was too busy making noise to appreciate the music or anything else.

I wasn't a bad student. Or rather, I was, but it wasn't for lack of smarts. I was real good at all things art, and I always liked algebra and history, too. I just didn't do well on tests. You couldn't get me to memorize a thing. It pains me to admit it now, because it's *exactly* what my teachers were always saying, but here's the honest truth: I didn't apply myself. I didn't care about learning. All I cared about was doing what I couldn't do at home, which was: whatever I wanted. And what I wanted to do was goof off, and daydream, and make smart remarks, or better said, stupid remarks that seemed smart at the time. And no, I don't remember them. Not a one. Which ought to tell you just how smart they were.

All that stupid talk didn't leave me a lot of time to listen. So I missed a lot. Misunderstood a lot. Like, for example, the civil rights movement, which kicked up when I was in junior high. I mean, I was *aware* of it. We always had newspapers lying around, and I'd look at the pictures, which were so graphic back then; if somebody was shot in the street, he was on the front page, close-up, lying in a pool of black blood. But I never read the articles. And my folks offered little explanation. And when my teachers tried to, I didn't listen. So I didn't get it. I knew about the lynchings, marches, boycotts. But I didn't get how it all fit together. How it related to Blackness. How it might affect me.

One of the very few things I did get, in those years, was a lesson taught by Ms. Whitney, one of my English teachers. She was a white lady, patient and kind, no older than twenty-five. One day, at the start of class, she walked around her desk and held up a sheaf of paper that turned out to be the script for the play *Tea and Sympathy*. She'd read it over the weekend, she said, and had found it to be very powerful, but since it dealt with issues of homosexuality, we probably wouldn't like it. She then placed the script on a table in front of her desk, walked to the chalkboard, and began with the lesson. Though I had never in my life read a play—hadn't even known you could—I now jumped from my seat and snatched the script from the table. I don't recall whether Ms. Whitney reacted. Don't even recall what I thought of the play once I'd read it, which I did that very night. Now, all these years later, all I remember about that day is how I felt and what I did when I got told, "This is not for you."

Sometimes, I wonder if I'd have paid more attention if I wasn't so small—if I didn't need to be so loud to take up space. Because I was *so* little. One of the shortest boys in school. There were these TV commercials with Charles Atlas where he'd be on the beach, getting sand kicked in his face, and then he'd go home and do his dynamic tension stuff and come back and beat his bullies. When I was at home, I'd do that, too: I'd do pushups and pullups, and I'd hold down one arm with the other and flex hard against it. But it didn't work. I stayed scrawny. When we played ball at lunch, I wouldn't get picked, and at night I'd cry to my mother. "Don't worry about that," she'd say. "You just find what *you're* good at." So I did. I found what I was good at, or at least what I thought I was good at, which was talking stupid. Maybe I was too short to shoot hoops, and maybe I didn't get good grades, and maybe I did get in lots of trouble (Ms. Harris, once when I'd been a real pain, walked me all the way home and up those hundred-forty-four steps just to talk to my folks, which didn't end well), but none of that mattered, because talking stupid got me what I needed, and what I needed was attention.

I bet I would've acted up less, too, if I'd had friends, real friends, outside of school. But real friendships were forged in the street, through lodies and handball, and I just missed too much of that to ever become friend material. When I did get to go out, I'd feel it: this invisible something the others all shared. They'd laugh at jokes I didn't quite get, come up with the same bad idea at the same time, and generally just walk a step or three ahead. And though I tried and tried, I never could seem to catch up.

Probably that's why I joined a gang. In sixth grade, I joined one with other boys from 128th. We called ourselves the Cimarrons, and what we did was: we hung out and told people we were the Cimarrons. There was another gang called the Diablos, and they were our rivals, though that never amounted to much more than nasty looks. Girls were in the gangs, too. They were called Debs: the Cimarron Debs, the Diablo Debs. One day, in class, a Deb was looking at my notebook, and I wanted her to know who she was dealing with, so beside my address I wrote: *Gang Block.* She didn't seem impressed, but when my mother found my notebook, *she* was. "What's this about?" she asked. I said I didn't know. And then she gave me an "uh-huh" and made me erase it and that pretty much put an end to my gang life.

There was one upside to my world being so small: I had to imagine. I had to slow down, look around, think. And where I often ended up, when I slowed down, was at the table, paging through my mother's magazines. She always had some lying around: *Ebony, Tan, Sepia.* My favorite part was the portraits. I was fascinated by how people looked, and how you, a person with a camera, could make them look. My favorite picture book was called *Monsters and Madonnas,* made in the thirties by William Mortensen. I'd found it on a library shelf. What had first caught my eye was the cover—a black-and-white of a naked lady—but what got me to check it out again—and again, and again—was the way Mortensen messed with his pictures. He fixed people up in weird costumes, and there'd be lots of guts and blood, and sometimes he'd retouch the images so there'd be these nasty beasts right there with the people. I'd learn much later that Mortensen was hugely controversial—Ansel Adams called him "the Antichrist"—but then, all I knew was: I *loved* that book. For a while, because of it, I thought I wanted to do movie makeup. At home, when the others were out playing, I'd take rubber cement and put it on my skin and fold it, make it look like a scar. Once, I showed up at school like that, and all of my school friends thought it was real. By the end of the day, rumor was that I'd been in some big knife fight.

Somewhere in there, I got my first camera, a Brownie Hawkeye. I had no idea how to use it, and the first pictures I took—of the dog, of my siblings—were lousy. Not just lousy. *Bad.* I didn't get to develop many of them, because my folks weren't going to spend money on the garbage I was churning out, but a few shots showed promise. One night in grade school, we had a lunar eclipse, and I went out to the fire escape and I set my Brownie on the rails, and at the moment of eclipse, I took a picture of the sky. The exposure ended up being long, long enough that you could see, behind the shadow of the moon, this little half-inch trail from its orbit.

Now, I pick it up, and it's just a little dot. It's nothing to look at. But then, it was the first thing I tried that really worked, that maybe felt like art.

I started taking pictures for the school paper, too, right around the time Sugar Ray fought Randy Turpin in England. Turpin beat him, and in the papers, Sugar Ray's face looked bad: cuts over his eyes, face swollen, blood everywhere. Well, my dad knew him, so one day, a week after the fight, he walked me the few blocks to Sugar Ray's office. I was ready, my Hawkeye around my neck. I think I was expecting some real gore, but when we got there, Sugar Ray just had a tiny cut over his eye, and otherwise he looked sharp: plaid jacket, pressed pants, not a hair out of place. He smiled, then picked me up and set me on his desk and started talking to my dad. And what'd I do? I watched. Didn't take a picture. Didn't do a thing. Couldn't. I was just flabbergasted. For a long while afterward, I felt like such a fool. I was there, Hawkeye in hand, and I didn't take a single picture.

One thing I did get pictures of? Pigeons. For a few years, I raised pigeons with this guy Johnny. He lived nearby and had a rooftop coop with twenty pigeons, and from up there, you could see other people on other roofs, tending their coops. Before feeding our birds, we'd let them out, and then we'd stand at the lip of the roof, waving a cane pole with a flag on the end, trying to get them to follow the patterns we made. This always and only happened in that sweet spot when school was done but my folks' work wasn't—when I could, for a sliver of time, get away with doing what I wanted, where I wanted. And I remember all of it: the smell of bird crap and bus exhaust, the flag slapping itself in the wind, the birds' bodies dancing across the sky, and that rare awareness that nobody knew where I was.

Maybe that's not quite true. We were never *alone* up there. Often, there'd be dope addicts, too. There was this guy who wore a tweed coat and was addicted to heroin; he and some others shot up atop a building connected to Johnny's. There was a covered landing where the stairs let onto the roof, and often, while Johnny and I were at our coop, flying birds, there'd be a few guys inside, shooting up. We had an unspoken pact: *you don't tell on me, I don't tell on you.*

My folks, if they'd found out, would've lost it. They meant to keep us far from guys like that. Our apartment was just a floor below the rooftop, so the rule was that we children, when home alone, weren't to open the door, ever, for anybody. They even installed a police lock, a big fat bar that ran from door to floor, the idea being: nobody was going to push the door in. It was overkill, I thought. On the rare occasion someone even came by—a salesperson or a neighbor—we'd all hush up and crowd the door and look through the keyhole and try to see who it was. Usually, all we could see was a bit of coat, maybe a hand, some rings on a finger. Once, though, someone knocked, and I saw tweed through the keyhole. My dad had a tweed coat, but that guy from the roof did, too. So I said, "Nobody's home." And then I said it again and again, until the tweed went away. We all ran to the window. I'd always figured Dad would test us like this, and now I figured he'd pop out on the stoop and smile up at us. He didn't, though. And when he got home, much later, he didn't say a word about the door. Neither did I.

It's funny, now, thinking about my father being so focused on the danger outside our home, given what was happening inside. The beatings were just getting worse. Lately, he'd started in on my mother, too, and that'd gotten bad, fast. They were always arguing, about things I couldn't have understood even if I'd been able to hear them, which I couldn't, because whenever they fought, we got sent to our room. One time, though, they were in their room, and he hit her. We all heard it, and then we heard her crying, loud. So Pamela and Rodney and I grabbed what we could from the kitchen— a broom, a knife, a rolling pin—and we crept through the dark apartment and pushed open the door. For what felt like forever, we stood there, huddled, silent, weapons raised, until finally my dad noticed. I can't imagine what must have been playing through his mind as he looked at us, his kids, banded together, our tiny weapons raised against him. He didn't say anything. Not then, or at any point afterward. He just pulled his clothes on and stepped out of the apartment. By nightfall, he'd come back.

The older I got, the less I wanted to be in that apartment. But I was still too young to do much about it, so I found other avenues of escape. Like stamps. I collected stamps. My favorites were the ones with big pictorials of places all over the world: horses in the Sahara, an Italian vineyard, a Parisian sunset. I'd look at those pictures and just dream of going. To Europe, especially. At the time, lots of Black artists were going to Europe— Baldwin, Baker, Wright—and though I was too young to get why, I knew there must be something good in Europe if all those Black folks wanted to go. Anyway, that just made me want more stamps. I'd find ads in the magazines, and I'd send for stamps, for as many as I could, never paying, until the company realized I was just some penniless child and cut me off. My collection got pretty impressive. And I'd look at it all the time, at the pictures of places so far from where and what I knew, and I'd tell myself, with a child's confidence, that someday I'd see all of them.

I only wanted what all youngsters want: for my world to feel bigger. So I collected more stamps. Kept flying pigeons. Spent weekends with why-can't-you-be-more-like-Larry, tinkering with teeny model airplanes: Mustangs, P-40s, C119s, F-4 Corsairs. And, of course, I stopped whatever I was doing and sat in front of the TV every time it played the commercial, the one with the flying jets and snappily dressed airmen, the one that said, *Join the Air Force, get your GED, see the world.* That message played over and over again on TV screens and radio waves to millions of youngsters who maybe wanted their little world to feel a lot bigger. And though I don't know if and how it landed with all the others, I can say that, for this one, sitting on his hands in a sixth-floor fish bowl, it hit pretty hard.

3
So Far from Home

In New York in those days, you had lots of choices for what high school you went to. Some had tough entrance exams, some didn't. Vocational schools, for example, didn't test hard, and there were tons of those, thanks to the unions, so strong back then. You had schools for aviation, automotive, cooking—my brother Rodney ended up going for cooking—and textiles and the arts, which, of course, was what I wanted. I was surer than ever that I was going to be an artist, whatever that meant, so I only applied to two spots: an arts-focused academic campus, the name of which I don't recall because I didn't pass its tests, and a vocational school called the School of the Industrial Arts. I was so excited about SIA. It was, to me, clearly the better school, the *art* school. So I never considered what now seems obvious: the academic one, had I gotten in, could've set me on a college track. If my folks were aware, they didn't say so. We never discussed my decision. I just made it. And that was that.

At SIA, they had you pick a major, and I chose advertising because it meant I'd get to draw a lot. During ad classes, we'd mock up layouts—I loved that, arranging paper-cut shapes, using brush and pen to make typefaces—and for homework, we'd carry three-by-five sketch pads and draw whatever caught the eye. What caught mine, as ever, was people. I'd sketch the faces of folks I saw at the park or on the subway or in photos from my parents' picture books. There was one I did of an old, toothless man, his mouth puckering into itself, that I was so proud of, mainly because Mom liked it.

But all of that got brushed aside once I took my first photography class. As soon as I stepped into a darkroom and started dipping contact prints in developer, I just knew it was for me. Soon, I was developing photos at home in the bathroom. I'd drop a board over the tub, lay out the trays, and kill the lights and work. The idea that I could drop paper in liquid and, poof, here was that thing I'd seen, an hour ago, a week ago—it felt like magic. I could've stayed in that bathroom for hours, just developing, but someone was always interrupting me, wanting to take a pee or a shower. And though I didn't have the words then to say what I now feel—that photography is a way of documenting time, unadulterated—I knew, absolutely, that I loved it. By the end of my first year, I'd taken it on as a minor.

I suddenly loved going to school, partly because of the drawing and darkroom, mostly because SIA was so far from home. The campus was down in Midtown near all the big TV and radio stations. There were zero other kids from my neighborhood, and the halls were full of Puerto Ricans and Cubans and South Asians and a whole lot of white kids, and the *music*—always, at SIA, there was music. The school had no gym, so for phys- ed, they brought in a pro dancer who taught us mambo, cha-cha, salsa, all that stuff. During morning class I'd inhale my food, and at lunch I'd join the other kids in the cafeteria, where we'd dance to music or make it ourselves—there was a piano, and one guy would play that while the rest would circle up with drums. I'd never had a drum, but suddenly I wanted one. So I found a nail barrel, bought a skin and painted it red, stretched it over the barrel, and heat-tuned it until it played right. Every morning I'd strap that drum on my back and wear it on the train, and often, that'd end up being the best part of my day. I'd just lean against a rail and run fingers over my drum skin and look at older folks in sharp suits and feathered hats and wonder where they were going and what they were thinking as they looked at newspapers or out smudged windows or right back at me.

The rule, still, was that I had to come right home and watch my siblings. Usually, I would. But twice a year New York gave tests, from which we vocational kids were exempt, and on those days, SIA might close for a half day or a full one. And so my school friends and I would just kind of forget to mention the closure to our folks, and then we'd meet in Midtown and from there go to a park or to an empty apartment, or maybe we'd just ride the subway, hopping from this line to that one, stretching fares as far as we could. One day a bunch of us went to the beach. I don't know which beach. Don't even recall whether I swam. I just remember leaving the apartment in the morning, swim trunks under my clothes, feeling giddy that I had a secret. I remember a dozen rowdy kids sprawled across a train car, laughing and joking and singing. I remember feeling, finally, like I was one of them.

My snatches of freedom, of course, weren't all wholesome. Even before SIA, when I was still stuck in the neighborhood, I'd found ways to get in trouble. I'd steal sweet potatoes from the grocery, then cook them over a fire in a vacant lot. Or I'd smoke cigarettes. (I got real into that for like a week, until this older guy, Sonny, saw me puffing a Spud in the stairwell and said, "Richie, you got to *inhale,*" which I did, then nearly coughed to death.) I tried selling weed, too, but that ended fast, thanks to my "partner" smoking up all of our product the day after we got it. And honestly, even if he hadn't, I doubt I'd have been able to deal anything. I was just too scared, less of the police than of my father, who loomed over every decision, just perched on my shoulder and whispered, *Yeah, man! Go ahead! You do that! Do that and let's see what happens!* And so even when I got to high school—where not a few classmates were slinging weed or sticking needles in their arms or running with gangs that'd moved well past bricks and sticks— even then, I kept out of trouble. Mostly, I just wasn't around for it. I lived far away. But the few times I *did* have a chance to do something, I passed, because I knew my dad would know, and I knew what that'd mean for me.

At the time I couldn't appreciate him for this. I didn't yet know that so many of my childhood friends would one day go to prison, overdose, murder, get murdered. I didn't know that I, as an adult, would have to stand over the caskets of hundreds of sweet youngsters turned hard men. Didn't know that, if my folks hadn't been who they'd been and done what they'd done, there's a real chance I'd have ended up in a casket of my own. At the time, all I knew for sure was that I wanted to escape them.

So, eventually, I tried to. I ran. This was when I was sixteen, not long after my father first hit me with a closed fist. I don't even recall why he did it. All I know is, he punched me, and I'd had it, so I left. My plan was to go to Philadelphia. Kids at SIA were always talking about going there to see the Penn Relays, and that sounded fine to me. That morning, I left home like normal, like I was going to school, and after a stop at the grocery, where I got a bag of ginger snaps and a quart of eggnog on my parents' credit, I set out for Philly. Pretty quick, though, my plan fizzled. For starters, I didn't know where Pennsylvania was. Or what train went there. Also, I had no money. So I just walked around East Harlem all day, and come dusk, I headed to our family's church, just blocks from home. Right before the doors closed, I slipped into the sanctuary and up to the last pew in the balcony, and there I slept.

The next few days it went on like this. I'd get up early, leave the church before I was seen, then roam the streets, looking out for parents and police. Come afternoon, I'd meet a school friend in a park by the Triboro Bridge, and we'd play ball until he had to go home for dinner, and then I'd go back to my pew. I wanted, badly, to feel happy, feel *free*. But at night, I'd lie there and look out the window at the warm lights of the home next door, and I'd just feel hungry and lonely and guilty. I didn't like what I was doing, didn't like letting my folks down. But it'd gotten to where I didn't feel I had a choice.

On the fourth day, I was at the park playing ball when I saw what looked like my dad's Buick parked at the curb. I ducked behind a tree and put on a new set of clothes—I'd packed some for just this sort of getaway—then bolted down East River Drive. I ran for a long time. When it seemed like I must have lost Dad, I turned onto Third Avenue and kept walking, head down, dizzy from exhaustion. I'd only made it a few blocks when I looked up and saw my mother. This time, I didn't run. I didn't even speak. She didn't, either. She just walked me to the station—she'd called the cops days earlier—and we sat, staring at a wall where—I kid you not—there was a poster, a little multiracial hand-holding scene, that I myself had drawn years ago for a contest during something called Brotherhood Week. When a cop finally came out, he lectured me, and when that was over, my mom told him I'd done the drawing. So he stroked me a bit for that and sent us on our way. And that was it. No follow-up. Neither of my folks asked why I'd run. I didn't tell them. So things just went back to how they'd been: them lecturing and beating me, me talking stupid and feeling I could only do wrong. Day by day, I felt more hurt, more angry, more sure of what I needed. And what I needed was to go. Anywhere. For good.

All this while, I was doing awful in school. Just *awful*. I was barely scraping by in geometry and chemistry, with their vexing formulas, and then there was my nemesis, French class. In junior high, I'd taken one year of French and one of Spanish, but the SIA folks thought it'd been two units of French, so they put me in an advanced class. I failed, badly. The next year, they put me back to second-year French, but it was too late. I was discouraged and, soon, was failing again. So I dropped French and took more art, which was fun but wasn't a great move, GPA-wise. I knew I was in danger of getting held back. And I didn't want my folks to know. So if they asked about school, I'd just tell them about photography.

I knew I wasn't a photographer, not yet. But I also knew, with a certainty I still can't explain, that I would be. Part of it, maybe, was this guy David, the only other Black boy in my photography class. He took beautiful shots: skyscraper shadows on parked cars, wrinkled women on benches, paint spilling down ladder rungs. I knew he was good, and I knew I wanted to be. So when it was time to get an internship, the summer after junior year, I went with David to two Midtown firms with openings for photographers. Together we went to meetings, showed our pictures, asked questions. It was a thrill, the idea of coming every day to a fifteenth-floor office to talk about and take pictures. But that never happened. Those firms rejected us. *Both* of us. Which made me so mad. If they'd just said no to me, well, fine; my pictures were junk and my grades were worse. But David? He was the real deal. He deserved a spot. And it seemed like the only reason he didn't get one was: the bosses of those firms were white, and he wasn't. I'll never know how much race played into that rejection, but I do know that the moment stuck with me. Those white men in those high-rises were standing in the way of my pursuing what I wanted. They had the power to do that. And I decided, then and there, that I wouldn't let that happen again. When I grew up, one way or another, I'd be my own boss.

It's hard to look back at that time and not see myself moving inevitably toward my future. But I just don't think sixteen-year-old me saw what was coming. Yes, I knew that my mom was growing more distant and my dad was growing more violent and I liked them both less and less. I knew my grades were abominable, and that that might soon mean more than ugly report cards and uglier lectures. I knew I was happiest when I was riding the subway or watching pigeons swarm the sky or dipping prints into pools of developer. I knew, more every day, what I'd begun to know in those Midtown offices: if I wanted to spend my life taking pictures—and I did—I'd have to make it happen on my own. And I knew from the commercials on the TV and the radio that there was a way for me to excuse myself out of Harlem and toward my future, a way to get my GED, see the world, and save money in the meantime. I knew all of that. But it didn't come together, not really, until the end of 1955, when my grades finally got bad enough that my principal sat me down in his office and told me he'd have to hold me back. I think it was those words that did it: *I've got to hold you back*. Hearing them just about set my nerves on fire. I was so embarrassed. And just done being held back, by anyone, for any reason. So there it was: the hinge that swung my life wide open. By the time I got home that day, I knew what I had to do. I kept my principal's words to myself. I kept going to school, like all was well, like I was going to graduate, like every day wasn't a gauntlet of shame. And finally, after months of walking halls with downcast eyes and trying to steer clear of my father's sharp tongue and balled fists, finally, on February 5, 1956, I turned seventeen, which—then as now—was old enough to do what I knew I needed to do, which was to meet my mother at the door of the apartment she'd just returned to after a long day at work, and tell her, "I'm joining the Air Force."

The Academy

January 2017

This morning, like so many mornings, I woke to an alarm in the predawn dark.

By seven, I was driving south toward Salem. By eight, I was at the Academy, listening to white men with badges teach curricula I could recite in my sleep. And after lunch, I decided to stick around for a talk on responding to critical incidents: bus stabbings, mall shootings, that sort of thing.

I'm wishing I hadn't.

I take a sip of coffee and rest my head against the drywall. I'm sitting in a plastic chair at the back of the room. There are thirty-some people in here. Mostly men, mostly white. Some I know well—Portland cops, Salem cops, Academy staff—and most of the rest I recognize, though I can't say where from. One of the only people I don't know is the facilitator. He's a public safety official, from Salem, I think. I liked him at first and was getting a lot out of his presentation, but an hour or so in, he started talking about civilians, about the people who, in the wake of civic catastrophe, want to offer food and drink to survivors, and in the weeks to come want to listen and provide support.

"Those people?" the guy had said, smiling. "We call them stray cats."

When he said that, several people laughed. I didn't. I didn't see anything funny about it. And then another cop started in about how citizen volunteers haven't been "vetted," and everyone nodded, and I sat back and

43

sucked my teeth. What I wanted to say: how about the cops who killed Tamir Rice and Oscar Grant and Philando Castile and Eric Garner and Kendra James and Michael Brown and so, so many other Black people? Weren't they "vetted"? Isn't it maybe the vetting that's the problem? I couldn't say that, though. I can't. Because the director's here, and I don't want to embarrass him and lose an ear I've worked hard to gain. So I just sit, quiet, biting back what's bubbling in my chest.

One of the cops just stole a glance at me. Guy in the last row. He made like he was stretching, but I bet he just wants to know: what's Richard think about this? In a way, that's encouraging. A white guy caring about my feelings—it's a start. But it's exhausting, too. Being seen. Watched. Always.

I sometimes wonder how these men talk about Black people when I'm not around. Like, what tags have they got these days for Black folks? I bet there's a dictionary's worth of new euphemisms, and I wonder which ones they use when I'm not around. Because—understand—there are no other Black people down here. That's right: zero Black people on staff at the institution tasked with training every Oregon police officer. There was a time, years back, when they had one Black guy, an ex-cop, teaching defensive tactics. But things were pretty siloed then, and he mainly stayed in his and didn't wander out. Before long, he quit. So now, again, it's just me. One Black civilian, one or two days a week.

I keep my eyes on Mr. Stray Cats, my hands in my lap. I keep my cool, or at least I pretend to. Over the years, I've gotten pretty good at reading a room, and my mood, and presenting myself accordingly. I've had to. It's never easy, though. My loudmouth hothead inner child, he's very much alive, and at least once a day I have to clamp a hand over his mouth and tell him, *Not now*.

Which reminds me: not long ago, I was at the club, talking with a guy I know, and we got into discussing what I do at the Academy. This guy, like most Black folks, feels talking to cops is the sin of sins, so he wanted to know why. Why do I do it? And I said what I always say: I put in my years throwing rocks at cops, until that didn't seem to be getting me anywhere anymore. And then I told him, again, about the rooms I sit in, the ears I've gained, the changes I'm trying to see through. This guy didn't seem real impressed—a sin is a sin, after all—but he did at least let up on me a bit.

"We'll see," he said. Which was and is deflating. Because I know *exactly* what we'll see. Maybe it won't be tomorrow, maybe not even next week or next month, but soon enough Portland Police will do harm to a Black body. And then I'll walk back into the club and run into this guy, and he'll be angry. He'll want to know why this stuff is happening on *my* watch. He'll assume that I, by virtue of being in the room with cops, am cosigning for them. And when I leave, he'll tell his friends I'm an Uncle Tom.

My coffee's empty. My head hurts. Thinking about that—about being called out by Black folks for my work on behalf of Black folks—hurts like few other things do. Because I'm no Uncle Tom. If I ever stay quiet, it's because, after decades of this work, I have a sense for when I will and won't be heard, when my words will inch me forward or blast me miles back. And I still speak up. If folks came to Salem, they'd see that. They'd see what I do when instructors mention the activists, two white, one Black, who were killed by the Klan in 1964 in Mississippi. Often, when discussing these murders—in a class called History of Policing—instructors lump the men together like their situations were the same. So I raise my hand and I add some things. I add that only Cheney, the Black man, was chain-whipped before being shot; that his body was so broken his family could only iden-tify him by his teeth; that it was a cop who pulled over the trio and passed them over to the Klan; and that this sort of police complicity in violence against Black people, on behalf of white people, is why Black people feel how we feel about police. And after saying all that, then keeping quiet for the rest of class, I'll linger, to talk to the instructor, compliment what I can, and encourage him to say what I'd said so I don't have to.

It's exhausting, doing all of this.

I do it *all* the time.

And yet, I'm an Uncle Tom.

Mr. Stray Cats is asking for final questions. I check my phone. Two-thirty. If I leave now, I can beat rush hour, but I shouldn't. I shouldn't leave. What I should do is take a lap around campus, let my blood simmer down to room temperature, then track down the director and let him know what I think about what I just heard. Over the years, I've had many such talks, and often they've borne fruit. Take the History of Policing. That class was my idea. I came up with it after sitting in on too many trainings that dealt with the *what* of policing but not the *why*. By that point, I'd done a lot of my own research. I'd read up on convict leasing in Charleston, lynchings everywhere, COINTELPRO. I knew the value of knowing all that. So I suggested to the director and the board that cops should learn their history, so as to grasp why civilians—especially Black ones—don't trust them. I had to suggest this many times, but eventually, it happened. They created the class. Someone wrote a curriculum, and they let me read it and weigh in. At first, there were issues—they'd talk a ton about Kent State and barely at all about Rodney King—but that was fine, because I'd circle back after class if I thought they'd missed the point or made the wrong one. My feeling was, the class *existed*. That was the big hurdle. I hoped I could just keep prodding the instructors toward teaching it better, keep suggesting tweaks to the director, until it was done just right. I still hope that, I guess. But ten years have passed. And just this morning, there was a new instructor, who botched the class so badly I don't even know where to start.

Everybody's standing now. Squealing back in their chairs, heading for the door. The room empties, until it's just a few stragglers standing in a half-moon around Mr. Cats. They're all smiling, laughing, asking questions I can't hear. And I'm leaning against the back wall, holding an empty coffee cup. I'm feeling heavy. I can't help but think about Tempe. About the umpteen other times I've leaned against a wall, watching a group of cops congratulate each other, waiting to get in a few words that'll probably get ignored. I'm not feeling right. I don't know what I might say if I get the chance.

I step into the hall and weave around clusters of people. Some nod, or smile, and a few reach out to shake my hand. I oblige, but my grip's weak. I feel like I'm back in junior high. Like I'm just outside of whatever they're in. I pass the desk, say bye to the receptionists, and walk out the doors. I'm pulling out my car keys when I see what I try not to see every time I come here. The slab of granite, as wide as I am tall, that holds the names of Oregon officers killed in the line of duty. The Wall of Heroes.

I stop walking, jangle my keys against my leg and scan the wall. I've got no problem with this wall. I know many good people who wear that blue uniform, and I know what they and their families put on the line day after day, and I believe that those who have died in service, with valor, deserve to be remembered. I scan the names—all 180 of them—until I've found the one I'm looking for. The name that doesn't belong. Not here, not anywhere.

Years ago, when I was still working closely with Portland Police, there'd been an incident. What happened was, police raided the clubhouse of this biker gang, and the raid went sideways, and one officer was killed. In the coming weeks, there was a memorial for the officer, and he got valorized in the media, and I was supportive, right up until it came out that, after this cop got killed, a fellow cop pulled drugs from his pockets. This "hero" had been planning to plant drugs. And the team's search warrants? They were falsified. When I learned all of that, I was livid. I'd been duped into honoring a crooked cop. A cop aiming to do the exact thing cops have done to innocent Black folks since forever. Other cops tried to defend him—to say that, regardless, he died bravely—but I wouldn't hear it. He could've died fighting Darth Vader for all I cared. My feeling was: I will not abide a crooked cop, nor an institution that protects one.

Now, though, here I am, staring at his name. It's just a few etchings in concrete. Could be paved over in a minute. That's what really gets me: this problem, unlike most others, would be so easy to fix.

I try to step away from the wall, toward my car. But I seem to be stuck. I've got a bone-deep urge to walk back inside and tell the director, again, that this man's name should be erased, yesterday. I know, though, that he'll say what he always says—"it's harder to undo something than to do it, let's focus on what's important, change takes time"—and no matter how I reply, he'll say it again and again. And really, I wonder what the point is. Doesn't seem like anyone besides me cares. The families of the other officers on that wall, they don't know what that name means, so probably I ought to just leave it, right? Just focus on something else and forget this small thing. But that, again, is the problem. There are so many small things about police that upset me. And none of them seem to be changing.

Here it comes: my eyes are misting up. I ought to go. I've found, lately, that once I start crying it's hard to stop, and I don't want anyone here to see it, not today, not again. The last time I cried down here—the only time—was years back, at the end of my last meeting as an Academy board member. I'd sat through the whole meeting, just listening, thinking about my seven years on the board, and just before we adjourned I said I wanted to speak. I hadn't planned anything. Didn't know what the words would be until I began saying them. And what I said was: never mind, for a second, the brutality against Black folks, because law enforcement leaders weren't even doing a good job taking care of their *own* people. They weren't giving them what they needed, I said, to make good choices in their work and in their lives. And then I started crying. I mean it: *crying.* Suddenly, everyone was leaning forward, listening with their whole bodies, with total attention. So I told them how upset I was. I was angry, I told them, because I—the only Black man, and the only civilian—seemed to care more about the well-being of officers than any of them. Then I wiped my eyes and sat. Afterward, they all came up, one by one, to thank me for my time and my passion. "Richard," a few said, "I get it." Whether or not that was true, I felt good. I felt, for once, that I'd been heard. And yet. Two years on, here I stand, a stray cat staring at a stone wall. And I don't feel heard. And I don't know that anyone's gotten anything at all.

Someone's calling my name. I turn to see a bald head and a waving hand. It's Rich. Standing outside the lobby entrance. Rich is one of my favorites. One of the few real allies I've got here. He must be in a rush, because he's just waving, not walking over, which is fine. I don't know what I'd have to say to him right now. So I just wave back until he drops his hand and slips inside.

I met Rich a few months after joining the Academy board. His was one of the first classes I sat in on. Back then, board members rarely sat in. I, though, had just come off two decades working closely with Portland Police—which was always citing the need for better training—and I was eager to see what was going on in the classrooms, so I asked the director if I could pop in. "This is your Academy," he said. So the next week, I showed up and stepped into some classrooms. At first, I didn't speak. I just watched. Even that made waves. Because suddenly you've got this old Black guy walking around and nobody knows why. People would come up and ask if they could help me, and I'd say, "Nope," and walk away. That's how it went with Rich. I strolled into D Facility, where they do defensive tactics, just as Rich was about to start class. As Rich tells it, as soon as he saw me, he was scared. He was teaching striking—not the most popular police activity—and now here was this Black man, watching. He asked if he could help me, and I said, "Nope," so he sucked it up and taught. After, I went up to him, and I could tell he was ready to be admonished. But I just started shadowboxing. And then I told him I was happy to have seen his class. I was happy cops were learning how to throw and block punches—learning to subdue someone without pulling a gun—because once guns come out, they rarely get put away, and if I *have* to choose, I'd rather have a black eye than a toe tag. From that day forward, we got along well. He liked my feedback, and I liked that he was open to hearing it, and I liked what he had to say, too, about recognizing implicit bias, about training and accountability, about what he felt was wrong with policing. In the years to come, I'd meet others like him, and I'd start referring to them as the vanguard: the ones who'd take charge when we started the revolution. Now, when I'm discouraged, I remind myself there are people like Rich, rising up through the ranks.

I'm still staring at the wall. I'm not sure how long I've been here. The director's got a window in his office, and it faces the lot, and maybe he is looking at me right now. I don't want to be seen. So I head for my car, with each step fighting an urge to turn around and storm inside and show them all what a stray cat really looks like. I slide behind the wheel and pull the car from the lot and wonder whether I ought to quit doing this. Just actually, finally retire. Spend my days watering plants and fishing for bass, telling lies at the club and maybe even taking some new pictures. I make my way to the freeway on-ramp, merge with the northbound herd. I'm positive I'd enjoy doing all of that, all day, every day. But I won't. I can't. Not yet. Not while I'm still so mad about so much. Not while I still feel so far from finding someone, much less many someones, to take my place. And that, I guess, is the real curse of this work. The more hopeless it feels, the more important it becomes to keep coming back.

And how are the children?
—traditional Masai greeting

I am committed to producing images that counter the stereotypes we often see of ourselves in much of the media. Our dreams for our children are no different than the dreams you have for yours.

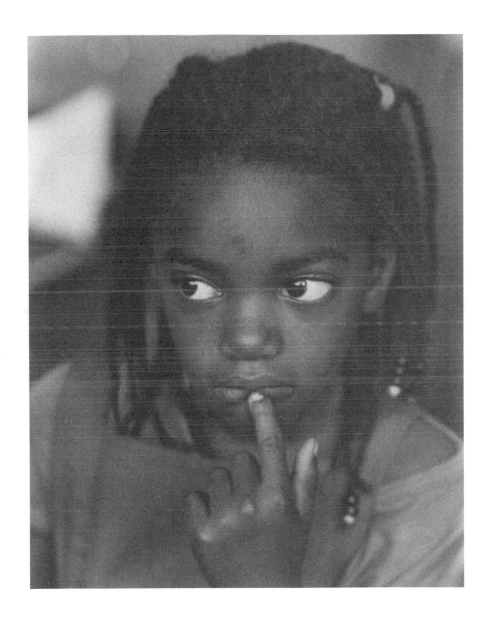

PART II

THE SORT OF PLACE YOU'D PULL PAST IF YOU COULD

The American South

1956–1966

4

Another Planet

During those final months in Harlem, when I was still a failing firstborn, still counting down to the birthday that'd hand me the reins to my life, I figured escaping would be the hard part. If I could just break out of that suffocating apartment, I figured, my life would open up. I'd be able to breathe. And if I could breathe, really *breathe*, what would there be to worry about?

I was seventeen years old.

My worries began the second I left LaGuardia. Despite all my day-dreams of flight, I'd never actually been in an airplane, and now that I was—in a plane, in the sky, bound for a base called Lackland in a state called Texas—I found myself dry-mouthed, shaking, frozen with fear. I spent the whole flight kissing the window and staring at the wing's dual engines, which coughed out violent plumes of smoke and fire. I was *positive* the plane was going to explode. Could think of nothing else. So I barely noticed—much less spoke to—the two recruits beside me, though they were also Black, also from New York, also bound for basic. I forgot about my mother, who'd hugged me hard at the airport, and my father, who'd avoided my eyes. I didn't think of my siblings or school friends, my lunchroom drum circle or rooftop pigeon coops. Didn't think of where I was headed, or why. All I thought as I sat there, suspended in air, finally free, was: I might die up here.

Soon enough, though, we were touching down in Atlanta for a layover. And I appeared to still be alive. So I swallowed my fear, and I peeled myself from the seat, and before long I was back in Richie mode: strutting through the terminal, goofing with my fellow recruits. I was looking sharp—tan suit, pink shirt, camel-hair overcoat—and I couldn't stop peeking at my reflection. I liked what I saw. A week earlier, I'd been in algebra class, my gut in a twist. I'd been stuck in that apartment, squirming under my father's thumb. Now, though? Now I was in Georgia. And I was bound for Texas, about which I knew nothing except that it was as far from New York as the Air Force would let me get.

It was awhile before our next flight, so we headed to the airport diner and took a table in the middle of the room. The place was plain—smelled like coffee and burnt bacon—and empty but for a few other tables full of white people. Pretty quick, a waitress came over. White lady, about my mom's age. She didn't speak. Just stood over us, holding a frowning silence I in no way understood. I broke it. Ordered eggs and bacon. For a second, she hesitated, then scribbled on her pad and slipped into the kitchen. If this left the other guys feeling weird, I didn't notice. I just kept on talking. Kept on right until the kitchen doors clanked open, and I spun to see two white men walking toward us, carrying tall beige screens. Without a word, they set the screens in a tight circle around our table.

As a youngster, in my Harlem cocoon, I'd heard about the racist stuff going on in the South. But it'd never felt real; the South might as well have been on another planet. So I didn't know what to do. I looked to the others, who were older, maybe wiser, but they were staring at their laps, silent. Seemed like the whole room had gone silent. And though I could see nothing but those screens, I had the sense that everyone in the restaurant was staring, breath held, waiting to see what would happen.

What happened was this: I erupted. I shot out of my chair and screamed at those screens. My whole body shaking. My voice like a foreign object. If you'd have asked me then how I was feeling, I'd have said I was mad. But I can tell you now that it was fear, pure and uncut. I'd never been so scared in my life.

At some point, the others must've slipped out. I found myself alone. So I did all I could think to do: I kept pacing and hollering for what felt like days. Finally, the screens shook apart, and a short Black guy wearing an apron stepped inside. He got a hand on my shoulder, started whispering at me, and I ignored him and kept raising hell until he said, "Look, you don't want these white folks seeing you eat anyway." Which just stopped me dead. Because he was right. I didn't want that. And I think on some level I'd been waiting for permission to shut up. So I did. And when the guy said he'd be off soon, and asked me to hang tight, I did that, too. I sat. I stared at those walls. I tried to imagine who and what was beyond them. And finally, the guy came back in and said, "Let's go," and we did.

By this point, I'd missed my flight, so the guy—a dishwasher, apparently—took me by a ticket counter to rebook, then led me outside. We were going downtown, he said, to kill time until my flight. And to get downtown, we had to take a city bus. As we approached the stop, he told me we'd need to sit at least a few rows behind any white people, and I nodded, but when we got on, the bus was empty but for the driver, and something in me just could not go past the second row. So I sat. The dishwasher touched my arm, asked me to come a few rows back. But I just shook my head and slid to the window.

Remember, this was February 1956. Two months after Rosa Parks became Rosa Parks. Smack in the middle of the Montgomery Bus Boycott. I knew about all of that, in the vague way I knew of most things, but as I sat in that seat, staring ahead, listening to the rattle and hum of the bus engine, I wasn't thinking of the movement. I wasn't trying to be part of anything. I was just a boy, and I was scared, and I didn't want to sit in the back of an empty bus. Maybe the driver saw that in me. Maybe he saw my fear and, in seeing it, felt something like compassion. I doubt it, but I don't know. I know only that he didn't say a word. Didn't even stare me down. He just put the bus in gear, and he drove.

As we bumped along, I stuck close to the window, trying to look calm, and when the first white passengers came aboard, I kept my eyes on the glass even as I felt them staring. None of them spoke to me, though. Nor did the white folks who got on at the next stop. Or the next. Or the next.

And before long, the dishwasher was at my side, squeezing my shoulder, beckoning me off the bus.

He led me into a pool hall. The place was dark and thick with smoke, and voices cut through music crackling from overhead speakers. Everyone was Black. It felt like home, but also, in way I couldn't have begun to describe, it didn't. The dishwasher set me up at a table with some older guys, then said he'd be right back and walked away. My father'd had a folding pool table that he often set up in our apartment, and he'd sometimes let me play, so now I did that: I played. I jumped in on a game of nine-ball with those older guys, and I shot until, again, I felt a hand on my shoulder.

The dishwasher was now flanked by several men. They led me to a back room, and once the door shut, they hit me with questions: who was I, and why was I in Atlanta, and where in New York was I from, and who'd I know there? I was confused and scared. But I couldn't show that. So I set my jaw and spat one-word answers. I was too naïve to wonder what I now assume: those men were with the movement and thought I was, too. Pretty quick, they must've wised up, because they stopped with the questions and showed me out. And before long, the dishwasher was putting me back on a bus.

It wasn't much of a goodbye. I think I just said something clever, tried to play it cool. And man, I wish I hadn't. I wish I'd thanked him. I wish I'd gotten his number so I could call him up now and tell him how often I wonder where that day might've taken me if he hadn't stepped in and slowed me down. Wish I could tell him that, in no small part because of him, I've dedicated my life to helping other Black folks, no matter what, no matter whether they even know they need it. But I was too young and scared to have that sort of foresight. So I just got on the bus, and I sat and kept every part of myself quiet, until I was back on a plane, rising up out of Atlanta, telling myself I'd never come back.

That flight offered no relief. It was nighttime now, and the skies had gone stormy. Wind gusts punched the plane's fuselage and raindrops wet its engines. I could barely breathe I was so scared, my new fear being that all that water would douse the engine's fire and we'd stall out and plummet down into whatever strange state we happened to be hovering over. So I just plastered my forehead to the plexiglass, stared at wet wings lit by dim green light, and wondered when or if this day would end.

Finally, after that stormy flight and a long, quiet bus ride, I arrived at Lackland Air Force Base, five hours behind schedule. I reported to a spare, overlit room, and I got in line with the other recruits and stood, weary, waiting to get my ID tags and bedding and bunk. Also in the room were a half-dozen guys, all white, who'd finished basic a month prior and who'd been called in to swarm us new recruits: to bark at us, breathe down our necks, make us feel like crap. Real quick, a bunch of them gravitated toward me. Southerners, it turned out, weren't fond of northerners, especially Black northerners, and extra-especially Black northerners from New York City, so one of the guys—a white dude who was even shorter than I was— started bumping me, yelling, trying to get me to drop and do push-ups. I stood my ground. Told him I wasn't doing any tricks. And he didn't like that. "You look like you think you could take me," he said, and I held his eyes and shot back, "I sure do." Before I could try, though, a bunch of other guys hemmed us in. "You fight him," they said, "you fight all of us." So I backed down. I sank into myself. I waited. It seemed like I was waiting for days, just trying to avoid eye contact, trying not to hear the things they were saying, until finally I reached the table where I got my tags and uniforms. At the end of the table, there was a Black guy presiding over a pile of bedding. I'd never been so happy to see a Black face. So I smiled, and I said something that seemed friendly, but he just scowled and asked where I was from. Before I'd even finished saying, "New York," he was tossing my linens on the floor, and telling me, in a thick Texas drawl, to shut up and get out of his face.

Wrinkled linens in hand, I stood with the rest of the herd, eyes on my feet. At last, we were led to our barracks. I wanted so badly to sleep, and I was so close, I thought, and kept thinking, until I saw the bunk beds. At which point my chest deflated. Because I just knew. I *knew* I'd get a top bunk. And for a bed wetter (still, at seventeen, I was), it didn't get much worse than a top bunk. I wasn't about to cop to that, though, so I did what I was told. I spun and saluted and yessir-ed. I made, remade, and re-remade my bed. And finally, once the beds were made, the lights dimmed, I lay on my back in my bunk, stared bleary-eyed up into the dark, and blinked back my dreams until dawn.

5

Survival Skills

Those early days in basic bleed together. Just a blur of loud voices and white faces, sore muscles and endless drills, long nights trying not to dream the wrong dreams and longer mornings trying to hide the stains on my sheets. I could tell stories—stories about shoe-shining and bed-making, about in-your-face quizzes on regiment number and posture and patriotism, about marching, pumping elbows and knees, spinning perfect ninety-degree turns like the robot you were expected to be—but honestly, I don't *remember* any of that. I just know it happened. And that, mostly, I liked it. There was something comforting about having to run and salute and keep my foot locker neat and mirror spotless. Something safe about melting into a faceless herd that marched and spun and sang full-throated songs in Texas rain. Something about that noise that quieted all the rest. It quieted the in-your-face race stuff, left everyone too tired to be terrible. Quieted my mind, too.

Other guys in my squadron would often be up late, crying in their bunks, missing their girlfriends, their moms, but not me. I knew I'd hurt my mother—I'd never seen her as upset as when I told her I was leaving for Texas in three days—but I couldn't feel much about it. Could barely get myself to write letters. And when I did, I rarely said much. Usually, I'd just ask for this coat, that shirt, maybe throw in an obligatory, "How's Rodney and Pamela and Gary and Jeff?" My mom would answer that question, and the ones I hadn't asked, in letter after letter—she wrote once a week—and she'd always ask me to call, which I occasionally did. But within minutes, I'd be itching to get off the phone. I just didn't like how it felt, being talked to like I was still a youngster, like nothing had changed or would.

Probably that's why I hated saying *sir* so much. That was my only issue with basic: they wanted us to say *sir* before and after every word and step and breath. I'd never even called my father *sir,* and now that I'd escaped him, I wasn't going to bow down to anyone else. So I came up with ways to not say it. I'd mouth it while others yelled. Or I'd say it at the start of a sentence but not at the end. Overall, I just tried to avoid talking with officers, with anybody, about anything. I tried.

One day, though, about halfway through basic, I was in the barracks with my squadron when I heard the clop-clop of booted feet. I went to the window, climbed onto a foot locker, rested my elbows on the sill, and watched the men march. They weren't doing anything fancy, but still, the sight and sound whisked me right back to Harlem, to when I'd marched at the Y and to that day when I'd stood at my window, watching the Hellfighters and wishing I could join them. I fell into slack-jawed reverie. So I didn't really even notice as other guys gathered around me, not until one of them gripped my shoulder and, in a reedy voice, said, "Get off my locker."

I felt myself being yanked down, so I wheeled my arms, got hold of a pistol belt on an overhead shelf. On pure reflex, I spun around and lashed out with that belt, and it struck the temple of the guy who'd tried to wrestle me down. He yelped and pawed at his face, then took a swing at me, which I dodged. We wrestled for a bit, but it was over quick. And that, I thought, was that. Just a little scrap. I don't even think he was bleeding. Within hours, I'd basically forgotten about it. I figured he had, too.

This was just a day before bivouac, the final stage of basic. The deal with bivouac was that you got supplies and a rifle and went out in the woods and honed your survival skills. I'd been looking forward to bivouac for weeks. But the next morning, as we marched out of the barracks, a training instructor pulled me from the line. Minutes later I was a room with the base psychiatrist. My superiors had heard about the scuffle, and they'd decided I was a Dangerous Person, so now here I was, sitting with this shrink, who started in about me attempting murder—*attempting murder*, he said—then asked about my mom and dad: how they'd raised me, what my inner child had lacked, all that therapy stuff. Man, I was dumbfounded. Because, sure, my upbringing affected me. But this? This wasn't about Mom and Dad. This was about some dude trying to throw me down and me defending myself. That's what I said to the psychiatrist. And he nodded, scribbled on his pad, and let me know I was free to go.

I threw on my backpack and bedroll and caught up with the group as fast as I could, and before long, I'd forgotten about that talk. Bivouac was just *fun*. All day we ran obstacle courses and built stick fires and crawled through yellow meadow grass and ran through a fake downed aircraft in real flames, and at night we slept outside in tents, which I'd never done before. I lay on my back in the warm Texas night, looking up at a big sky full of bright stars, just bewildered that I was where I was.

Bivouac ended, though. And as soon as we got back to base, before I'd even showered, I got pulled into a room with a few officers with star-studded uniforms, and they sat me down and told me they'd come to a decision: I couldn't continue in the Air Force.

I didn't say much. Couldn't. All I could think was, I'd left home and come so far and worked so hard, only to get held back again? Man, it hurt. And knowing it was my fault—that I'd messed up—made it worse. But I did as I was told. I packed my things, headed to these isolation barracks for guys with "mental problems." I'd learn, later, that these barracks were mainly populated by men who'd been outed as homosexuals, but that day, all I knew was that I'd been told to go there, and stay there. So I did. I went, and I lay on a bunk, fighting tears, trying to figure out how I'd explain this to my folks.

By nightfall, I'd come up with a plan. We'd just gotten our assignments for the second phase of basic, and I'd been placed in Biloxi, Mississippi. I'd been planning to ask for a reassignment—I knew by now that Biloxi, Mississippi, was the last place a Black man wanted to be—but my new thinking was: if I could get to Biloxi, keep my head down, maybe this would blow over. The next day, I went to personnel to process out. I made it through all the steps—arranged travel, signed out, turned in bedding— but afterward, as I was walking across the base, one of the men who'd told me I was done—my first sergeant—came up and grabbed me by the arm and told me I wasn't going anywhere but home.

I was sent back to my original barracks to await discharge. They were empty. Just stripped beds and bare floors and cold concrete walls. I peeked upstairs, where there were private rooms for TIs, and those were empty, too, so I sat in one and waited for whoever was coming to get me. By morning, no one had. Not by dusk, either. I began to relax, and after sunset I snuck out. There was a servicemen's club, which I'd had little time to visit during basic, but now, time was all I had. So I sat in on games of Whist. I bowled. I met guys about whom I recall little, except that one of them taught me to dump peanuts into my Dr. Pepper. I leaned against the wall and watched in wonder as big white men sat in a circle, plucking banjo strings and crooning harmonies to songs with names like "Wildwood Flower."

Nobody came for me the next day. Or the next. It was starting to seem like they'd forgotten, and I wasn't sure what to do about that, so I just kept hiding out by day and hanging at the club by night. Going to the club, of course, cost money. And soon I didn't have any. What I did have was a washing machine in my barracks, and I'd noticed that its snake—the tube that ran from coin slot to coin box—wasn't secure. So one day I yanked out that snake, then set the end in a butt can and hid the can behind the washer and told everyone my barracks had the base's best laundry. Then I had money again. Not a ton, but enough to spend every night drinking peanuts and Pepper and playing Whist and bowling. I was, I thought, getting good at bowling. One night, I had a particularly great game, and so I called my dad, collect, to share the news. And Dad, who was in a league, who regularly broke 250, whose voice sounded weirdly froggy, said, "You're calling me at one a.m. to tell me you bowled a ninety-five?"

Finally, after two weeks of this, some TIs came in to inspect the barracks and found me. Hours later, I was before a panel of angry officers. They told me all I'd done wrong, and they asked me why I should get to stay in the service, and I just crumpled. To that point, I hadn't believed I was going to get booted. It'd just been words. But now it felt very real. So what I did was, I cried. I begged. I told them why I'd quit school, why I couldn't go home. I told them I'd do whatever they told me if they'd give me one more chance. And to my everlasting surprise, they did. They told me they'd let me move to the second phase of basic. I could even do it there at Lackland, they said. But if I screwed up once—if I missed one *sir*, mis-made my bed, messed up at all—I'd be gone, done, period. I don't think I'd ever been so relieved. So I thanked them. I made promises. And I kept enough of them that, eight weeks later, I was graduating basic, leaving Lackland, bound for a tech school and a new beginning in Illinois.

6

The Ghost of a Stripe

Scott AFB lay just east of St. Louis, but it felt to my teenage self like Nowhere, USA. All I could see, wherever I looked, were cornstalks and powerlines and an endless beige horizon. And that was just fine. After four months of basic, I was happy to be someplace quiet, somewhere I wasn't getting berated dawn to dusk, where I could start to do whatever it was I'd do with the rest of my life.

I'd gotten assigned to communications, which meant I'd be studying airborne radios. I didn't know much about radios, but I'd always liked to tinker, and just generally, I was happy to have ended up in the radio shop—in any shop—because most other Black guys at Scott—and there weren't many—had gotten placed in the motor pool or the chow hall or some other crap service job. In those years, that was just how it was: though the Air Force had been integrated for nearly a decade, we still didn't have a single Black general, and overall, Black airmen were still treated as second-class, or maybe third or fourth. So I felt lucky to have ended up in the radio shop. I intended to stay there.

To fix radios, you had to understand electronics, which, as it turned out, involved a bunch of geometry. I thought I'd escaped geometry when I left school, but now here I was, back in a chair, staring at a worksheet and listening as every pencil but mine squiggled along. It was a familiar feeling, being the one who didn't get it, and I had an urge to do what I'd always done: talk stupid, give up. But this wasn't school. This was the Air Force. If

I talked stupid or gave up, I'd get booted or banished to the chow hall. So I applied myself. I tried. I kept trying. And though I wouldn't say I ever got *good* at math, I did well enough to keep up until, finally, we put down the pencils and picked up radios.

My job, eventually, would be to fix radios in planes flown by pilots-in-training, so my education mainly involved taking old units apart and reassembling them. And sitting at a table, digging into heaps of metal and wire and making things work, it came naturally. I felt like I was back building tiny planes with why-can't-you-be-more-like-Larry? Now, as others scratched their heads, I hummed along. It was a new feeling, being the expert, and I liked it, and in the years to come, I'd wonder how life might have looked if I had gotten to do this sort of thing more often as a boy—if I'd gotten to use my hands, solve real problems, instead of just memorizing crap I never cared about in the first place.

If I wasn't in the shop, I was at the club, playing pool and ping-pong and pinochle with guys I'd met in the barracks. The ones I liked best were Roy Hicks, a guy from Chicago with a tongue even sharper than mine; an older white dude, Stanley, who'd served in the Navy and was covered in tattoos; and this stocky brother about whom I remember only that once, while we were riding in a cab in St. Louis, he started talking with the driver, also Black, in what sounded like gibberish, but they kept on until eventually I realized they were speaking Korean. There were others, too, and if pressed, I could give you a hazy detail about each, but really, it wasn't about the individuals. We moved as a herd.

Most Fridays, we'd all board the base bus and head to St. Louis, usually ending up at Peacock Alley, where we'd listen to jazz and eat fancy food with fancy people. Saturdays, we'd head right back, for the YWCA dance— I'd be on the floor for hours, spinning and shaking with girl after girl, until the music stopped, at which point I'd get shy and stare at my feet—and afterward, we'd head to another club or two before catching the last bus back to base. Sundays, we'd return again, to sit in Morningside Park and see this husband-and-wife soul duo, who, though they were good performers, didn't seem too special, because this was 1956, and nobody'd yet heard of Ike and Tina Turner. I loved that moment when the bus would pull into St. Louis and I'd step off and look up at that great glistening arch and feel far from home, in the best of ways. Years later, I'd learn that a Black man not much older than me had been lynched not too far from the Illinois station where I got on that bus. But at the time, all I knew was that I was on my own, in a strange new place, with guys who finally felt like friends. I was doing just fine.

And I made sure to tell my parents so, in the few letters I sent. I bragged about my grades (I had a fifty-three, the average was forty-two); I shared that I'd applied for overseas duty, not understanding how much this might hurt my mother nor how little control I'd end up having over where I went; and I gave them the rundown on drill team, my new favorite thing about the Air Force. I wrote about giving performances all over southern Illinois, about getting inspected by three-star generals, and, of course, I wrote about the uniforms: white helmet with a gold star, jump boots, bloused khakis, a shirt with a braided rope adorning the shoulder.

I left things out of my letters. Like my demotion. How that happened was, one day during a drill team performance in cold, slanting rain, my teeth started chattering and my lungs went cloudy, so I went to sleep early. I woke feeling worse—warbly voice, scratchy eyes—so I rolled over and kept sleeping through breakfast, lunch, and my post-lunch detail, my thought being: skipping just once, for illness, was no big deal. The next day, though, I got pulled into the first sergeant's office, and he said I should've gone to the hospital, or at least called in. Since I hadn't done that, he had no choice but to take away my single stripe. Now, I was no longer an airman third class. I was back to basic.

That demotion kicked my legs out. I felt stupid and small, like I had when I'd gotten held back in school. I wanted that stripe back, bad, so for the next thirty days—you were eligible, after a month, to get a stripe restored—I nailed every detail, worked hard and fast. But those thirty days passed. Then forty, fifty, sixty. And no stripe. My first sergeant barely acknowledged me. I tried not to take it personally, but I couldn't help but notice there were a bunch of other guys who'd screwed up—been lazy, mouthy, late—and they'd all kept their stripes. And the only difference seemed to be: they were white.

I kept working hard, though, kept biting back my resentment, and soon it was November. Nine months after leaving home, I was graduating, a certified Air Force radio man. By now, we'd gotten our base assignments, and mine was in Enid, Oklahoma. Oklahoma wasn't exactly what I'd had in mind when I was a youngster, dreaming of seeing the world, but it was somewhere new. As I boarded the plane, in full uniform, I just felt proud. I'd left Harlem, landed on a planet called the American South, and I'd become a man, an *air*man. I thought about all of that as I sat on a plane full of white people, staring at firing engines I didn't trust, rubbing my fingers over the ghost of a stripe. And then I shut my eyes and braced myself for flight.

7

Paper Cup

It was nighttime when I arrived in Enid, Oklahoma. From the window seat of the puddle jumper I flew in on, it didn't look like much—just a few lights sprinkled over the dark—and its airport was tiny and empty, save for a few employees who'd come in, on call, to receive our flight. I'm sure there were others on that plane, but in my memory, it's just me stepping onto the tarmac; just me, shivering in the surprising cold; just me, walking into the bus station, also empty, except for the white clerk who took one look at my face and showed me to a back room with old benches instead of plush chairs. This was the same treatment I'd gotten in Atlanta in that airport diner, but now, nine months on, I didn't get angry, didn't scream, didn't react. I just took a seat on a bench. I waited. And an hour later, I stepped off a bus and onto the floodlit grounds of Vance Air Force Base.

Enid wasn't far from San Antonio, which had been warm, so I figured Enid would be, too. But that first morning, I was shivering and miserable. I could see, in the soft dawn light, that there was nothing out there. No hills, no trees. Just barren land blown clean by wind. That morning, too, I saw my first tumbleweed. Just a big ball of dirty grass, bouncing between barracks. "Oklahoma snow," I'd call it, once I learned to have a sense of humor about the place.

Vance was a pilot training base, its runways teeming with T-6 Texans and T-33 Shooting Stars and Mitchell B-25s, and my job was to keep their radios working. Maybe I should've been nervous—I was the only Black guy in the shop, not to mention the youngest and least tested—but right away, I took to the work. On all planes, the system was the same—one box for pilot, copilot, and navigator, and on blimp-like B-25s, for tail and turret gunners—and if a plane's radios went down, you'd go box by box until you found the problem. It was simple work. And kind of humdrum, since the planes were between missions: cold, empty, quiet. Sometimes, though, during exercises, a pilot would have a radio problem, which could force him to abort, and an abort was capital-B Bad. In this case, we'd get a call, and one or five of us would run out into the cold and wind and rain and scramble aboard the plane and try to divine the problem. Meanwhile, the pilot would be strapped in, watching, waiting. These were called "pilot standbys." And I *loved* them. I loved climbing around on huge roaring machines. Loved knowing a clock was ticking and it was up to me to beat it. And man, I was good at it. Good enough that, before long, and even though I was young and green, I got pegged as the go-to for pilot standbys.

On the job we wore one-piece fatigues, and the ones I got issued were too big. I wasn't about to go to work looking like a circus clown, so I cut out the stitching on the sewn-in belt, folded the fabric over itself, and sewed it back up; I religiously shined my shoes, too, and every week I took my uniforms to the tailor, paid fifty cents to get them starched. I did all of this because I wanted to look sharp, like Mr. Gill, like a man deserving of respect, but it's like they say: crap rolls downhill and someone's got to catch it. And since I was youngest, Blackest, and lowest-ranked, I found myself at the base of Crap Mountain. While other guys drove box trucks and did neat construction jobs, I landed the worst details; if there was a window to be washed, a toilet to be scrubbed, I was the guy. At first, I rolled with it, but as time wore on, I got frustrated. I'd been eligible for promotion for months, and was trying to show I deserved one, but my NCOIC—an Arkansan named Pugh—didn't notice. He was too busy playing daddy to this white guy, Atkins, who was always coming in late, reeking of booze, barely working, none of which stopped Pugh from having him over for dinner, saying he'd someday adopt him. Before long, Pugh recommended Atkins for a second stripe. Meanwhile I kept scrubbing toilets, stripeless.

Pugh had this toy poodle with fur the color of a dirty sock. He'd bring it to work, and it'd crap all over, and he'd ask me—always me—to scoop it up. "I'm not cleaning your dog's crap," I'd say, and though he never made me, it bugged me that he asked. Bugged me, too, when he put me on coffee detail. Understand, I'd never been a coffee guy. Didn't like the taste, the smell, or the nervy jolt it gave you. But now, every morning, I'd have to brew a pot for the whole shop. I told Pugh I wanted another detail. He told me, "Tough shit." So I set out to make some *awful* coffee. I'd use the same grounds for days and days. And if I did add new stuff, I'd just dump it onto the old. Soon, the filter looked like a mud pit and smelled like vinegar. Still, the guys drank it. So I began taking money from the pot they paid into. First, it was a quarter per brew. Then, when no one objected, I started taking dollars. At this Pugh finally gave in. Pulled me off coffee and gave me some other detail. And though now I can see that I might've gotten a stripe quicker if I'd just made the coffee, all I could think back then was, I *won*.

That, though, was just my job. Every night I was free to do what I wanted, and mostly what I did was hang at the club. There were always dice games going, the same ones I'd seen older guys play in Harlem: street craps, Cee-Lo, that sort of thing. I'd liked watching, and I must've paid attention, because I kept winning. It wasn't a fortune, but it was enough to buy, on installment, a diamond ring, a Hamilton watch, a Browning shotgun, and the other things I felt I needed to feel like an adult. Like a car. I won a car. Now that seems wild, but in the moment, when I raced against this guy from Baltimore, won, and took the keys to his 1950 Chevy, all I could think was, how do you drive this thing? I wasn't about to admit I'd never done so, so I took the keys and left, all casual, and later, when no one was watching, I gave it a go. I didn't know what a clutch was, so at first it was a lot of grinding and stalling, but before long I'd figured it out. And though that guy would soon buy back his Chevy—I'd use the money to get and soup up a '51 Ford of my own—there was a week or so where I just drove that first car around base, radio cranked, backfiring the engine and laughing.

With my winnings, I also bought my first real camera. For years, I'd coveted a Rolleiflex—the best there was—but when I went to the store, the guy just looked me over and said, "You don't need one of those." He suggested an Ikoflex, which had the same lenses but was way cheaper. So I got that. I got a nice case, too. And there my camera stayed. Fancy equipment or not, I was scared to take pictures of people. Whenever I stuck a camera in someone's face, I felt like an amateur. And I didn't want anyone thinking that about me. So I took few pictures, and just none of the guys I ran around with.

There was Garrison from Chicago, who painted planes; and Sam Brown from Baltimore, who worked in flight sims; and John Dexter, a Detroit native and formidable boxer; and Laverne Smith from Vallejo, who repaired aircraft and was an all-around kindred spirit. Some days, when Smith was in his repair truck and I was bored in the shop, we'd play chess over the radio, and every morning one of us would pick a word from the dictionary, which we'd practice using all day in hopes of growing our vocabulary. Every one of those guys, too, was on the base basketball team with me—finally, I'd hit my growth spurt—and that, maybe above all, was where the friendships were cemented. We'd practice together on base, play games in underlit gyms in one-intersection towns, trace vulgarities into steamed windows on the bus rides home and spend the whole next day bragging about this block, that crossover.

And every weekend, we'd clear off the base and head for Enid. Oklahoma was a Klan state, not far removed from the 1921 Tulsa massacre, so Enid, like many Southern towns, was segregated. In my years there, I barely went downtown—one visit to the theater, where I had to sit in a separate balcony, was enough. Mostly, I hung out in the Black neighborhood, East Park. A rail line split East Park from the rest of Enid, and the base bus would drop us at the tracks, and from there we'd walk.

East Park was a small town with all the trappings: brick schoolhouse, ice cream parlor, leafy park, steepled churches, and, of course, bars. There were three bars: a big, loud one where we'd go, late-night, to dance; a wood-framed place where I'd get smoked baloney sandwiches before catching the night bus back to base; and a basement bar, named after its proprietor, a gruff old guy called Unc. Unc's, that was the spot. It was nothing special—just a dim room with booth seats and a cobwebbed jukebox—but we'd end up there every night. Unc sold bootleg, and after closing, he'd often let us pile in his car and go along on moonshine runs. I wasn't much of a drinker, so usually I'd just sit with the others, and as they guzzled bootleg, I'd drink their orange soda chasers. They'd razz me for that—for being a soda-drinking baby, stealing what they'd paid for—so finally, on a night when the razzing went too long, I stood and went to the bar and slapped down a five and said, "Unc, gimme a squeeze." By the time he'd come back with my change, I'd emptied an eight-ounce bottle. I remember sliding into my booth seat, getting a few shoulder slugs. Feeling a little dizzy, and then a lot dizzy. That's about it.

Nights at Unc's, I was often with Garrison, Sam, and Laverne, but I had white friends, too. Like Carl, this big redhead from Louisiana. He'd always take me fishing, and once, he brought me down to the Rattlesnake Roundup, the gist of which was: throngs of people walked around in the sun, catching snakes, and the best snake-catchers got awards, and at the end you'd sell your catch to the organizers. I was the only Black guy. Just a kid from Harlem, tiptoeing through dried-up creek beds, breathing sage-tinged air, and listening for rattles. At first, I was scared. But once we'd caught our first snake and got it into a laundry bag, I relaxed, and soon I was having fun. Carl and I ended up with a half-dozen snakes, and we decided to keep them—all of them—as pets. Back in Enid, on a bored afternoon, I let one loose in the barracks. The idea was: I'd pin the thing and milk it for venom, like I'd seen done on the show Zoo Parade. That went just about how you'd expect it would. We got rid of the snakes soon afterward.

Mostly, I enjoyed Carl's company—he taught me to fish, laughed a lot, knew how to tell a good lie—but still, he was a Southern white guy, and he never seemed to grasp what that meant. Like, one time, we stopped at an A&W drive-in, and a white waitress came out, and we both asked for burgers and root beers, and when the waitress brought our orders, his root beer was in one of those frosty mugs, and mine was just in a paper cup. I was so upset by that. Just sat in silence, seething, my appetite gone. But Carl? He dug into his burger and slurped from his mug like nothing had happened at all.

That memory has stuck with me, probably because it was one of the few times I can recall biting back my anger. Most of the time, if someone did me wrong, I'd speak up. I'd speak up at Vance, about why I kept catching crap details, and if white folk, anywhere, tried to call me "boy," I'd ask if they knew who they were talking to. "I'm an *airman*," I'd say. "Airman Brown." This amazed the other Black guys I ran with, most of whom were from the South, who'd grown up learning to expect and ignore "boy," and so the more I did stuff like this, the more I got dressed up in the jacket of being political, being a radical. I liked that jacket. I made a point of wearing it as often as I could.

While that attitude had its merits, it wasn't helping me in the communications shop, not at all. I'd now been at Vance for two years, but despite my expertise, and despite the arrival of several fresh-faced kids, I was still stripeless, buried at the bottom of Crap Mountain. Partly, this was my fault, and I knew it. I knew I ought to mouth off less, say *sir* more, show up for my details, even if I felt I didn't deserve them. But I was still so young. I couldn't make myself behave how I knew I probably should. And so you can imagine how I reacted when, one day, out of the blue, I got pulled from my shop and put in a building across base, where a new crop of NCOs was getting trained. My new job: to be their custodian. It was one hundred percent busy work: mopping floors, changing linens, and cleaning butt cans, which I hated since I didn't smoke. And the worst part? Three of us were on that detail, and we were all Black. I was just sick with anger, and I did not hide it. I skulked around the barracks, did the jobs half-ass or outright refused them. I started bringing my record player, and while I worked, I'd listen to Ahmad Jamal, who'd just put out *Live at the Pershing*. But whenever the director of the training academy came in, he'd make me turn the music off, then give me some new nothing job. Well, one day, while doing one of those jobs, I came across a hutch of rabbits. I liked rabbits. So I grabbed one, took him inside and put him in a straw-bedded box. For a few days, I fed him grass, petted him, took care of him. But inevitably, the director caught wind. So he tossed my bunny out and hauled me into his office and started laying into me about my demeanor. During his speech, his lip twitched, and I thought that was funny, so I mimicked it. And at that, he just shook his head and told me what I wanted to hear: I was done at the academy. The next day, I was back at the radio shop, still stripeless, still thinking, *I won.*

From there, things only got worse. A few weeks later, I was in East Park, in one of the bars, when the teenage son of the owner sat down beside me. He was drunk and loud, and I was in no mood, so I said, "Seems like you're drunk." Well, the owner was sitting behind us, and she popped up and told me not to disrespect her son. I mouthed off, and suddenly she was opening her coat, and there was a pistol inside. I got up and left, but she followed me, gun raised, yelling. The guys who were with me managed to settle her down, and we left, but from then on I only went to two clubs.

And then one Friday night, I was sipping soda at Unc's when some white folks came in. White folks were always coming to Black bars, which bugged me— if I couldn't go to their house, why were they in mine?—but I'd mostly gotten used to it. At some point I ended up in a booth with a white lady. It was her and me and a few guys I didn't know. We were just sitting, talking, laughing, like always, but some white men at the bar kept looking over, sneering. At one point, one yelled to the woman, "C'mere, you little n——r." She laughed but didn't leave. And then a bunch of cops burst in. The bartender—not Unc—pointed at our booth, and the cops came over and said they'd had complaints about public intoxication, which was odd, since no one was drunker than they ever were at Unc's. At first, they left me alone—just cuffed the others and took them out—but then the bartender, for reasons I never learned, pointed at me and said, "Him, too." I told the cops I hadn't done nothing, but they weren't hearing it. As they were hauling me out, someone asked what was going on, and I said, "These damn cops are arresting me!" So that's how I got charged with public intoxication *and* profanity.

I had to stay in jail overnight. It was terrible. Everyone was hammered. One of the white girls was screaming and bawling. The place smelled like sweat and piss and fear. Roaches everywhere. I was still in my suit, and I wasn't about to sit on one of those nasty benches, so I just stood. I stood all night. And I'm telling you: you don't know how long a night is until you've spent one standing in a room full of drunks, in a jail run by white folks. I was released eventually, and in the days to come, I'd be asked—by fellow airmen, by officers—what'd happened. And I'd tell them the truth:

I didn't know. I didn't know why the cops had been called. Probably I should've gotten a lawyer, but no one told me to, so I went to court, where I pled not-guilty to drunkenness but guilty to profanity because, in my home, saying "damn" was a punishable offense. Looking back, I still feel angry about all of that: angry, especially, that no one thought to help me. I know it wasn't anybody's *job* to take care of me. But I also know that if I'd been a white airman, the whole base would've had my back.

I didn't tell my folks about that night. Didn't tell them hardly anything. My mother was still writing near-weekly letters, about how my siblings were doing and who of my friends had overdosed or been shot or gone to jail, but I rarely responded. Didn't call much, either. If I did, it was only to ask her to send clothes, records, or savings bonds, which the Air Force was still sending home. I didn't miss my family. I felt about home like I'd once felt about the South—like it was some distant planet, like whatever was going on there didn't concern me. All I cared about was where I was. And where I wanted to go. And why it was taking so long to get there.

It'd been two years since I'd lost my stripe. Every time I found myself mowing a lawn, or saw a young white guy with no skills and two stripes, I just got more bitter. If Pugh gave me a crap detail, I'd tell him I wasn't doing it, so then he'd have to give me another, and another, and while working those details, I'd think about my Harlem daydreams—about what I'd hoped for and where I'd ended up—and I'd feel pretty bad. So one day I just did it: I told Pugh I deserved a promotion, and if I didn't get one soon, I wasn't sure why I should stay in the Air Force. I'm not sure what I expected. But here's what happened. Pugh said, "You're right."

Not two weeks later, I had my stripe.

I knew right away that this was one of those growing-up moments. Knew I'd learned a lesson. And I was glad for it. But tired, too. So tired. Because my lesson hadn't come easy. And because I now knew that if I wanted something—no matter how easy it seemed to come to others—I'd have to take it.

8

A Real Person

February 13, 1960, marked four years in the force and the end of my initial enlistment. With zero hesitation, I re-upped for another six. My plan, the one I'd hatched as a squirmy Harlem kid, hadn't changed at all: I was going to put in my twenty years, learn whatever I could, and sock away enough cash that come 1976, I could quit working forever and focus on photography. Admittedly, I hadn't snapped a single photo since leaving Harlem. But I knew somehow that when the time was right, I'd start again, and I'd never stop. And meantime, on the military's dime, I was going to see as much of the world as I could. The day I reenlisted, I told my first sergeant for about the thousandth time that I was ready for transfer, as soon as possible, to anywhere besides Greenland. And then I took all of my leave—I'd by this point accumulated a full month—and boarded a plane bound for New York.

Since leaving Harlem, I'd been back once or twice, for visits so short I barely recall them. Now, though, I had all sorts of time, and more importantly, I had two stripes on my coat, four years under my belt, some hard-earned swagger. Whether it was because of all of that, I don't know, but from day one things just felt different, especially with my father, who was now asking me questions like he thought I might be a real person. And while I appreciated this—appreciated being seen, finally, as I saw myself—I didn't exactly sit around and soak it up. I was twenty-one, flush with military cash, free of responsibility. I spent that month doing what I'd long dreamt of, which was whatever I wanted.

I'd brought along this guy, Douglas—he'd come to Enid halfway through my tour, and we'd become fast friends—and all month, we lived it up. We rode the subways, saw the big sights, hit every jazz club: Birdland, the Blue Note, the Half Note, Smalls Paradise. Smalls, that was Wilt Chamberlin's place. At some point, we met him—I don't recall a thing I said, only that I had to look up so high it made my neck hurt—and saw some great acts at his club, including Cannonball Adderley, whom I mistook for a preacher because he wore a black suit and a white thing around his neck that looked like a cross (Douglas later explained it was his sax strap). We caught Cannonball again at the Five Spot, and saw Yusef Lateef there, too, maybe a half-dozen times, eventually striking up a sort of friendship with him, such that whenever we walked in, he'd play a piece off *Happyology*, my favorite of his records. My sister sometimes came out with us, and one night at Birdland, her earring fell off, and we all crawled under the table, and as we were pawing around on the sticky floor, searching, a fourth person joined us, holding a lit match, and I looked up and saw that it was Ahmad Jamal.

I remember those nights like they were last week. Standing in small, low-lit rooms that smelled of cigar smoke and cologne. Rubbing shoulders with impossibly hip people. Watching the very same musicians I'd listened to during my worst days in Enid, and feeling their horns and keys and strings and hi-hats wash right through me. Walking to the subway with Douglas, recounting the night and scheming on the next. Sitting in a train car, bones vibrating, ears ringing, thinking: years ago, in my sixth-floor cage, I'd imagined that life might feel exactly like this.

And man, I just loved the chance to show Douglas a good time, given all he'd shown me. The year before, he'd taken me home to New Orleans, where he taught me to fashion knives from hacksaw blades and to hand-weave nets, and took me fishing pretty much every day. And just generally, back at Vance, Douglas was kind of a mentor to me. He came to my basket-ball games, talked me down when I got too riled up, and gave me all sorts of smart advice. There was one day when I'd come back to the barracks, fuming about having caught another nothing job—sweeping a swept floor or mowing a mowed lawn—and Douglas, who was fixing one of his nets, just looked up and said, "Look, it's your mouth gets you in trouble. You don't want to do something? Don't. But don't *announce* it. If it's busy work, the only way they'll know you didn't do it is if you tell them so." At first I was too stubborn to listen. But eventually I relented, and I tried what he'd suggested—nodded when I caught crap details, then quietly skipped doing them—and just like that, the crap details stopped coming. I appreciated Douglas so much for that: for helping me get out of my own way. And so I was happy, here in New York, to be returning the favor, to be showing him something he might never have found on his own.

Besides my family, Douglas was really the only person I hung out with. There just weren't other options. So many of the boys I'd grown up with—boys I'd watched, longingly, from my sixth-floor window—were just gone, erased from the city. So-and-so had overdosed. Such-and-such had shot somebody. Or been shot. It was so, so sad when I thought about it, which, mostly, I didn't. I was still a youngster, a hair past twenty-one, and I just wanted to enjoy being where I was, living big in the city I'd always wanted more of. On some level, though, I think I knew that had I not left to join the force—had my cooped-up childhood not compelled me to—I, too, could've ended up erased.

One night, Douglas and I stayed out till nearly dawn. It was a weekday, so as we walked home from the subway, the streets were empty, the quiet broken only by our laughter. When we turned the last corner, I looked up, as I always had, to see if there was anyone at our window, and I thought I saw someone. But a second later, I looked back up and nobody was there. We crept in, went to bed, slept late. But not long after I woke, my mother took me aside and told me I needed to be more respectful of my father, who'd stayed up all night waiting for me, then got up at six for work. In the moment, I think, I shrugged it off. But that image—my father, sitting up—it stuck with me. I think that's when I began to see him as I'd wanted him to see me: as a real person. Someone who felt things, who was trying his best. I can't say I stopped resenting him entirely. Not yet. But on some level, I understood his sternness, his rules. Even almost appreciated them.

9

Outcomes

About a year later, about halfway between here and there, I pulled my Ford into the lot of a two-pump gas station. It was a run-down building, sagging into itself, the sort of place you'd pull past if you could. I couldn't. I needed gas. As I waited for the tank to fill, I looked my car over. I'd added chrome lake pipes and lowered the back end until it nearly kissed the ground, and it was full of records, clothes, everything I owned. When the nozzle clicked off, I headed in, and at the counter an old man was giving me a leer I'd long since gotten used to. When I paid and asked for a bathroom key, he just thumb-pointed over his shoulder. "Back there," he said. So I went outside and did my business in the dirt, then walked to my car, feeling relieved, as I always did when leaving places like this. As I was sliding in, though, I noticed my leather coat was gone. It'd been on the seat, and now it was gone. I shut my eyes. Talked myself down. This was a white man, and we were in a white nowhere, his nowhere, the sort of nowhere that could swallow up men like me. So I got in my car and fired the engine, pulled from the lot and drove. And soon, too soon, I was in Denison, Texas. My new home.

After a mostly uneventful fourth year in Enid, the Air Force had an-nounced, abruptly, that they were closing Vance. For a moment, I felt deep joy—*finally*, I was leaving—but then I got my new assignment: a base

86

called Perrin, in a state called Texas. I'd told my superiors, over and again, that I wanted Greece, Germany, Saudi Arabia—wherever, so long as it was far away—but here I was, back in Texas. It'd taken four hours to drive from Enid to Denison. I didn't feel like I'd gone anywhere at all.

It was, at least, an easy transition. Denison was bigger than Enid, and the Texas twang was a bit twangier, and there were a few more trees, but otherwise, little had changed. I was still in the barracks, still working radios, still one of a few Black guys on a mostly white base. Given all the growing I'd done at Enid, coming to Perrin almost felt like cheating: I knew what this place was and how to make it work for me. And having just seen Benjamin Davis become the first-ever Black Air Force general, I felt a little more hopeful than I had in Enid. So I dove in at the shop. I made sure to show my NCO I was a serious man, deserving of responsibility. I accepted my details and did them well. Overall, I just strove to enjoy my work—and when I clocked out into the Texas night, I strove to enjoy that, too.

Seeing how I had that flashy car, it wasn't real hard to make friends. Before long, I had a pair of Geralds (Ford and Burke) and one Edwin Ransom. We were all from New York except Burke, who'd grown up in Georgia. Burke played drums for a rhythm-and-blues band, and sometimes we'd join him at his gigs in one-horse towns (I made myself band manager, which meant little, though I did print some neat business cards). Mostly, though, we'd just cruise downtown Denison, which had bars, or go to Sherman, which was dry but had a Black community center that held dances. One night, we headed there to see Bobby Blue Bland. I'd just installed these Lancer hub caps with amber lights in the wheel wells that flashed as the car rolled along, so we drove around Sherman, then headed to the show. We were there for hours, dancing, talking—by this point, I'd figured out how to talk to girls—and when we finally left, I was feeling good, right up until I saw my car. Somebody'd chopped the locks off my valve stems and stolen those Lancers, left me with four flats and no hubcaps. I climbed into the car and I sat, silent, in the dark. My plan was: if the person who'd done it came back, I'd whip his ass. After a few hours, I called a tow truck.

At one of those dances, I met a girl from a small town south of Sherman. We dated for a while, and it was nice except for the drive to her house. I was *always* getting pulled over. Like I said, I'd lowered my Ford's back end, and since she lived in a dry county, I'd get stopped by cops who wanted to look in my trunk, see if I was hauling moonshine. Which seemed crazy to me. I mean, if I'm hauling bootleg, why would I do it in such a flashy car? Well, it kept happening, and I think they got how silly it was, because they began apologizing. "Airman Brown," they'd say, "we're sorry, we know you're not a bootlegger, but your car, it's . . . we've got to check." And though it never felt threatening, it was pretty annoying. Anyway, at some point I lowered the front end, too. And they stopped stopping me.

In those years, at least, the cops were less an issue than the civilians. Not a few of the male civilians hated us airmen. I couldn't blame them. Denison and Sherman were small cities, where little changed, where there wasn't much money to be made, and then here we came, every weekend, with fresh faces and military money. We were more desirable. We symbol- ized a way out. The men, at least, saw it that way. Black or white, they didn't trust us, ever. I'd feel it whenever I was in town, in the way guys looked at me, in what they did and didn't say. A few times, it boiled over into fights, and a year after I got to Texas, a civilian shot a guy from base. Killed him. We all went to Sherman less after that.

We didn't waste much time on Denison, either—the only club I recall was rimmed by a moat-like ditch and catered to an older crowd—but we were always going to Dallas. Come Friday, we'd pack in the car—me, Edwin, the Geralds, whoever could fit—and we'd take off for the hour-long drive. By this point, I'd traded the Ford and gotten a '54 Mercury, which I'd decked out with a nice radio, plush seats, and a console bar with space for two bottles and six steel cups; by the time we got to Dallas, we'd be feeling good, the windows would be down, and we'd be singing. This guy Laverne owned a home there, and we'd stay with him. Fridays, it'd be a big party at his place; Saturdays, we'd cruise town, maybe see jazz at the Omar Khayyam, a little club with great local acts where you'd take your shoes off and sit cross-legged on pillows on the floor, which seemed like just the coolest thing; and on Sundays, always, we'd be at the park in our best suits, talking with whichever girls we'd met, making plans for the next weekend.

One Saturday night in Dallas, Edwin and I went to see Ray Charles. We were wearing matching outfits—we did this a lot—and halfway through, when Charles started playing "What'd I Say?," we crept from our seats to rows on either side of our section and stumbled down the steps, slipping, tripping like we were sloppy drunk. Soon, everyone around was looking and laughing. When security came for us, we slipped into the aisle and started dancing the twist—this was when the twist was the thing—and then melted back into the crowd. And the next day as we were walking downtown, still in our suits, two girls stopped us, starstruck, to ask how long we'd been part of Ray's show.

I just *loved* Dallas. Went there whenever I could. It was no New York, but it was a city, a place where you could disappear for a night, no matter who you were. I wish I could've said the same for Sherman, for Denison, but in those cities—puffed-up towns, really—you never forget who you were or how you were seen. And so you mainly stuck to the Black neighborhoods, and that was fine. Occasionally, though, you had to go downtown. You wanted to find a record, get a watch fixed, whatever. And no matter how your day had been going, when you got there, you couldn't help but hear every person, every passing car, every sidewalk crack whispering, *Go home, n* ——. The best thing, really, was to avoid the place, try to forget it existed. But eventually, inevitably, it'd remind you.

Like in 1963, when a Black guy from Perrin won Airman of the Year. Per tradition, the Air Force had a celebration for him at a nice restaurant downtown—white tablecloths, prime rib, that sort of place—but when this Black airman showed up, the doorman wouldn't let him in. Said he had to use the back door. To go to his *own* celebration. Word about that got around base in no time, and when I heard about it, I was just furious. I didn't even know the guy, but I felt like it'd happened to me. So I decided I'd organize a demonstration. I'd never done anything like that before, and in hindsight, I guess it seems like a pretty big deal. But then, it didn't. Then, it was something I was going to do.

I huddled up with a few others, and we made a plan, and the gist was that a bunch of airmen would go to that restaurant, and when we got turned away, we'd get in our cars and drive laps around the lot, until it felt like a parade or maybe a funeral procession. Soon, we had a lot of guys on board. I was getting excited. But a few days before the protest, an hour south of us, JFK got shot. And one of the airmen who'd been helping us plan—a white guy from New Hampshire—he knew people who knew people who knew MLK's people, and MLK's people said that, in honor of JFK, they were putting a moratorium on all actions. So we put ours off. Waited a few days, then a week, then two. Eventually, it faded away. At the time this was hugely disappointing, but looking back, I think I just feel proud. For the first time, I'd gotten beyond myself, tried to do something for Black people. And though I wouldn't have called it activism, and I definitely didn't see it as a win, that was then, and I was still pretty young, too young to grasp that activism isn't always about outcomes.

And anyway, it wasn't long before I got another go at organizing. The impetus, this time, was dancing. Every week, the club held dances, and the base would bus girls in from Texas Woman's University, and that was nice except all the girls were white, which meant we Black airmen never got to partner-dance. I loved dancing, and I was good at it, so I asked—I did, and a few other guys, too—if the base would consider bringing in some Black girls. That went nowhere fast, so I decided, again, to plan a demonstration. At the next dance, when the women showed up, I pulled a few aside and shared my plan: as soon as the band played a fast song, all the Black guys would ask white girls to dance. No hugging, I said, just dancing. They were for it. When the time came, we all asked, and they said yes, and we danced for a minute, maybe, but then the music cut, and the lights came up, and the white woman who ran the club stepped onto the stage. "The dance is over," she said. "Go home."

Next thing I knew, I was at the base police station, answering questions. The club's director, I guess, had fingered me as the agitator. So the police laid into me, let me know how *dangerous* my little stunt was, and that there could've been real problems, and so on. I didn't speak much. Just let them say what they needed to say. Even when they mentioned the thing at the restaurant—"We know about that, too"—I kept quiet. I knew they were just trying to intimidate me. And I wasn't going to let them. In the end, nothing happened. They said I was free to go. I said alright, didn't say *sir*, and left. And then, as soon as I could, I went on down to TWU with a few other Black airmen and we met some Black girls and made a plan. The day of the next dance, when the base bus showed up at TWU, those Black girls just got on with the white girls—the driver either didn't care or know better—and rode up to Perrin. When they arrived, we were waiting, and we escorted them off the bus into the club. All night, we danced. Sure, we caught stares from white airmen and the owner. But the band kept playing. Nobody gave us crap. And it went like that for the next dance, and the next, and the next.

But then time did what it does, and one morning I woke up and realized I'd been in Texas for five years. And in the South for almost ten. For ten *years*. I'd been doing whatever I could to stay something like happy—partying, driving with the guys to small-town funk shows, gambling at the club, and going out when and where it felt safe—but I was starting to struggle. Because that little Harlem Richie, he hadn't gone anywhere. He still sat on my shoulder, always, and if things got quiet, he'd whisper in my ear, remind me of why I'd joined the military and how far I was from where I wanted to be. And where I wanted to be was somewhere, *anywhere* else. "Anywhere but Greenland," I'd say to my NCO, whenever I could, with a forced smile. And my NCO, he'd nod, but he wouldn't say the words I needed to hear. And then a month would pass, and another, and another, and I'd get even more miserable, desperate, bored.

Even in my work, I was bored. On the one hand, I liked knowing that I could fix any and every radio system, blindfolded, and I liked being the shop's de facto trainer, liked being seen and respected and appreciated for my expertise; but on the other, I needed something, anything, to change. So when I heard one day that there was about to be an opening in Perrin's missile shop, I beelined it to personnel and threw in my name. Two weeks later, it was goodbye radios, hello missiles.

Overnight, I found myself back at the bottom, doing humdrum crap work. But the thing about the missile shop was that even crap work was cool. We worked in secure situations with clearances, and we were always passing through checkpoints, like in the movies. And the *danger*, man. After a half-decade of radios, I was now working with explosives, propellants, warheads. Given my expertise with electronics, and what I was learning was an uncommonly good work ethic, I moved up quickly. Before long, I was put in charge of an evaluator system, checking compatibility between missiles and firing systems. It was a complex job, involving fancy instruments and a ton of record-keeping, but the long and short of it was, I made sure the plane and the missile were talking. If they weren't, that was a problem, and I'd make sure it got fixed. I'd keep tabs on the components, too: the warhead, fuse, and rocket motor all had an explosive component, and as they aged, they could become unstable. I tried to prevent that.

And I guess it's like they say about watched pots not boiling, because not so long after I'd switched to missiles, at the end of a week when I'd truly enjoyed my work, word came down that I was going to be transferred to another missile shop. In the *Philippines*. I didn't know a thing about the Philippines, but man, I was elated. No, I wasn't going to Paris, like James Baldwin and Langston Hughes, but I was headed somewhere far away, far enough to reignite my dreams, to remind me that I was an artist, biding time as an airman. So I said goodbye to Edwin and the Geralds and the rest. I stuffed all I owned into my latest car, a red Corvair. And I drove away from the South, over the Rockies, and out to the coast. Once there, I parked my car on a freighter and myself in a plane. I sat in my seat, eyes on the ocean below, thinking of my stamps with their pictorials of places I'd never been. I thought of every bright day I'd spent indoors, looking at those stamps, aching to step into them. And then I shut the sunshade. I sat back in my seat. And I slept till the tires touched the ground.

The Club

April 2017

It's ten to nine on a rainy Thursday, and I'm here, again, at the club.

I wasn't planning on coming to the club. Not tonight. Just ten minutes ago, I was in my car, radio off, driving through the dark toward home. I was feeling sour, having sat too long at the Nabvets social, where I got into it again with Albert, who loves to vent about racist cops and racist laws and racist racism but all but calls me a house Negro if I try to talk solutions. When I left, I told myself that for once I'd go home, go to bed at an hour befitting an almost-eighty-year-old. As I drove, though, I started getting that feeling. The weepy feeling. The one that seems, as of late, to strike whenever I slow down. And then I guess autopilot must've taken over. Because here I am, walking into the club.

Already, half the tables are full, and most of the stools, too. My friend Bob's sitting over by the taps, and just past him, grinning down at a phone, is a youngster I know from way back. I recognize most of the rest, too, even if I can't quite say where from, so I make my rounds, say my hellos and my hey-how-you-doings, and when that's done, I head for a stool, my stool, at the high table near the front door. I pull off my coat and cap, and for the first time all day, I relax. There's a bop tune—Mingus, maybe?—playing over the speakers. Blue lights splash the red brick walls. On the stage in the corner, three guys are running cables, tightening cymbals, and I know all of them, though I don't know that I could tell you their names. The drummer gives me a nod. I nod back. And as I do, Beth appears from the kitchen, and when she sees me, she trots out from behind the bar to give me a hug.

"*Mister* Brown," she says, smiling.

I've known Beth since she was three feet tall. Met her in the eighties, when her family hired me to take their picture. In the years to come, I saw her here and there, and then, after her daddy died—too early, of cancer—I just made it a point to be involved. I caught a few of her soccer games, gave advice if she asked, and once she was old enough, I began inviting her to join me in my work. She became a regular on this foot patrol I ran, even joined me for sit-downs with Portland Police. She left town at some point for Atlanta and was gone awhile, but a few years ago, she came back. Now she's tending bar, driving a school bus, finding her way back into the work. Just last week, in fact, a fellow driver had approached her about organizing a union, and she wanted to know what I thought about that.

Now, we chat, we catch up. But there's not too much to catch up on, seeing how I was here last night, and the night before. Lately, I always seem to be at the club. And it's not about drink. I've never been much of a drinker. Maybe I'll have some wine, or a rum and coke, but just as often, I'll stick to water. Because I'm not here to catch any buzz. Or, rather, I am, but it's got nothing to do with alcohol.

I follow Beth to the bar, and she pours me a glass of red, and as I walk back to my stool, I hear cymbals rustling and the whack of a tom and the band is off, the sax player riding a melody I know I've heard. Just like that I'm flashing back to New York—to Small's, to the Five Spot—trying to figure out who I've seen play this song. And here comes that buzz. Needles and waves, forehead to toes. This place, it gets me feeling like myself. The music, the sea of Black faces, the ones who know when and how to show respect to us who came before—it fills me up. Feels more like home than home.

Solae's, this club is called. It's the sole Black-owned bar on a street that used to brim with them. Alberta Street. For decades it was a main artery of Black Portland, full of, on the one hand, barber shops and burger joints and soda fountains, and on the other, dope sales and drive-bys and activists working to stop both. In those years, Alberta was the street that white people would drive ten minutes out of their way to avoid. Now, though? I barely recognize it. Just a bunch of coffee shops and bike shops and vegan bakeries and artisanal ice creameries and who-knows-what-else. It's something new every day. And honestly, I don't pay attention anymore. If I'm on Alberta, I'm probably at the club.

Funny thing is, I've only been coming out, to this or any club, for a few years. My first four decades in Portland, I just did the umpteen activist things I was doing, and then I went to sleep. One night a few years ago, though, I was working on a project that involved the guy who ran the Elks Club, and he suggested we meet there. Well, I hadn't even gotten off my coat before some guy came up and started shaking my hand, going on about all I'd done for him back when he was stuck in that gang life. Only then did I recognize him as one of the dozens of boys I'd met at the House of Umoja, a residential facility for gang-affected youth where I used to spend time. That same night, two others came up, with thank-yous and do-you-remembers, and I also ran into folks I'd coalitioned with on this police issue or that school boycott, as well as a woman whose family I'd photographed. I went home feeling *great*. I'd never thought I was the sort who needed affirmation about my work—nothing, at least, beyond support I'd get from folks I was working with—but now, I was thinking: how did I *ever* do what I do without getting some backslaps and attaboys? So, a few nights later, I went back to the Elks. Then I went back again. And when Solae's opened, I started stopping in quite a bit, and also frequenting Daddy Mojo's down on Fremont. Before long, I was out most every night, catching up with troubled boys turned good men, getting treated much like I, as a boy, had treated men like Mr. Gill.

Now there's a hand on my shoulder, and a young woman wearing cashmere and bangles is saying, "Hey, aren't you Richard Brown? The photographer?"

I shrug and say, "I was."

I don't think she hears me, though, because now her eyes are going soft, and she's smiling and saying, "I *remember* you. You're the one who documented Black Portland."

I know this is a compliment, but still, I wince. Because it's never been my goal to just be some documentarian. Sure, I get it: my pictures likely will become a document of how Black Portland was in the eighties and nineties, and that's fine. But that was never my aim, and I want people to know. I want them to know I wasn't a documentarian, then. I want them to know I'm an artist, always. Still, I haven't taken a good picture in years, and that's no one's fault but mine, so I smile at this kind woman and ask where we met and what she's up to now, and then we hug and I get back on my stool.

When I go to take a sip of my wine, I find the glass is empty. Already. This is why I don't drink. I'm not a sipper. I always finish what I've ordered before I've tasted it, so for the sake of my wallet and my liver, I rarely have more than one. Still, I want something to hold onto, so I head to the cooler to pour a cup of water. As I pour, I try to take in the music—the band's playing "Caravan," one of my favorites—but I just can't. I'm stuck on what that woman said about my pictures. I'm drifting into myself, into my thoughts. And my thoughts, as usual, are leading me to my basement.

My *basement.* Just the thought of it jacks up my pulse. For years, that place was such a haven. In one corner I had my darkroom; in another was the shop where I built photo frames. I had a model car workstation, too, and a little setup for fixing amplifiers. Sure, there were always lots of boxes and books and what-not, but that stuff was mostly shelved. The basement was where I *worked.* Now, though? It's a disaster zone. It's like my life avalanched all over itself. If I want to find a frame I made in 1987, I have to dig through clothes I wore in 1959, letters I didn't send in 1973, curricula I taught in 2006. Then I'll start reading the letters, or trying on the clothes, and at some point I'll look up and realize I don't know why I even came downstairs. So then I'll tell myself, Richard, you got to get organized. You *got* to. And I'll pick a day to do that. But then that day will come, and an hour in, I'll have only made more of a mess, and something in that mess will have unearthed a feeling I've tried to forget, and suddenly I'll be in tears, in my basement, alone. So then I'll quit and come back to the club.

I'm on my way to my stool when Lawrence stops me. Seems like every other time I come here, I see Lawrence, a big man with a big smile and, usually, a big beer. I met him years ago in a program for Black men on parole, which I did and still do facilitate; I call it "the group." Back then, Lawrence was a Crip, a dope seller addicted to his product, a man trying but failing to get out of that cycle of offending and reoffending and re-reoffending. He stayed there for a long time. And then, one week, he was just gone from the group. At the time, I doubted that meant anything good, but one night a year or so back, I ran into him here. And man, he was glowing. He proceeded to tell me all about his job—he'd gotten into remodels—and about the home he'd bought with his wife, and about how he felt he owed *all* of that to the group, and to me. He still says that, every time we see each other. Now, he's leaning in, talking fast, about how he and his wife just found out that they're about to have their first child. And that news is enough to bring back that good buzz and flush out whatever I'd begun building up. So I smile, and I ask him about boy-or-girl, about what names are on his list, about what else is good, and then he hoists his glass and I hoist mine and I turn for my table and run right into Damon.

Damon, he's another guy I know from way back.

He's my protégé, too, though he maybe doesn't know it yet.

I give Damon a hug and a hey-how-you-doing, and he says he's doing fine. For a bit, we chat about a record he just found—he's into jazz, too—but soon, we're talking shop. Talking cops. Damon's the only other Black civilian I know who does deep work with police. So we talk about that. A lot.

I met Damon, like Beth, when he was little. Took his picture at some Urban League event. I know this because a few years ago he called me and asked me to coffee and showed me that picture. He said he'd never forgotten how warm I was with him when I took it. As he got older, he kept an eye on me, on what I did and how, and overall, I ended up being a big reason he got into his work. He's got a consulting outfit, and he gets hired in Portland and beyond to do trainings on implicit bias, on ethics, on the stuff I find important. Does it well, too. He's smart, and he's got a good compass, and he knows there's nothing new when it comes to cops and Black folks. So, when he's struggling? He calls me. We talk. I give him advice. I also, from time to time, tell him I think he ought to get himself on the board of the Academy. I tell him he's got the mindset and know-how. I tell him he'd be perfect.

Now I tell him that again.

And Damon just smiles and says, "Someday, maybe I will."

I want to tell him what I've told him many times before—that it doesn't have to be for him what it is for me, that he can do what other board members do and just attend four meetings a year, that the point is, we need a smart, savvy Black person there, in the room, while decisions are being made—but I bite back those words. I remind myself that I took *my* time getting to where I am. And that it was important for me to move gradually and I guess it is for him, too. So I just nod and say, "Alright, then."

We talk for a while longer, and then he's got to go, so I give him a shake and return to my stool. I'm feeling good, like I always do after seeing Damon. I like that he asks questions, *real* questions, and listens to the answers. Many youngsters, I find, don't do that. Take this sister I spoke to last week. She said she was running for school board and asked if she could count on my support. I had never *met* this woman, but here she was, asking me to cosign, sight unseen. So I told her what I thought. I told her she had to do more than just run. I told her she had to do the real work, the years-and-years work, the organizing and coalitioning, such that, the next time she came to me with a clipboard and a cash bag, I'd be able to say I'd been watching and I'd liked what I'd seen. Well, she didn't like my ideas. She felt I was being brash. Which, hell, maybe I was. I come on strong, I know that. But I learned, years ago, that folks will take offense no matter how you say what you say, so I've stopped trying to make things sound nice. And anyway, my intentions are good. My feeling is, I'm eighty years old, and if I've amassed anything by this point, it's information. This sister, though, she didn't want information. She wanted a rubber stamp. So in the end, I gave her one. I gave her my name and a twenty. I gave her my card, too, and told her to call me. And I hope she will, after she loses this election—which she will—so we can talk about how she might do that work that'll get her elected next time.

The sax player's in the middle of a dizzying solo, all scales and squeals. I watch him for a while, then turn and look outside. My stool is in front of the window that faces Alberta, which is why I sit here. I like that I can see what's happening—in the bar and on the street—all at once. And what's happening on the street is, two white people are trying to decide if they're going to come inside. It's a man and woman, middle-aged. They're standing under an umbrella, and something about the way they're leaning close and talking at the ground tells me they probably just looked at me.

Probably they're discussing, in one language or another, whether they'll feel more guilty walking in or away.

And now my face is going hot. Because a few weeks ago, in this same spot, I saw two white girls holding a banner, longer than I am tall, that said, *Is Portland racist?* Two white girls, standing outside Alberta's only Black bar, asking *that*. As soon as I saw it, I stormed out and asked the girls what they had in mind, standing *here* with that banner. One of them said they'd been downtown, and the answer they'd gotten there was that nobody thought Portland was racist. So they came here. At that, I lost it. I asked if she had any idea what she was doing—if she was aware that she'd just asked me to rip out my guts and dump them on the table just so she could have a look. Then I spun and went back inside. The girl, to my surprise, followed me. She said she wanted to talk. So I obliged her. I told her exactly what I thought of her project, and I kept telling her, and before long, she was crying. Which made me feel bad. I tried to console her, and I told her it wasn't personal, it was just that I'd grown so tired of being asked questions by white people who had no plan for what they'd do with my answers. It took awhile, but she composed herself. She said she'd come back soon, sans banner, to talk. And I told her I'd welcome that, and that she ought to bring her teacher, too, because now I had an assignment for her: how about, instead of sending white kids to ask Black folks to do a show-and-tell with our mangled guts, *you* do the work, in *your* class, to help these kids understand how gentrification happens, and why, and why white people only want to talk about it when it's ten years too late?

That was a few weeks ago. I haven't seen that girl again. I doubt I will.

The couple's leaving. I can't tell if that makes me happy or depressed. Can't tell how I'm feeling at all. I try to focus on the music, on what's around me, but time passes, and keeps passing, and even as I hear more songs I love, as I get hugged and attaboyed by more men whose lives I don't recall changing, I find myself doing the thing I can't stop doing these days: I start tearing up. Before I know it, I'm sinking out of the club, down into my chest, into those dark halls I've managed to steer clear of for so long. I stand up, shrug into my coat. I know I need to just do it: spend time with my basement, myself. I know that. But first—I need some air. So I step out of the club, and into my car, and I drive.

PART III

NO DESTINATION BUT THE DRIVE

Here, There, and Everywhere

1966–1976

10

Light Casualties

One morning, a week after arriving in Angeles, the Philippines, I was getting ready for work when I saw some boys huddled in a half-moon outside
my apartment. They were staring at the fish tank I'd placed near the window. Didn't seem like they'd seen me, so I set down my coat, and I watched
them watching. In Harlem, we'd kept fish. Guppies and swordtails, mollies
and platyfish. Sometimes one of the bigger fish would try to eat a baby,
and my siblings and I would swat the tank, screaming, until the aggressor
fled and hid under an upturned pot. There wasn't any such drama here
in Angeles, but still the boys were riveted, watching the tank like it was
television. As they stood, looking in, I thought about those long Harlem
days, looking out. I thought about what I'd wanted and how far I'd felt
from getting it. And then I stepped outside, and I waved at the boys, and I
told them what I knew about my fish.

It'd taken nine years and a placement in the Philippines, but I'd finally gotten an off-base apartment. The place was a two-bed, and I shared
it with a younger guy named Smiley. I'd only just met him but he felt like
family, in no small part because he, too, was from Harlem—his dad, a
boxer, had sparred at the same YMCA where I'd met Jackie Robinson. Our
landlord, Arvin, also happened to be Angeles's chief of police, and I don't
know whether he just liked me or was grooming me for favors or both, but

within days of my arrival, he'd hired this guy, Danilo, to be my handyman and chauffeur. I declined the latter—no way was anyone else driving my Corvair—but said yes to the rest, because I liked Danilo and liked feeling I was helping him get along. Smiley and I would play him records and tell him about America, and he'd show off his karate moves and insist we let him teach us (we didn't), and we'd all sit on the steps, telling stories, as kids gaped at the fish tank and red jeepneys whizzed by.

Still, I sometimes felt like I'd never left Texas. Every morning, I'd drive to an American base to inspect American missiles; most nights, I'd sit at the servicemen's club with Americans; and when I ventured into Angeles, I'd often end up at a bar full of Black airmen—eight thousand miles from the South, and still there were Black bars, white bars, and tracks between. I'd learn, later, that this was common—where our military goes, our racist structures follow—but back then, it blew my mind: their city, built to our flaws. Filipinos hung out on both sides of the tracks, but they weren't saints, either. Their country had a long history of prejudice toward Indigenous Negritos, and everywhere you looked, there was a billboard, a newscast, a skin product whispering *light skin is better.* One night at one of those Black bars, a Filipina told me a white veteran had told her that Black people still had tails.

The farther you got from base, though, the less you felt all of that stuff. So whenever I could, I got out of American Angeles and met Filipinos on their turf. Manila was only a few hours away, so I'd often drive down and just get lost. I remember streets full of open-top busses and rumbling jeepneys, horses hauling carts stacked high with grain, Coca-Cola signs on every corner, and music everywhere. There was a huge Latin scene—mambo, cha-cha, tango—and *everyone* was a good dancer. One day, I ended up in a town between Angeles and Manila with my friend Sylvester—a Mississippian with a secret fear of bats—and in this town, they were having a celebration. At some point, tango dancing started, and these old folks got out there. It looked like they were a thousand years old, but *man*, could they move. For hours and hours, it was hip swishes and dips, kick steps and elegant twirls. And the whole time I stood to the side, camera around my neck, failing to summon the nerve to snap a picture.

I at least had the equipment. Everything was cheaper overseas, so I'd gone on a spree, gotten a Mamiyaflex outfit, a 35mm setup, and all sorts of darkroom gear. There was a hobby shop on base with a photo section, and I made friends with Jack, who ran it. He'd grown up in a village not far from Angeles, where he'd take me sometimes. It was pretty country—mud-brown rivers, lots of palm trees—and if I'd been into that, I could've gotten some nice pictures. But I was only ever drawn to people. And I was still too timid to photograph them. Sometimes I'd use a telephoto lens I'd picked up, but all the creeping around made me feel like a sniper. So usually I kept the camera at my side, and I kept telling myself what I'd been telling myself forever: there'd be time for pictures when I retired.

I ended up spending a lot of time in Jack's village. It was pretty tiny, pretty remote. Few cars, no stores, just rice paddies and terraced crops and thatch-roofed homes on stilts. One day, they had a christening, or maybe a wedding, and out of a few hundred people, I was the only American. A band was playing, people were dancing, and there were tables full of fruits and meats. Mostly, it was chicken and pork, but there were some red cuts, too, on a platter off to the side. I put some on my plate. Months earlier, at Clark Air Force Base, we'd had a briefing on Filipino food, and what I remembered best was that Filipinos, supposedly, didn't have a word for hot dog; if you ordered one, you might get a hot *dog*. Now, I tried to ignore that. My feeling was, wherever I was, I'd eat what the people ate, drank what they drank; if I got sick, oh well. I still don't know if that meat was dog. Just that I ate it, and it was tough and sweet.

Meanwhile, at work, I found myself in a familiar spot: after three years as a missile man, I'd learned all there was to learn, had become de facto trainer to white men ten years my senior, but still I was stuck at two stripes, watching those men get promotions I deserved. This time, rather than let my feelings fester, I went to my NCO, a guy named Perry. He was small, like I'd once been, and he clearly had angst about it. I recall being in a meeting with him; someone said a thing he disagreed with, and he stood, instantly, and started going off, and you could see that, as he went, he was figuring out what he wanted to say. I liked that: I liked how he took space for himself. Anyway, I said my piece, and he agreed that I was getting a raw deal. So he dug through reports filed by airmen seeking promotions, and he found that some guys had duplicates in their portfolios. The reports gave you a score. Those guys' scores had been doubled. Right away, Perry brought the error—which, we knew, was no error—to his superiors. They made a small stink about it, but in the end, no one could or would explain what'd happened. So nothing changed. The white men kept their promotions. And I got a new thing to resent.

And resentment-wise, I was at capacity. This was 1965—a time when Black people back home were getting hung and beat and bit and hosed while white politicians debated whether we ought to be treated like people—and I was just more aware of all of that than ever before. Partly, this was because I'd become a news-reader, but the headlines, they weren't the half of it. It seemed like every Black man on base had a story, or a dozen stories, about getting mistreated. Stories about sitting in the back of a bus or the backyard of a diner; about getting called n—— by a six-year-old with pigtails; about hiding in the bushes from a truck full of white men; about being harassed, arrested, abused by cops. I had stories, too—about the Atlanta airport, the Enid jail cell, the Denison dance—and I told them often. And the story I told most, it was one that'd just happened, while I was back in New York.

I'd gone there on leave just before flying to Angeles. Mostly, it was a good visit. I saw jazz, bought clothes, tried to not be a stranger to my family. One day, though, my cousin Alan wanted to see an apartment, and I had that Corvair, which I was always looking for an excuse to drive, so I picked him up and off we went. As we drove, we talked, mostly about the Nation of Islam, which Alan and my brother Rodney had joined and about which I knew little. Just after we crossed the Brooklyn Bridge, two cars came up on either side of us, and a voice, amplified by a bullhorn, told us to pull over. So we did. Two plainclothes cops stepped out of those cars and up to mine. "We've got a report," they said, "on two Black men in a new convertible." Then they asked us to step outside. I did what I was told in silence. But Alan? Alan thought their report sounded vague and racist, and he told them so. Next thing I knew, we were at the station in separate rooms. As I sat in mine, I could hear Alan next door, cursing the cops out. When they came for me, I gave them my Air Force ID and told them my leave papers were at home, and they took my card and walked out. Only then did I notice that the station was silent. No Alan yelling. No nothing. I sat there, imagining where Alan might've gone, where *I* might be going, until finally, a cop came back in. He said he'd been trying to validate my identity, and it'd taken a bit, but now I could go. So I did. I didn't play music on that drive home. Didn't tell my folks what'd gone down. But I did think a lot, in the months to come, about those hours in that station. I thought about how I, the cooperative one, had sat in a cell. And Alan, who'd fought back, had been released.

All of that to say, I wasn't feeling gung-ho about the United States. And that was unfortunate, because I had the growing sense that I'd be called, any day, to fight a war in its name. The Gulf of Tonkin thing had happened pretty much the day I arrived, so US troops were now pouring into Vietnam, just a hop and a skip from Clark. Given everything, my feeling was: why would I fight people who never did a thing to me, just because white men in Washington told me to? I was not—am not—a nonviolent person, but I was against that war, one hundred percent. Scared of it, too. My missile shop sat between the hospital and the flight line, and though the radio was always saying we had "light casualties," every day you'd see busses speeding by, loaded with wounded troops. ("Must be the enemy," we'd joke, though no one laughed.) I'd decided I wouldn't fight. If my number came up, I'd leave the service. Period. Sure, I'd have to forego my pension, find a new job and a new life, and all of that'd suck, definitely, but at least I wouldn't have to break my moral code, or get killed, or both.

One day I went to the air terminal to see off a friend who was headed home. After his plane took off, I turned to leave, but I stopped when I saw a young Black Marine in full dress uniform, sitting in a bank of seats along the wall. Me being me, I chatted him up. Turned out the guy was headed to Vietnam. Headed *back*. He'd been there four months already, been wounded three times. And still, he was going back. This Marine, he was twenty, maybe. And he was just one of those guys who earns your respect instantly. I had so many questions for him, but before I could ask, he got called out to his flight. So we said goodbye, and I wished him well, and long after he left, I stayed there, staring, thinking. I didn't know what motivated that guy to keep going back. Just that he was going. And thousands more were, too. Thousands of good kids, American and Vietnamese, doing what they felt they had to and dying for it. And all I could think was, if I was the best missile man in the Air Force—and I'd decided I was—then I had a *responsibility* to go over there, use my skills, help end this war. Now, I look at that, and I see so much arrogance: *I* was gonna end the war, by myself? But in the moment, I felt it strongly. I thought, I can sit here, criticizing. Or I can step in and try to help stop it.

A few weeks later, I was boarding my own flight to Saigon.

Let's be clear from the get-go: I didn't have *that* Vietnam experience. I wasn't Rambo. I didn't crawl around in the jungle, ducking bullets. Really, little in my day-to-day changed. I still worked in a shop, inspecting American missiles. I still lived on base and hung out at a servicemen's club. I even still got out, when I could, and explored Saigon. On days off, I'd often take a taxi downtown, walk around in shorts and sandals, and see where I ended up. I ate all sorts of street food, fell in love with Vietnamese coffee, and made friends with this Muslim Indian, Tariq, who worked as a tailor at a shop back on base. Sometimes after he finished with his work, he'd drive me around Saigon on his scooter, and I'd forget, for a little while, that I was there for a war.

Inevitably, though, I'd get reminded. One day I was walking the Street of Flowers, and I heard, from far off, this awful grinding. The sound got louder and louder, but I didn't grasp that I was hearing tanks, not till they were rounding the corner. The tanks were flanked by men in black pajamas. Enemy soldiers wore black pajamas. Across the way there was a barbershop, so I dashed in, and it was like a Western—as soon as I opened the door, everyone spun and stared. Heart thumping, I asked for a manicure, then sat down. By this point the tanks were rolling by the shop. Everyone else ran to the windows and waved, but I just sat, staring at my reflection. As soon I could, I went back to base.

Even on base things were tense, because at any time we could be attacked. One night a guy came speeding up to the gates on a motorcycle, then blew the thing up; I don't think anyone else got hurt, but I doubt anyone slept that night, or the next. And a week later, when I was on the base bus after a night in Saigon, a voice came over the radio, telling the driver to drop to his parking lights, stay above forty, flash high beams at the gates. Turned out that hours earlier, a guy with a pack had appeared, then vanished. The thought was, it was an enemy combatant carrying explosives, so the base was on high alert. The bus got quiet. And when we got to base, the driver ferried all of us right to our huts. I recall bursting in, heart hammering, and finding the other guys just drinking and playing cards, loaded guns lying at their feet. They knew about the danger. They'd just long since gotten used to it.

I never got used it. Was jumpy, always. I'd never been a heavy sleeper, but now if someone so much as rustled their sheets, I was up, alert, blood pounding in my neck. Our beds were wrapped in netting—the bugs were atrocious—and I'd untuck mine slightly on one side, so that I could roll out and get under the bed if I needed to. Well, one day, we heard that some Indigenous folks—US allies—had been attacked in their village. I didn't think much of it, not until that night when I woke to see the silhouette of a man, near-naked, leaving the hut. He was a big man. And it looked like he was wearing a loincloth. For minutes like hours, I lay on my side, cradling my M-16, staring at the door. Finally, it opened. And I saw, in the light spilling in from outside, a tall white man with a towel around his waist. I let out all my breath. It was a new guy who'd arrived during the night. I hissed at him, asked what he was doing, and he told me he'd taken a shower. I pulled back my sheets and showed him my M-16. Well, he never again took a midnight shower. And I never again had to cuddle my gun. But I never did learn to sleep well in Saigon, either. Couldn't shake the fear that someone was out there, watching, waiting. So when my tour ended a month or so later, I didn't even think of staying on longer. I just took a flight back to Clark, climbed into my bed, and tried to remember how to sleep.

It was a pretty triumphant return at first. Maybe a month after I got back, I was named Clark's Airman of the Year. And that, after years of no stripes and no respect, felt amazing. Sure, I wondered, and still wonder, if it was just a look-good—if the Clark higher-ups decided they ought to hand a trophy to a Black man—but I didn't dwell on that. Because I *deserved* it. In the Clark missile shop, like the Enid communications shop, I'd become the expert, the guy you went to if you didn't understand. And I'd made all sorts of tweaks that'd led to safer inspections, quicker inspections, and overall more satisfying work. So, though I was honored, I wasn't surprised. My overall feeling was: *about time.*

Before my award had begun gathering dust, though, I got pulled from my shop and put on a detail in a barracks full of young airmen. My job was to watch over the Filipino staff—make sure they cleaned the bathrooms, mopped the floors—and after a week, I'd be back to missiles. I wasn't thrilled, but I had three stripes, and everyone with three stripes caught a detail like this, so I should, too. That first day, I reported to the barracks, briefed my crew in. And then I just lazed around. Nobody came to check on me—not that day or the next—and it was seeming like they weren't going to, so one day I just gave my orders and went home. I kept on doing that. It was a cush setup, and I was enjoying it, but something felt off, and the more I thought on it, the odder it seemed that nobody was monitoring me at all. And then, the day before I was to return to the missile shop, I got word that they'd extended my detail another week. So I went to Perry and shared my concerns. He said he'd look into it. Hours later, he called me to his office. And that's how I learned I was under investigation.

For days I racked my brain, trying to figure out what I might've done. All I could think of was that back in Saigon, I'd given my friend Tariq a radio for his birthday. You're not supposed to buy gifts for people outside the military. I'd known that. It hadn't seemed like a big deal. But now, I was sure that was it. For days, then weeks, I just sat, waiting for the call, the questions I knew were coming. Finally, Perry—who'd been checking in daily—decided to act. For some time, he'd been planning to promote me, make me an inspector of Clark's special weapons, a job for which you needed top-secret security clearance. And so now he put in the promotion papers, thinking that he'd force the hand of whoever was behind this. And it worked. The next day, I got a call from someone in the Office of Special Investigations, asking if I could come in for a meeting.

I hadn't been in the waiting room for two minutes before I saw a face I recognized. White guy, blue eyes, billboard forehead. I'd seen him once or twice standing outside Tariq's place. By the time I was called into the office, my whole body was slick with sweat. There were three men, all white, sitting behind a desk. The room silent but for a whistling air conditioner in the window. The guy on the right spoke first. Asked if I'd ever been to Wichita Falls, Texas. Which was just not what I was expecting at all. Relieved, I said, "No," but then he narrowed his eyes and asked, "You sure?" I was about to say yes, but I recalled, hazily, having gone to play ball once at a base in a town called Wichita Falls. So I told him that. He nodded, asked if I'd met anyone there. I shook my head. We'd stepped into some bar, I said, but we didn't like it, so we left. The guy just stared, then repeated, "You're *sure*?" I told him I was, and he nodded, then opened up a file. He wanted to discuss the incidents—*incidents*, he said—from my tenure at Vance and Perrin. They knew about the dance hall protest, the restaurant demo, all my on-base antics. Before I could even begin to respond to any of that, he asked if I knew any Muslims. I paused, let his words settle in, then said that yes, my brother and cousin were Muslim. And yes, I'd been stopped with my cousin, in Brooklyn, but it'd been the cops' error. All three men now began blasting me with questions about how often I talked to that cousin, if I'd been at this meeting or that march. And though I told them the truth, over and over, they kept asking, for what felt like hours.

I didn't yet know about COINTELPRO. Didn't know about any of the awful, unlawful things the FBI was doing to suppress dissident voices in those years. I didn't know about the wiretaps, the agent provocateurs, the letters encouraging Martin Luther King Jr. to kill himself, the memo with the order to "pinpoint potential troublemakers and neutralize them." All of that would come to light in the seventies, but now it was 1966, and I was in a metal chair in a hot room on an island eight thousand miles from the Pentagon. All I knew was that I was scared. I was angry. I was Airman of the Year, and I'd done nothing wrong, and still, I was here. I answered their questions, though. I said what I felt I had to say to get out of that room. And finally, I did. They let me go. Before long, I got word that my clearance had gone through. I began reporting to my new post, and as the months passed, I began to forget about that meeting, those men, their files. I was busy, consumed with my new job. And I was still so naïve. Too naïve to really wonder what was in those files. And to grasp that, once they'd been opened, they'd never really shut.

11

Black Skin and Wire-Rimmed Glasses

A year later, on this or that Sunday, I sat in my idling sedan with a few new friends, looking out over a frozen lake speckled with shoddy little sheds. Ice shanties, they were called. On weekends, white guys would sit in them all day, drinking beer and pulling fish through augured holes. White guys in Michigan did lots of stuff I didn't understand: ice fishing, ice climbing, snowshoeing, snow skiing. I recalled a time when I, in my Harlem walk-up, had longingly paged through picture books of snow skiers. Now, I had no desire to snow ski or ice fish. Now, I just liked to watch white men do it, from a warm car, for an hour or two, before moving on to whatever came next.

It'd taken me a while to warm to Michigan. When I'd arrived on base— a sprawling complex called Selfridge, on Detroit's suburban fringe—I'd been depressed, which had less to do with where I was than where I wasn't. I *really* missed Angeles. After two years there, I'd grown close with a lot of good people, gotten comfy in my little place with the big fish tank, and overall just locked into a nice rhythm: days in the shop, nights at the club, weekends in this rural town or that Manila tango club. Leaving all that behind was hard, especially because I knew by now that I was no good at staying in touch. I'd even lost contact with Douglas, a guy who, for a time, felt like the best friend I'd ever had. He'd visited once when I was in Texas, and we'd talked on the phone some, but then I got shipped to Clark, and life did what life does, and one day I woke up and realized we hadn't spoken in five years. All that to say: I knew leaving Angeles meant saying goodbye, forever, to everyone and everything there. So for a week or two, I moped. But I'd never been much for nostalgia. And I knew this was what I'd signed up for all those years ago, when I'd sat at a window, dreaming of seeing the world. Michigan, I reminded myself, was a part of that. Michigan was part of the world.

It maybe wasn't the most *exciting* part, though. Mt. Clemens, the cookie-cutter suburb just west of Selfridge, had nothing for me. And though Detroit did—I'd visited back when I lived in Enid, and loved it—I didn't go there often, either, besides the rare trip to see a show. I just didn't feel welcome. I'd arrived months after the '67 riot, when the city still felt like a war zone— crumbling concrete, shattered glass, blocks burned to the ground—and the police presence was suffocating. In late 1968, Martin Luther King Jr. and others from the Poor People's Campaign had a rally at Cobo Hall, and I went, but I didn't even get to see them speak because before the thing even started, a bunch of cops showed up on horses, then spun them ass-end toward us and backed us into the hall, where more cops were waiting with big guns and black batons. Before those guns and batons could come out of their holsters, and before I could see how I might respond, I left Cobo Hall and went back to base.

And that, maybe, was the biggest thing keeping me from Detroit: I enjoyed Selfridge. Within weeks, I had a gang of friends, and we were always up to something on or near base. We'd hang out by Lake St. Clair, or drive winding back roads, or play pool and talk smart at the club. I spent a lot of time at that club—more than at any other base—and at some point, somehow, I got hired on as a bartender. I had zero experience, and I still wasn't much of a drinker, but as soon as I started that job, I got real into it. I had a special knack for eyeballing a shot. I was good enough that the club owner, some nights, would set out a rocks glass and bet other patrons that I'd pour two ounces, exactly, and I made sure he never lost. The part I liked the most, though, was all the people. I loved chatting others up, hearing their lies, telling them mine—loved being in the mix, in the center of things, at the heart of what really felt like a community, even if it was just a bar on a base in a Michigan suburb.

I felt like I was thriving, too, in my work. Six months after arriving at Selfridge, I got promoted again, this time up to sergeant, which meant some management responsibility. Finally, I got a say in how the shop ran. And having now spent five years in missiles, I had a *lot* to say. For example, the shop was basically an assembly line. One guy would inspect the delivery system, and another would run electrical tests, and they'd stay in the same stations, day after day, for years. Which, in my opinion, stunk. It was boring and inefficient. Way back when I was in Texas, I'd suggested we instead create teams who would inspect an entire missile system together, so everyone could learn everything. Well, my superiors didn't listen. Not in Texas or in Angeles. Finally, though, at Selfridge, pre-promotion, I was able to convince the NCO in charge of my shop to give it a try. And lo and behold, productivity *and* morale shot way up. Every guy in the shop just *loved* it. After a week, though, that NCO reverted to the old way. He never said so, but I knew the reason: he hadn't thought of it himself. I was pretty upset, but I understood by then that saying so would get me nowhere. So I kept doing my job. And I waited. And a few months later, when that NCO transferred out and I got promoted and tapped to take over the shop, the first thing I did was reinstitute my system.

Not too long after that, on a day when I was feeling particularly good about my work, about myself, about everything, I found myself walking into a Kmart in north Detroit. I guess there must've been a sale on, because I recall there being a bunch of tables set up in the aisles. One had baskets of sunglasses, so I took off my gloves and picked through the pile; I had a few pairs already, but none matched with this suit I'd just bought. This being Kmart, I didn't have high hopes, but I kept digging, through the aviators and rickety clip-ons, looking for whatever I thought I was looking for, until, at some point, as I dug, I felt the air shift around me. I looked up to find a tall white man, standing close, his eyes on mine. Before he even opened his coat, I knew there'd be a badge on his belt.

He told me to keep my hands on the table, then stepped even closer. I tried to hold myself still, to not look nervous, to not look any way at all, even as I took note that this part of the store was now empty—it was just me, this guy, and three more men in matching coats fanned around us. In a voice just above a whisper, the cop told me that his department had a wanted poster with my face on it. My blood was beating hard, my ears ringing, but I said what I knew to be true, that I wasn't on any poster. Now the cop wanted to see my ID, so I reached for my wallet, slowly, then thumbed it open and handed it over. The cop pulled the ID card from its sleeve. He looked at me, and then at the card, and then at me again. Something in his eyes flickered, just for a moment, and then he folded the wallet and handed it back and said, "Well, Sergeant Brown, thank you for your cooperation." And before I could respond, or even catch my breath, he produced a four-by-six from his pocket. "This," he said, "is why we stopped you." I took a look at the picture. And despite the knot in my chest—or because of it, maybe—I almost laughed aloud. I mean, Stevie *Wonder* could've seen it wasn't me. The guy in the photo had black skin and wire-rimmed glasses, but otherwise, the two of us were *nothing* alike. I didn't say that, though. I just nodded, and I let the cop thank me again, and I walked away.

I was out the door in seconds. Out the door, down the street, and speeding back to base, punching the wheel, vibrating with anger. For the rest of the night—the rest of that decade—I told any Black folks who would listen about how I'd been stopped for shopping while Black, and how crazy wrong that cop had been, and how completely I'd kept my own cool. As time passed, though, whenever I thought about that day, what would really begin to stand out was that cop's demeanor: his voice so soft that, at times, I'd had to lean close to even hear him. If he'd been an ass, like the cops that'd stopped me and my cousin, like every cop in every cop story I'd ever heard, who knows how I'd have reacted? Maybe I'd have exploded, raised hell, gotten beat up or locked up or shot. But it hadn't gone like that. Because he'd treated me like a person. He'd made a mistake, and it had cost me a lot of time I could've spent feeling something other than anger, but he'd treated me like a person. And the older I got, the more I'd come to understand how rare this was. Eventually I'd take this memory and tuck it in a cubby separate from the rest. And years on, in a different city, a different season, I'd pull it out and use it as an example of how cops, even when they're wrong, can get some things right.

12

Speed and Other Limits

It was a fifteen-minute drive from Ramstein to Mackenbach, if you skipped the autobahn and took side roads, which, in my four years in Germany, I almost never did. Sure, I liked that backroad route through hilly fir forest, but the few times I took it, all I could think was, man, I could be on the autobahn. So, usually I was—I was out on that civilian superhighway, where everyone always drove ninety, where a commute felt like a race, where I often got passed by people wearing helmets and Nomex suits. I now drove a '68 Triumph with wire wheels and sleek lines and an engine that begged to be opened up, and whenever I could, I did. Music up, windows down, I'd drive to Mackenbach and Kaiserslautern, to Munich and Nuremberg—and as I drove, I'd think about the states, about speed and other limits, and about how good it felt, going so fast and knowing I'd never be told to slow down.

My Harlem dreams, finally, had come true: I'd made it to Europe, to Germany, to just a few hours from the Swiss town where James Baldwin wrote "Stranger in the Village." Which, more or less, is what I was: one of few Americans—and the only Black one—in a small foreign town. Mackenbach wasn't much more than a smattering of homes, a butcher, and a bakery. I lived in a flat in a house beside a leafy park. Most nights I'd stay home listening to records and drinking coffee and eating cheesecake, and on Saturdays I'd walk to the bakery and buy a loaf of black bread still hot from the oven, then sit in my yard sipping tea and eating buttered bread and watching young men play soccer. And if I ever did want life to get louder, I'd hop in the Triumph and head to Kaiserslauten—to buy clothes, see shows—or I'd just stay on the autobahn, cruising, no destination but the drive itself.

That's the first thing I think of when I think of Germany: driving. Ramstein had a racing club, and I joined right away. We mostly just drove parking-lot cone courses or sat at the club, drinking drinks and talking cars, but still, we covered our cars in decals and bought matching fuchsia jackets. I wore mine always, everywhere. And it never got old, seeing the looks I'd get and knowing that, at a given moment, I really might be the only pink-jacket-wearing Black man in the entire country.

We went on little field trips together, too, up to Hockenheim or Nuremberg Ring, where we'd watch the pros. One weekend, we rented a short track and spent the day racing each other. I'd never felt anything like the rush of ripping around that course, so I decided to enter an actual race at a local track. Of that race I recall only that by the time I was done, my leg was shaking so badly I could barely walk. Also, I lost. I lost that race and every other one I entered, save for a slalom where it was just me and a guy in a Corvette, which had too much power for a finesse event. That was the thing: I wasn't a bad driver. In slaloms—in races more about skill than speed—I did okay. But on straightaways, I'd get blown away. The Triumph just wasn't a race car. No matter how well I drove it, and how much money I threw at it, it'd never be one. None of which stopped me from trying. After one race, during which my engine pretty much exploded, I met this German racer, an older guy who went by the name Horse and who happened to be a mechanic. He took one look at the engine, and since it was so clean—I power-washed the thing religiously—he offered to work on it. From then on, I'd go to Horse's house every weekend, and we'd strip and replace and tweak and overhaul until nightfall, when we'd drop our tools and drink crock after crock of the fermented wines and brandies he kept in his crawlspace. None of our work did me any good. I kept losing, and the Germans at the tracks kept shaking their heads at my Triumph and telling me I ought to get a *real* car, a German car. But what I remember far more than any race are those long afternoons I spent tinkering and drinking wine and telling lies in that old German's garage.

Eventually, though, I'd have to leave Horse's place and return to Ramstein Base. And, man, the prejudice at Ramstein was awful, even worse than what I'd seen in the South. I was forever hearing stories from fellow Black airmen about their struggles. One guy, a fireman, after getting promoted to inspector, was so badly harassed by white guys who'd wanted the same job that he'd taken to sleeping with an axe. And then there was the deal about Afros. This being the seventies and the height of Black Power, most every Black man, myself included, wore an Afro. Well, Air Force code stated that your hair had to fit under your hat. Afros didn't. So we were made to get them trimmed, often by white barbers who didn't know a thing about Black hair. If you refused, you were punished. A few guys even got threatened with court-martial. And it was that insult, I think—that insult on top of the persistent structural disparities and the ugly individual acts and the weight of weathering all of this and more for years and years and years—that resulted in a group of us sitting down one night, and then many nights after, to have long, looping conversations that eventually led us to form the Black Action Committee.

Our goal from the first was to help Black guys—especially younger ones—feel some pride. It started with a Sunday get-together in the town park: just a chance for Black men to enjoy each other's company, like Black folks always had. Soon, there were weekly meetings, and study groups where we'd discuss books on race and racism and Black history or just talk about what we faced on base and how we might respond. Afros, for example. What I tried to stress to young guys was, choose your battles. The Air Force wasn't going to change its dress code just because some Black guys wanted it to—not yet, at least—so the trick was to learn how to move within it. When you go to bed, I told them, you throw on a cap and pack your hair in tight so it'll fit under your hat in the morning—but as soon as you get off, take your comb and blow out that Afro as big as you want. And I'd remind them that it's a *job*. That's all. So you work that job, and you do it well, but from the moment you leave until you clock back in, you live like you're out of the military. You don't ever let it define you.

It felt pretty good, giving advice to young guys—having advice *to* give—so as the months passed, I got even more active with the BAC: I helped put on a suit-and-tie-dance, organized some sickle-cell anemia screenings, and got deep into voter registration. McGovern was challenging Nixon, who I loathed, so wherever I went, I carried a stack of forms, signed up as many Black folks as I could. None of this stuff, of course, was world-changing. But I do believe that in our small way the BAC, along with thousands of other groups around the world, helped push the Air Force toward taking its race problem seriously. Suddenly, Ramstein was holding all sorts of talks and trainings; they were bringing in a Black barber to give the white base barbers tips on how to trim Afros; and the wing commander, a good man named Colonel Georgie, was pulling together a "civil rights committee" charged with holding trainings and conducting investigations into race-related offenses, which—because of my efforts with the BAC (by then I was chairman, whatever that meant)—Georgie asked me to join.

If I had to pinpoint the time in my life when I really started thinking of myself as an activist, I might say that it was then, there, on Ramstein Base. Sure, I'd done what I'd done in Oklahoma and Texas, and I guess I could call that activism, but in the moment that hadn't felt political—it was just me being pissed off. I'm not sure, exactly, why things shifted in Germany. Maybe it was the sense, at that time, that everyone, everywhere was in some broader revolt. Maybe it had to do with feeling, finally, like I'd amassed some power. Or maybe it was just seeing young Black airmen, and seeing myself in them and recalling many moments when I'd felt so scared, so alone. All I know for sure is, when I was goading my fellow airmen into voting, and when I was making flyers for this rally or that dance, and when I was sitting with white men talking about what to do about the racist actions of other white men, I knew I was working toward something that felt a little bigger than I was.

Maybe if I'd still been living in Sherman, Texas, or Enid, Oklahoma, or somewhere else I didn't want to be, this would've been that moment, the one when I stepped into my activist future and never looked back. I don't know. Because I wasn't in Sherman, Texas. I was in Germany, in the land of fast cars, good cheesecake, and good people. And I only had a year left on my tour, after which I'd be sent to who-knew-where. So what I did was: I let myself off the hook. I let myself enjoy myself.

There was a solid Turkish population in Germany, especially in Kaiserslautern, where I met a Turkish woman I ended up dating for a time. Whenever we hung out, she'd talk about Turkey—the food, the architecture, the people—and she kept saying we *had* to go to Turkey, and before long I said, "Okay." I took a month's leave as soon as I was able, and we took off in the Triumph. I'd driven across the states several times, but none of those trips had prepared me for this one. In under twenty-four hours, we passed through five—maybe six?—countries, over umpteen mountain ranges, through all sorts of small towns, and each time we crossed a border, it felt like entering a new world. The radio was one of the best parts: we had it on and off the whole time, and though it'd usually be static, as we approached a town, we'd sometimes start catching horns and accordions and warbling voices, music like nothing I'd ever heard. Since the Triumph was just covered in stickers, and I myself was wearing that pink team jacket, pretty much everyone we came across seemed to think I was a pro rally driver. We rarely went long without somebody—another driver, a youngster on the road shoulder, an old lady on a small-town sidewalk—clapping and cheering.

The original plan was to spend half the trip in Turkey, then go to Greece, but once we got to Istanbul, that was the end of it. My friend was right about Turkey. I loved everything she'd mentioned and way more. We stayed in this hotel, the Acropolis, owned by a family she knew who'd come from the country's eastern, tobacco-farming region, and though they spoke almost no English, from day one we got along so well. The old man, the proprietor, loved my Triumph, and told me to park it right up on the sidewalk in front of the hotel. And then he gathered a bunch of us on the hotel's front porch and pulled a watermelon from beneath the steps, and together we ate it with thick sweet Turkish coffee, not really even talking, just taking big bites of melon and sipping coffee and nodding and smiling.

We'd end up repeating that watermelon routine pretty much every day, and afterward we'd play game after game of backgammon and drink our weight in Turkish coffee. I *loved* Turkish coffee. Just everything about it: the taste, the cups they served it in, the rituals around it. One night we were at a restaurant, and I noticed that someone at a nearby table was holding a cup upside down and talking all animated, making his whole party laugh. I asked what that was about and was told it was tradition to tell a fortune when you emptied the coffee. So I did one, on the spot, for the old man. Just made something up. Everyone laughed, said I was a natural, so from then on, I didn't miss a chance to play fortune-teller. People ate it up, too, every time. I liked to believe this was because I was so good, but I wonder whether they were just surprised to see a Black man in Turkey, doing anything at all.

You didn't see many other Black Americans in Turkey. Almost none. I'd learn later that Turkey does have a small, mostly coastal Black population—the Afro-Turks, descendants of slaves brought over by the Ottoman Empire—but during my weeks in the country, I felt pretty much like it was just me, alone. And not in a bad way. Turks, across the board, were kind to me. One evening I was out in a small town near Istanbul, just exploring, and I ended up in a restaurant, chatting with an old—I mean *real* old—Turkish guy who spoke some English. Turned out he'd only met one other Black person, ever. We kept talking, and he invited me to his place for dinner, and on the way we stopped to buy beef, a near holy meat in Turkey, only eaten on special occasions. Back in his home, the old man molded the meat into little balls, then served them on a platter, raw. I was queasy at first. But just like with the maybe-dog meat in the Philippines, I told myself: I'm here, and I'll eat what they eat. So I ate the meatballs. And they were so good. And then the two of us sat, talking about Turkish history and Muhammad Ali, until late in the night. And that was how it felt in Turkey. I'm sure the country had its prejudices, its ugliness. But for me, it was just good. It was a respite from how my life often felt.

I stayed in Turkey as long as I could, until the very end of my leave, but finally, after morning coffee on the hotel steps, I said my goodbyes—to the family and to my lady friend, who'd decided to stay—and then I hopped in the Triumph and sped off. I didn't make it very far, though. Just a few hours north, at the border with Bulgaria, I got detained, along with a Middle Easterner in a Mercedes. The border police brought us to a shed, where there were bays with dugout trenches, and while one guy tore through my trunk, another climbed under and began inspecting the frame. I was anxious, because I'd brought a few hookahs and a liqueur called *raki*, and I didn't know whether that was legal, and also I'd had some work done by Turkish mechanics who knew I had Turkish friends in Germany, and who seemed solid but could've maybe planted opium to smuggle back. Also, I was a Black man in a nice car, detained by light-skinned police. And I'd been around long enough to know what that often meant.

At some point, though, I noticed that the Middle Easterner looked almost bored. Seemed like he'd done this before. So I tried to keep calm, too. And soon, the men finished their search, gave us a nod, and led us back to the border, which was now empty of traffic. As we sat, idling, one of the men walked up between our cars, and after a pause that lasted a little longer than it needed to, he threw up his hands and shouted, "Gentlemen, start your engines!" Well, my engine was already running. And the man was smiling. And when he yelled, "Go!," I hit the gas and took off, smiling as my tires screamed.

I know that I shouldn't draw any big conclusions from that. Maybe I just got lucky. Maybe that day, and so many others, in my Mediterranean travels and my German home, I was just fortunate enough to meet the right people and avoid the wrong ones. I kind of doubt it—a whole generation of Black artists before me had come to Europe to get treated better—but really, I don't know for sure. I do know that I liked how my life felt over there. I was happier, maybe, than I'd ever been. And so those years sped by, as the best years tend to. I kind of forgot about everything else. I forgot about my old friendships, and my family, and for surprisingly long stretches I even forgot to remember how hard it was being Black. Because in Germany, often enough, it almost wasn't.

When the time came, I didn't want to leave. I really didn't. But I only had two more years of service before getting my pension, before starting to live my long-awaited artist's life. I knew, now, that I wanted to live that life in Germany. And I knew, with what felt like total certainty, that I would.

13

Twenty Years

One night a week or so into my post-Germany leave, I was at my mom's place in Brooklyn, nodding off in front of the TV, when a bulletin came on about a winter storm in North Dakota. I'd learned recently that I'd be serving the next two years—my last two —in North Dakota, so I leaned in and turned up the volume. As images of whiteout snow and flashing ambulances played on the screen, the newscaster explained that the night prior, an old couple had gotten stranded in their car for hours, and by the time someone found them, they were both frostbitten so badly that the ER doctors had to take out their blood and heat it up and put it back in. In the end, said the newsman, the woman emerged with mild scarring; the man lost only a toe. For a minute, I just sat, taking that in: *only a toe*. Then I turned off the TV and went to bed. As I lay on my back, staring at the street-lit ceiling and listening to the pleasant racket of the city, I thought, *two more years*. Two more years of Air Force life, and then I'd get the reins, get to decide where and who and how I wanted to be.

One thing I knew: I wanted to be a better son. While in Germany, I'd fallen out of touch with my folks, having gotten too busy racing cars and eating cheesecakes and living my life to think too much about theirs. By now they were both retired, and separated—my only thought about that was, *finally*—so I spent my leave shuttling between their places. And man, I was struck by how vibrant their lives were. Mom volunteered at an old folks' home, spent plenty of time with friends old and new, and regularly bussed to Atlantic City, where she'd sit at the slots and spend out her coin bucket and not a cent more. And my father was always fishing, bowling, playing cards, golfing, telling anyone who'd listen that his son was a *sergeant*. He was clearly proud of me. Both of them were. If I'd been holding onto any old resentments, they just vanished. My parents, they were just people. People who were and always had been trying their best. And so I made the most of my time with them. I took walks and cooked with my mom. I sat around and talked with Dad. I saw my siblings quite a bit, too; I dropped in a few times on Pamela, who was in the Bronx teaching high school and smoking about a hundred cigarettes a day, and went out often with Gary to see jazz shows or visit the old neighborhood. The days, though, passed by fast, too fast. And soon enough, I was packing my bags, making familiar promises to call and write, and boarding a flight bound for Grand Forks AFB.

That newscast had scared me quite a bit, so a few days before leaving, I'd bought a heavy topcoat, fur-lined boots, and fleece mittens, all of which I tugged on before stepping off the plane. I might as well have been wearing a Speedo. That cold ripped right through my layers. Within seconds, my beard was icing up, my eyeglasses freezing over. I couldn't see a thing, breathing felt like inhaling fire, and as I shuffled down the tarmac, head turtled to my chest, I thought, eighteen years and four stripes and *this* is the thanks I get? From there, I was shepherded into an orientation, where I was shown a photo of a one-story building surrounded by snow, with an oddly short flagpole in the yard, and another photo, with no snow, of a taller flagpole and the same building, which, I now saw, was two stories tall. I walked out with a "survival package," with blankets and hand warmers to keep in my car. And that very day, package in tow, I drove to downtown Grand Forks, where, through sheets of blowing snow, I saw a bunch of white people walking around in T-shirts.

The next day I headed in for a meeting with the first sergeant. I was figuring we'd just be talking about my role, my responsibilities, my ideas— but as soon as I took a seat, he reached into a file and pulled out a telegram from the Department of Defense. He proceeded to say what'd been said before: that Washington had questions, the same questions they'd been asking for years. And I just sat there, fuming. At other points—in Angeles, especially—those questions had terrified me. But now I was a sergeant, two years from retirement, too solid in myself to feel too bothered. So I told him, "Look, you just go ahead and do whatever you do to someone who won't answer questions no more. Because I am done." And that, as it turned out, would be the last time I'd ever have to have that conversation.

Though I never did get used to the cold—even now, just thinking about it hurts—I did meet some good people in Grand Forks. There were a bunch of older guys on base—mostly white, but a few Black men, too—and for years, they'd had a running poker night, or, better said, poker weekend. One guy, an Asian from Hawaii whose name escapes me, lived in a trailer off base. We'd all go there on Fridays, start playing poker around dinnertime, and as the hours passed, the stacks of chips would rise and fall, and we'd all get into our cups, and time would just sort of stretch out and lose its shape, until someone would look out the trailer window and murmur something about sunrise. If you got tired, you just stepped back from the table and dozed off on the couch or corner recliner, and before long, there you were again, cradling a warm coffee cup to your cheek, trying to decide whether to bluff or fold.

Over the years, I'd gotten to be a good gambler—I'd kept at it, in the years since winning that car in an Enid dice game—and so I did well at poker and made myself some money, which I used to buy more photography equipment I still never used. I told myself then that *wanting* to take pictures was enough. It made me see things differently. Made me see them, period. I was always looking for the contrasts, the best framing, the faces that held the most mystery. And maybe that's why I ended up enjoying Grand Forks as much as I did. That and the fact that, since it was a college town, there were actually some fun clubs and not-bad jazz acts. I don't know. What I do know is, just as I was starting to get the place, get my bearings, word came down from up on high that the base was closing.

So I did what I'd done so many times before: I said goodbye to good friends. I loaded my life into my car. And I drove, bound now for McChord Base in Washington. For years I'd heard good things about the Northwest—more than one airman had said I ought to do whatever I could to get shipped to Oregon—but I was now a year away from retiring, and the prospect of building another life, anywhere, just made me tired. So once I got there, I didn't. I didn't go out much in Tacoma, Seattle, or Portland. Didn't take long drives through the Cascades or the Olympics. What I did, mainly, was wait.

And while I was waiting at McChord, what I enjoyed doing most was offering advice to young Black airmen. I told them all the stuff I wished somebody'd told me when I was getting started: which battles to fight, how to climb Crap Mountain, why to pay a few bucks more to get your uniforms starched, and what to do with your Afro. If any of them asked me what I, Sergeant Brown, was going to do when I was done, I'd smile and say, "Nothing." My plan, I told them, was to move back to Germany, where I'd spend my days sitting in the yard, reading the paper or listening to music or just watching people run this way and that, doing things I no longer had to. And once I'd done that for long enough, I told them, I'd stand up, and I'd start taking pictures, and I'd never stop. Man, it felt *so* good telling youngsters about that. About how, twenty years ago, I'd made a plan and I'd stuck to it, and now, I'd spend the rest of my days doing what I wanted without worrying about getting paid.

I was beyond ready to step into that life. So when my superiors, a month before my time was up, asked if I maybe wanted to stay on, maybe serve a few more years in South Korea, I said, "No." When they proposed a retirement ceremony, I shook my head and told them to just mail me my papers. And when the clock struck five on my last day, my room was clean, my car packed. The only thing left to do was stop at personnel and swap my old ID for a new one. In the photo on that new card, my Afro was blown out wide, my jaw tight, eyes smiling. *Richard Brown*, the card said. *Retired*.

The Street

August 2017

It's a muggy summer night, and I'm out on Alberta, carrying my camera
and weaving through the Last Thursday throngs. Last Thursday, it's this
monthly art walk, kind of like a First Friday but with fewer wine spritzers
and more fire dancers. Seriously, I just walked by two teenage girls twirling
flaming batons. Over the last hour, I've also seen a jug band, a capoeira
circle, a guy blowing giant bubbles at giggling kids, a hundred-some ven-
dors hawking who-knows-what, and a duck on a leash.

Twenty years ago, on this street? It was a rock in a pipe, a needle in
an arm.

But now? A duck on a leash.

If I think about how this came to be—if I remind myself that it was
Black activists who cleaned up Alberta, only for Alberta to end up owned
and operated by white folks who seem to know very little about who and
what come before—I'll get upset. So, mostly, I don't think about it. Because the time to stop gentrification here has passed. It is gone. And I have
grieved it plenty. The way I feel about gentrified Alberta isn't far from how
I felt about Enid, Oklahoma. I'm not going to waste my time and spirit
grumbling about what and how it isn't. I'm going to make what I can of
what it is.

I lean on a streetlight and peer down at my camera's viewscreen. This
camera is new. It's a Leica. I bought it because last week I went to my

basement, planning to get my life in order, but what I did instead was look at pictures. Boxes of them. As I looked, I got to feeling bad, because it'd been eons since I'd taken a picture worth the paper it was printed on. So I went and did it: I bought this digital. Other photographers, for years, had been talking about digitals, saying I *had* to get one, and I'd resisted, because it'd seemed like learning a new language and I liked my native tongue just fine. Now, though, I was clearly in need of a boost, so I told myself, *You're a born learner. You'll learn this.* And I still believe that, even as I stand here, toggling through menus that may as well be written in French.

I drop the camera and walk. I've got to say, I'm surprised at how many Black folks are out. At the moment, I can see two Black youngsters, laughing into cupped hands, and just past them, a mixed couple considering bridge photography. Earlier, I passed a few kids dancing on cardboard, and I've seen some old-timers, too, sitting on benches, watching. Now here comes a tall brother with a girl on his shoulders. Walking right toward me. He reminds me of a guy I photographed years ago for my series on Black men. I like how he and his girl look, rising up out of the crowd. So I point my camera to his right, like I'm shooting something else, and I snap one picture, then more, all the while turning slowly toward the guy and his daughter. Suddenly, he sees me and frowns. With his daughter still on his shoulders, he digs a hand in his pocket. And then he pulls out a phone and takes a picture of me.

I look up and shrug as if to say, "guilty as charged." He doesn't smile. Just keeps walking. Folks these days seem to be different about pictures. Maybe it's the Internet? How photos can be taken here, posted there, just like that? I don't know. Don't care, either. I'm not posting anything. I'm just practicing. So once that guy has passed, I flip through my shots. And I smile. Because I got a good one.

I keep moving. The sun's dipping toward the West Hills, the light warm and thick, like it's being poured over the street. I get a picture of teens dancing to reggae. And another of myself, reflected in a window. As I take my shots, I run into a guy I've known since he was a toddler, and a white lady who says we met in a photography workshop. Both say they're glad I'm still taking pictures. I say, "Me, too."

On a bus bench in front of what used to be a pharmacy, I see a woman with a girl on her lap. She's twirling her finger through the girl's hair. Something about their posture whisks me back to Nicaragua, where I spent time in the eighties taking pictures. I sidestep out of the crowd, crouch, and line up a shot. But as I'm taking focus, the woman sees me. She stands, hoists her girl onto her hip, and walks away. I drop my camera and wonder again if people have changed, or if maybe I'm just that rusty.

As I watch the two of them walk, the girl hugging tight to her mom's shoulder, I'm reminded of this thing I read yesterday about the Maasai people. Usually, when people talk about the Maasai, they describe them as a fierce warrior tribe—the first thing that comes up if you google them is *Why do the Maasai drink blood?*—but this article said that Maasai people say in greeting, *Kasserian Ingera,* which means, "How are the children?" When I read that, a buzz ran through me. Because it sums up exactly what I think a community ought to be about. If we can't respond to that question—as do the Maasai—with, "The children are well," we are failing. I've always felt that way. From here on, instead of "How you doing?," I'm going to say, "How are the children?" I think I'll add it to my business cards, too—if I ever make them—and I'm definitely putting the article in my newsletter.

Have I even mentioned my newsletter? Every week I make one, a ten-pager full of writing by and about Black folks—Black history lessons, profiles of Black doctors and students and soldiers, essays about reparations and prison reform, Black movie reviews, Black comics, whatever I can find—and I send it out on Thursdays at one or two in the morning to three or four hundred people. When I started, fifteen years ago, it was just for the guys in that group I facilitate. But anytime I'd mention it to anyone else, they'd ask to get on the list, so now it goes to all sorts: old friends, old mayors, fellow vets, fellow activists. Cops, too. The higher-ups at the Academy get it. And I think they read it. So I make it a point, whenever we've had an argument about something, to include some article that sheds some light.

It's getting darker. I doubt I'll get more shots tonight, but that's okay. It's good, being out here, trying. I've been feeling this way a lot lately, even when I'm down at the Academy. They've begun, finally, to weave in teachings on implicit bias. And though I wish it hadn't taken so long—I've been saying forever that we've *got* to get officers to accept they've grown up on racist ideas, to think on how this affects everything they do—I'm glad it's now part of the curriculum. And I like the new guy teaching History of Policing; he doesn't shy away from talking race, and he creates space for me, too. And I'm noticing, more than I usually do, how many times a day people stop me in the hall to chat me up and ask how I'm doing and thank me for all I do and have done. And like I said, after years of telling myself I don't need any of that, I'm coming to accept, lately, that yes, maybe I do.

I'm two blocks from Solae's, and I already hear music. I'd been figuring on stopping in tonight for a quick hey-hello-how-are-the-children, but now, I can guess what'll happen if I do that. I'll stay. I'll stay for hours, sipping water or wine, talking with everyone and their mother, basking in the attention, and though that'll feel good, just like any drug does, I'll get home late, and it'll be another hour before I can sleep, and then tomorrow I won't want to get up and go fish with James.

That's another thing I've gotten back into, finally. I've been fishing. My friend James has this place on the Columbia, a floating home. And lately I've been going there, casting off his dock. I run light tackle, so I've mainly been getting bass, crappie, perch. And that's fine. I don't keep much. I'm not that kind of fisherman. Not anymore, I'm not. Now, I'm the kind who sits and stares and listens to water lap against dock pilings and then looks up and realizes an hour has passed. I treat fishing like it's glorified thinking. Thinking with a prop. Thinking in a place that's brighter than my basement.

The light's fading. I am, too. The street's still full of families, but I'm seeing more beer and less art, and maybe I'll just go home now. Lately I've been liking going home early. Living slow. Doing what I want, when I want. For years I've said my activist work is what I want. And I've meant it. But now? Now, I might really want to be retired. I don't plan to start watching *Matlock* and playing bridge. It's just—I want to take more pictures I won't print, catch more fish I won't keep. I want to relax.

I'm about to head for my car when I hear my name. I look up. Beth's standing on the sidewalk outside Solae's. Part of me just wants to wave, move on. But it's such a nice night, and I figure there's no harm in enjoying a few minutes of it with one of my favorite people. So I walk over, and we hug, and we talk, and pretty quick, the small talk turns to big talk, about how she's working so hard on this bus-driver's union but she's not sure what their demands are or how they should be voiced. I'm offering ideas, and she's asking questions, and at some point she checks her watch and says it's time to head in and am I coming? I almost say no. I almost say, I've got a date with my basement. But I'd like to keep talking. And it's a nice, nice night. And you never do know how many more of those you'll get.

Three hours later, I'm still at the club.

If you educate a man you educate one individual,
but if you educate a woman you educate a family.

—Fanti proverb

Black female role models are everywhere, in all walks of life. Well, you say, how come I never heard of them? There's an African proverb I like, and I like to change one word: "Until the lionesses have their historians, tales of the hunted will always glorify the hunter."

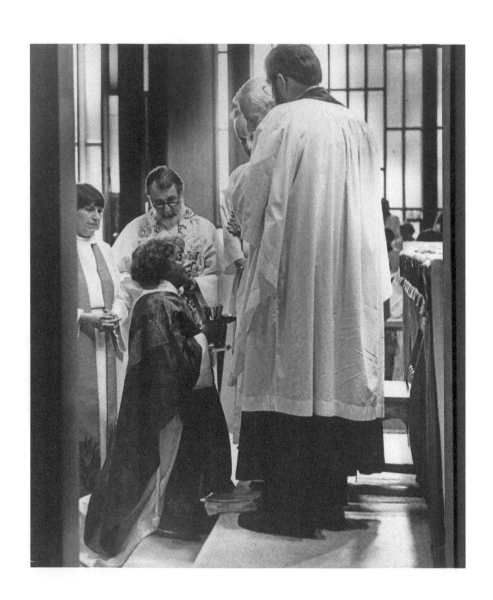

PART IV

PICTURE TAKIN' MAN

Portland, Oregon

1976–1982

14

Like a Little Bird

One Tuesday, a month after my joyride out of McChord, I found myself in a government sedan, driving unlined asphalt through farmland. To my left was a grove of fir trees. To my right, a vineyard. Ahead and behind, it was wheat, and past that, blue clouds and blue mountains. It was pretty country, not unlike the land near Mackenbach, and I could've pretended I was there, maybe, if not for the binder beside me, the spine of which read: *Oregon Soil Conservation Service.* Inside that binder were words about dirt. Words I'd soon be quoting to some farmer, whom I half-expected to ask, "Are you lost?"

I was beginning to wonder that myself.

The short version: I'd decided, in the weeks before my retirement, that I didn't have my act together enough to just up and move to Germany. Not yet. First I needed to get my mind settled, get things sorted. I knew I couldn't stay near McChord—Tacoma wasn't for me—but I'd spent a bit of time in Portland, enough to have gotten to know folks there, including Carolyn, a woman I'd met at a party and then visited several times. So I'd decided I'd go to Portland. Just to hang out. Just for a time.

For the first few days, hanging out was just great. I'd sleep in later than I ever had in the Air Force. I'd have breakfast with Carolyn and her daughter. I'd take long walks on leafy streets—carrying a camera but never using it, because I was still shy, and I had my whole *life* to take pictures, so why rush?—and at dusk, I'd sit on the porch, and I'd watch the world go by, just like I'd said I would.

It was on the eighth day, I think, that I started to panic.

Looking back, I see how predictable it all was. Did I *really* believe that after decades of rigid structure, I'd waltz, worry-free, into so much open space? I think I did. I believed that. I believed it up until the eighth day, when I found myself standing at the window, bored, having done all I could think to do, feeling even worse than I'd felt as a youngster, because now, it was me, cooping myself.

So when Carolyn, days later, mentioned that a friend had mentioned a job opening with the Department of Agriculture? I applied. And three weeks after retiring, I was back at work.

My title was technician, my employer the Soil Conservation Service. My job, basically, was to support farmers in rural Oregon, help them prevent soil erosion, soil acidification, soil salinization. Let me tell you what I knew about all of that: nothing. Sure, we'd had tomato plants on the fire escape in Harlem, and I'd potted philodendrons in the Philippines—but I didn't know a thing about dirt. What I *did* know? I knew systems. I knew protocols. And the SCS had a lot of both. So from day one, I leaned on them. I memorized the rules. I invoked them in my talks with the men whose farms I visited. And since those farmers were used to working with technicians who'd gone to their same high school—men who'd known them for decades, who freely bent the rules—they were never happy to see me.

One of my tasks was to administer a drainage subsidy program: farmers couldn't cultivate until the land was dry, and our subsidies helped speed that process via the installation of drain pipes. I met with several farmers, and all of them wanted a million pipes. Well, my handbook said farmers could only get so many pipes, spaced widely. So, if a farmer asked for a ton of money to install umpteen pipes with no gaps between, I'd tap my book and say, "No." And if a farmer told me every *other* technician had approved his requests, happily, since the dawn of time, I'd say, "I'm not other technicians." So then those farmers would call the SCS and ask for someone more *sympathetic*.

And I just wasn't—I wasn't sympathetic. How could I be, given the stuff coming out of those farmers' mouths? Always whining about how the government would have more money for rural people if we didn't waste so much on inner cities, on welfare. On *welfare*, they said. None of them ever quite said so, but it was beyond clear: they were talking about Black people. I liked to remind those farmers that the only reason I was on their land was to dole out government money that'd keep their farms afloat, and wasn't that the very *definition* of welfare? At that, the farmers would go quiet. And I'd go back to my office, where my boss would be waiting, wanting to talk about a call he'd just gotten.

Come quitting time, I'd drive from the office to the inner city, where I lived. Carolyn's house was just off Alberta Street in the heart of Albina, a small oval of land that held almost all of Portland's Black community. Albina wasn't what those farmers made it out to be: some nasty, hopeless slum. Sure, the housing was in shambles, and the parks were often full of young men with nothing to do and nowhere to be, but it was a community. You saw Black folks everywhere, laughing and chatting on sidewalks and porches, clustered around every bar and barbershop, filling every church pew.

I didn't know yet how Albina had become Albina. I didn't know the city had been all but empty of Black folks until the forties, when tens of thousands came to work in Vanport, a huge new shipyard town on Portland's northern fringe. Didn't know about the flood that, in 1948, left Black Vanporters homeless, adrift in a city that wanted nothing to do with them. Didn't know about the years of redlining that left Black people living atop one another in Albina. Didn't know that the city went on to neglect everyone and everything in Albina, that police referred to it as "Tombstone Territory," as a place they could and would ignore. I didn't know about the vibrant community Black folks still managed to build—the Jumptown jazz scene, the Cotton Club, the dozens of Black-owned shops lining Williams Avenue—nor did I know how it all got swept away by city decree, to make room for sports arenas, highways, and hospital expansions that never happened. I'd soon learn about all of that, and much more, but then, all I knew was: Albina was where Black people lived. So I'd live there, too.

My fourth month in town, I started house hunting. I was still planning on Germany, eventually, but in the meantime, I wanted a home, somewhere I could really settle into. And before long, I found one on the north edge of Albina. It had three bedrooms, a basement big enough for a darkroom, and a garage fit for a Triumph. Everything I needed. On a spring weekend I moved in, and in the days to come, I got settled. I put my records here, my cameras there. Built planter beds, a little radio shop, and a basic darkroom. And once all of that was done, I resumed doing what I did in those days: nothing.

I mean it: I did *nothing*. I didn't go to clubs. Didn't take pictures. Didn't take weekend drives, or go to church, or to the park. I didn't make friends, either, not even when Carolyn enrolled her daughter at the Black Education Center, a private, Black-run school that was focused on Black history and culture and dependent on community support. Sure, I ushered at BEC fundraisers, painted a bathroom. But I didn't really get to know anyone. Didn't even try to. I just worked. Sat at home. Worked more.

And at work, likely because of complaints about my by-the-book approach, I got transferred from one Portland suburb to the next, Oregon City to Hillsboro. In Hillsboro, though, it was the same deal: white farmers asking for handouts while whining about welfare, and me telling them what I thought about that. Before long, the farmers were asking to work with my coworker, Eldon, who'd been at the SCS forever and acted like their buddy. If I picked up when they called, they'd ask for Eldon. I didn't like that. So one day when I got one of those calls, I said, "Eldon's dead. What's up?"

I got transferred again and ended up in a downtown high-rise, working as a liaison between the state office and the field. In my new role, I made maps that tracked the work we did, and I talked with techs, supported them. I had a feeling they'd created that job just for me—they were tired of me pissing off farmers, so they made me a liaison—but that was fine. I liked the new job a lot. Every morning I'd take the elevator to the fifteenth floor, and I'd settle into my cubicle, and there I'd stay. No more farmers talking about welfare. Just me, in my office, making maps. I was happy there, and I got along with folks, but still, if anyone talked crazy to me, I'd put a stop to it. One day I was in my cubicle, whistling—I was a good whistler, like my dad before me—and my boss walked by and said, "Better be careful, somebody might be up here hunting birds." Which bugged me. So I leaned back and said, "Well, if you see that person, you let them know this bird's got a gun, too." Then I kept whistling.

Somewhere in there, I began spending a bit more time at the BEC. I'd help with upkeep, paper drives, whatever. I was growing to like the folks who ran the place, especially Ronnie Herndon. Ronnie was from Kansas but had long ago moved to Portland to go to Reed College, where he'd co-led a campaign to create a Black Studies program. I could see right away that he was a good man: warm, smart, full of fire. I admired his work. But I didn't want any part of it. I had it in my head that I was retired— even while working at the SCS, I did—and that meant I wasn't getting involved, with anything. So when Ronnie came by the house one day to talk about an organization he and some others were founding, called the Black United Front, I stopped him short. "I'm retired," I told him. And that was that. And Ronnie didn't try to push it. He just thanked me for my time, said he'd see me soon.

Part of my declining had to do with photography. Finally, I'd started taking pictures. Through the BEC, I was always hearing of events—block parties and barbecues, marches and rallies—and at some point, I just started showing up, camera in hand. I was still shy about getting in people's faces, so at first, I mostly took long-range shots, quickly. And those pictures just sucked. They were poorly composed, blurry, boring. Which was frustrating. I mean, I'd built this darkroom, and it felt like such a waste, using it to develop photos no better than what I'd taken as a teenager. So at some point I made myself swallow my discomfort. I moved closer. I started taking pictures people knew were being taken.

Portland's not a big town. Black Portland, especially, isn't. So it wasn't long before I met Jimmy Robinson and P. C. Perry, two other Black photographers in town. I don't recall where we met. They were just those kinds of guys; if there was an event with Black folks, they'd be there. Anyway, we started hanging out, and at some point we decided to have a joint exhibit. We knew the galleries wouldn't have us—wasn't a lot of enthusiasm for

Black novices in the Portland art scene—so we just did it ourselves. We built pegboard stands, mounted prints, and one Sunday, we went to Mt. Olivet church and set up in the lobby. I'd chosen some prints I'd taken abroad. From the Philippines, mostly. I was nervous, showing them, but folks *loved* it. So the next week we did it again, at another church. And then another. And so on. Setup and teardown often took longer than the show itself, but who cared? We were getting seen.

And then one day, not long after meeting P. C. and Jimmy, I was at this barbecue, trying to take some photos, when I felt a hand on my shoulder. I turned to find a woman holding a notepad. She looked about the same age as my mother and had that same air of total poise and grace. She introduced herself as Kathryn Bogle, said she was doing a story for the *Portland Observer*, which I'd heard of but never read. She wanted to know if could I take a picture for her. I said yes. Said it like it was a question I was asked all the time. I honestly don't recall a thing about the photo I ended up taking. Don't even know whether it made the paper. All these years later, all I remember about that day is that it was the end of one thing and the start of another.

From then on, anytime Ms. Bogle was reporting a story, she'd call, and if I wasn't at work, I'd hop in my van and speed over. Suddenly, I had a free pass to get pictures I'd always known I wanted: an old woman peering up at her umbrella; two kids on tiptoes before an ice cream stand; a young man, telling stories, smiling with his eyes and his hands. My pictures were still far from perfect—I had so much to learn about composition, exposure, and the art of photographing Black skin—but they were pictures, in a paper. And I'd taken them. And for a while, that was more than enough.

The more time I spent with Ms. Bogle, the more I realized how lucky I was to know her. That woman was a walking history book, and as we drove, she'd tell me stories. She'd grown up in Oregon, in an era when the state had few Black folks due to its hinterland location and horrific racial exclusion laws. At seven, she'd been in Portland's Rose City Parade on the "Colored Float"; after finishing high school, she was denied admission to every business school, then struggled to find work, this being a time when Black men only got hired as porters, and Black women didn't get hired at all; in her thirties, she'd written an essay, "An American Negro Speaks of Color," that got printed in the *Oregonian,* the first time the paper ever paid a Black writer. Since then, she'd done and seen it all: she'd helped find shelter for Vanport flood victims; she'd seen Sammy Davis and Etta James play the Cotton Club; she'd marched against the "public works projects"—freeways, stadiums, parking lots—that tore through the heart of the Black community; she'd seen the rise of the Portland Black Panthers, the Irving Park riots, the Model Cities project, the Black backlash against forced displacement and police brutality; and along the way, through good, bad, and in-between, she'd met just about every Black person in Portland.

The more time I spent with Ms. Bogle, the harder it became to show up at the SCS. Every day I'd fidget in my cubicle, wishing I was out with my camera. My office was downtown, fifteenth floor, so all I had to do was look out the window to see if anything was going on. Well, one day at break time, I took the elevator down and took a walk. It was pretty dead out there, but after a few minutes, I came across two little girls, one Black, one white, giggling and drinking from the same fountain. So I took a picture of that. Days later, it ran in the *Observer.* I think I'd maybe had a few photos printed already, but it's that one, of those girls, that I recall as my first newspaper picture—or at least, the first one I was proud of. And so, in the months to come, I kept sneaking out whenever I could to take more.

The whole setup was working well until one Friday when my boss asked me into his office and told me that the agency, for budgetary reasons, needed to eliminate my job. *Of course* they wanted to keep me, but the only opening was in the field, in Baker City, on the other side of the state. I knew he was bluffing: that Baker City job didn't exist, and he just wanted me to quit because he knew he couldn't fire me. But no way was I going to let him railroad me into doing what he wanted. So I said I'd think about it. And then I let the waiting game begin. A week passed. Then two, four, seven. I kept sneaking out, taking pictures, quietly doing my job, and at no point did my boss say another word about Baker City. I knew he'd been bluffing, so I decided to have some fun. I called a meeting of my own, and I told him that I had a pilot friend (this was true) who'd offered to fly me to Baker City on Mondays and back on Fridays (this wasn't). I could start next week, I said. At this, he got a few shades paler. Said *he* needed to think about it. For another week, I let him. I let him think. Let him squirm. Let him get all tangled up in his bluff. And finally, when I felt he'd had enough and I'd had enough, I walked back into his office, whistling like a little bird. And there, for the second and last time, I retired.

15

Human Interest

Back when I was a youngster dreaming of being a photographer, what I thought about, mainly, was what beginners think about: the end product. I thought about how my pictures would look gracing the pages of *Ebony* and *Jet*. I imagined galleries full of people taking in my framed work. I told myself I'd be the next James Van Der Zee or Gordon Parks—an *artist*, with a vast body of work, endless acclaim, and the adoration of billions—and if I ever gave thought to the actual taking of pictures, I think it just played like a noir film starring me in an overcoat, walking quiet streets and waiting to stumble upon that perfect moment. Suffice it to say, I didn't imagine myself standing in Northwest drizzle, waiting for a city official to show up for a press conference. Didn't imagine hoping for a photo decent enough to earn me five bucks, a byline, and a home on page two of a tiny newspaper.

Overnight, I'd become the *Portland Observer*'s number-one photographer. Numbers two, and three, and twelve, too. Before me, they'd just had Ms. Bogle and the others, using little point-and-shoots, so I was in demand. Every day I'd drive around the city, scrambling to shoot it all—hearings, rallies, funerals, ball games—and come nighttime, I'd go to my darkroom and develop. Or at least I'd try to. Those first few months—or years—all my photos came out too light, too dark, or just bad. Part of it was, the *Observer* paid five bucks a shot, which wasn't enough to justify making a contact sheet, so I'd just scour negatives, pick and print only the best-looking photo. But I also didn't know, not yet, that to get good photos of Black folks, I'd need to expose for their skin, not just the light in the room. So in my early photos, the scenes were sharp, rich with contrast, but the subjects were lost in shadow.

Still, the *Observer* was happy to have me, and the feeling was mutual. I was proud to be a part of a real *news*paper. Ms. Bogle and the rest always bit into the meat of the story, the stuff other papers left out, so I knew that if I got a photo of youngsters playing ball in a schoolyard, it'd likely end up beside an article about Black organizing against forced bussing. And the people—I met a *ton* of people. A small paper like that thrived on its ability to get folks in its pages, and it was my job to get human interest photos, to snap shots of folks out having fun. It was nuts, really, that I hadn't thought to do this decades before. But that's how it goes: your dream job is often the one you wouldn't know to dream of.

Seemed like every waking hour, I was now doing something related to photography. If I wasn't taking pictures, I was in my basement, developing; if I wasn't developing, I was at my desk, trying to come up with captions; and if I wasn't doing that, I was sitting in my van holding a police scanner, waiting for a voice to crackle through the static and tell me where to go next. One night I was heading home in my van—a sharp van, which I'd just had painted brown and orange—when I heard over my scanner that the cops were doing a prostitution sting near a big hotel: they were trying to catch johns, using women as bait. I was blocks away, so I popped off MLK onto side streets, still listening as the cops described a john who'd run off. I kept taking laps, listening, looking for that john and anything else I could photograph. It sounded like the cops were holding johns in the hotel, and I was thinking of trying to go there, get a photo of whatever was unfolding, when I heard a voice say, "I think we got another one in a brown and orange van." That's when I went back home.

At the time, that was the extent of my interaction with cops. I'd show up at their crime scenes, take pictures, and leave. I didn't want a thing to do with them. On top of my own run-ins, I'd now heard thousands of stories from other Black folks about being abused, for no reason, by police, so I mostly just steered clear. I was, though, still Richie—still a hothead, or at least a ham—so despite what I knew about cops, I'd sometimes have to mess with them. Once there was this anti-racist action at City Hall, and skinheads showed up, and at some point, a cop came up to me and asked if I'd take a picture of the skinheads for him. I don't even know why he wanted one. I didn't ask. Just told him no. And from then on, any time I'd see that cop in his car, I'd act like I was taking a picture of him.

I had so much to learn, still, about taking pictures. Seemed like I got some new schooling every day. There was this one evening, after a day spent photographing the circus, when I headed to a ball at a Black sorority. The women were in twinkling gowns, the men in suits and ties. But me? I was wearing my circus getup: button-down and slacks. Earth tones. Right away, a sister came up and said, "You could dress up a little." Which came as a shock. If there was one thing I knew, it was how to dress. I told her that. I told her, too, that I'd come from the circus, and I couldn't control my schedule, and then I huffed off, took my pictures, and left. Later, though, I admitted it: she was right. From that day on, I made it a point, always, to tailor my looks to whatever I was doing. I'd keep a sport coat or three in the car, wear a collared shirt that'd match them all. And if I had to be more dressed than that—if I needed to be in funeral brown, wedding tuxedo, whatever—I would be, period.

Around that same time, I found a book on Erich Salomon, a German Jewish photographer. Salomon had been active in the twenties and thirties, and he took these amazing, unposed photos: of Herbert Hoover, mid-Depression, frowning over a lit cigar; of Supreme Court justices in deliberation; of exhausted dignitaries at The Hague, slouching on couches. He was so clever and fearless in getting his shots. He had this camera, an Ermanox, that could shoot in dim light, and he'd hide it in whatever disguise the occasion called for: under bowler hats and floral arrangements, in briefcases and arm slings. Even when not using those ruses, he'd have just the right clothing and posture, so that no one ever wondered whether he belonged. During a UN meeting that led to some disarmament pact, he waltzed in and took the seat of an absent delegate. People called him the Houdini of Photography. The phrase "candid camera" was coined by a reporter describing his technique. I admired that technique so much. And slowly I began to emulate it. Before long, if there was something worth seeing in Portland, Oregon, I'd be there, dressed Harlem sharp, coaxing folks into forgetting my camera, and then using it.

Using a camera all day, every day, was expensive. The *Observer*'s five-bucks-a-photo fee didn't even cover the cost of film. And though I'd begun doing my own framing, I was spending a lot on prints for my shows with P. C. and Jimmy. So in hopes of breaking even, I opened a studio. Richard Brown Photography, I called it. Simple name, simple everything. Just me, my cameras, and my darkroom. The idea was, I'd shoot weddings, graduations, and portraits. I'd earn a bit while also making portraiture accessible to Black folks who couldn't pay the grand theft fees charged by other guys in town. I'd be, I hoped, for 1980s Portland what James Van Der Zee had been for 1930s Harlem.

James Van Der Zee—he was my biggest inspiration, then and now. I'd first heard of him when the rest of the world did, in 1969, when his work was included in a Met installation called *Harlem on My Mind*. I was in Germany at that point, but I heard about the show, and about the protests by Black folks from Harlem, many of whom found the show to be a prettied-up view of their home, made by and for white people (there were zero Black folks on the show's advisory board). I understood that anger, but I didn't feel it. I was just transfixed by Van Der Zee's pictures: immaculate black-and-whites of middle-class Black folks getting married or baptized, talking strolls or dance lessons, just living lives. And the crazy thing: back in the thirties and forties, before he'd become the toast of the highbrow art scene, Van Der Zee had just been a for-hire photographer with a storefront over on 135th, a few blocks from my family's apartment. A few years after I'd learned about him, bought all his books, gotten obsessed, my mother mentioned— like it was nothing—that he'd shot my auntie's wedding. I'd been looking at his pictures my whole life. And I didn't even know it. And now, those pictures were up at the Met.

So I printed business cards, handed them out incessantly. And though the work didn't come easy, it came. Suddenly I was a wedding photographer, spending weekends in churches and ballrooms. And at first I liked it. It was a real challenge, trying to get posed shots that appeared candid— trying to make you believe that the bride, at her own wedding, might be found staring out a window, hand to her lips—and I tried to take photos that told a bigger story than cake slices and forced smiles. I'd always get a shot, based on a Ford commercial, where I'd pull everyone together after cocktails and have them all jump and scream. That was fun. Less fun was spending days in my basement, editing pictures, pulling a story together. And then there was the money, or rather, the lack thereof. More than a few times, the folks who had been so excited about pictures before the wedding were less enthused afterward. So they'd stall on meeting. Then they'd stall more. Often enough, I'd end up eating the bill.

I was mostly okay with that—I wanted to help Black folks, not profit off of them—but I still felt I needed to earn something, protect my retirement, and in hopes of figuring out how, I signed up for a workshop about weddings and portraits put on by the Oregon Professional Photographers Association. I'd taken several classes, but none like this one, which cost four hundred bucks and not-so-surprisingly ended up being me and a bunch of big-name Portland photographers. They all came in with giant samples of their work—wall hangings, like billboards—whereas I just had a stack of eight-by-tens. Well, the guy in charge, Don Jack, took one look at my work and said it was fantastic. His feedback? I just needed to start charging more. And while that was encouraging to hear, I didn't want to charge more, not if I was working for Black people, so I began considering other options.

There was a guy at the workshop who owned a big studio, and he let it be known he was hiring. And though I'd told myself for years that I'd never hire myself out to someone else, I now decided to suck it up and try. My thinking was, this guy worked on a much larger scale than me, and if I joined his crew, I could make money and maybe learn something. So I set up a meeting, showed up with my best photos. A few minutes in, the guy told me that my photos were great—he echoed Jack's critique—but he didn't have a spot for me. It was because of my *equipment*, he said. His photographers—who, like him, all happened to be white—used a certain brand of camera. I didn't. I couldn't see how that mattered, if my pictures were up to par, which he'd said they were. But he didn't budge. I ended up walking away feeling like I had when I was a sixteen, angling for an internship in a Midtown high-rise.

Not long after that, I dropped weddings and focused on portraits. I knew I loved them and knew I needed to improve, so I studied Van Der

Zee, practiced a ton, and joined a group, the Portland Photography Forum, hoping it'd help me grow. The PPF, though, was mainly made up of guys who used medium- and large-format cameras to take pictures of trees and rocks. This was the heyday of Ansel Adams, so that's all anybody cared about: trees and rocks. For a time, I made an effort—went on field trips to the Cascades and coastal dunes, took a few shots I liked—but I never got it. The Adams acolytes loved to wax about their photos of desert sunrises and windbeaten pine, about what their photos *signified*. And I loved to tell them what I thought: they were full of it. They only made up their stories after taking the pictures. Maybe, I'd say, that was why they took pictures of rocks: rocks couldn't speak, couldn't dispute the stories you shaped around them. But people? People talked back.

And my life, in those days, was all people. Alongside my studio work, I was still putting in long hours at the *Observer*, so while the Adams acolytes were in the woods taking nature pictures, I was in the city on deadline, capturing Black folks of all ages doing what they did: picnicking in Alberta Park, and jumping double-dutch in parking lots, and playing Jeff High football games, and thumbing through soul forty-fives at the House of Sound, and getting barbered at Jesse Rogers's shop, and celebrating tenth birthdays and fiftieth anniversaries, and lighting Kwanzaa candles, and arriving at church dressed like royalty, and swapping lies on porches, and grilling meat at daylong block parties, and pouring into the streets for this or that protest and then celebrating when those protests bore fruit, or even if they didn't, because things weren't gonna change overnight, but that was no reason to stop having parties.

It's hard to convey just how many people I met in those years. Maybe just look up the 1980 census, and whatever Portland's Black population was, subtract twenty, and there you go. If Black folks were anywhere, doing anything, I'd be there, taking pictures. And those pictures would end up on the pages of the *Observer*, the paper read by most every Black Portlander. And once people realized I was the guy who could get them there, they'd come up to me on the sidewalk, or in the grocery aisle, and ask if I'd take their photo. Usually, I did. Then we'd get to talking, and I'd learn that their auntie ran the bake sale at Mt. Olivet, or maybe their little brother was the guy who barbered my hair, or maybe they were headed that very day to a block party down on Shaver, and did I want to come? Usually, I did. And before long, it got to where I could walk into a room, scan the faces, and recognize every one.

And then there was the Black Education Center. By this point, I was spending a ton of time at the BEC, and some other parents—Ronnie, Joyce Harris, Avel Gordly, Charlotte Rutherford, Charles Myrick—were becoming good friends. We'd meet up on Sundays, and we'd chat while huddled over picture books, using crayons to color white skin brown. We'd throw parties whenever a Black artist came to town. We'd hold paper drives and painting parties and curriculum meetings that'd bleed into political discussions and back again. We often put on BEC fundraisers, too, to keep up with rent and pay the teachers better and get more books for the kids. For one of those fundraisers, we held a masquerade ball where folks dressed as famous people from African American history. The week prior, on a giant sheet of butcher paper, I'd painted a life-sized reproduction of James Van Der Zee's storefront, and I set it up as the backdrop for a photo booth. All night I took pictures of folks, and they kept on saying that my drawing was so good, so realistic, and that I ought find a way to show it to Van Der Zee himself.

So I did that. A few months later, I went to New York for a visit—my first in years—and one of the first things I did was look up James Van Der Zee. His name was in the phone book. I called, and I spoke to his wife, who told me he was ill but I should still come over. So I gathered up my work and headed to Manhattan, where he lived. I was giddy as I ascended the floors, overjoyed that I'd get to meet him, thank him for his work and show him mine and hopefully get him to sign some books. When I arrived, though, his wife told me he was too ill to see me—couldn't even get out of bed—and that he never received guests in anything less than a suit. And I sympathized with that. I gave her my books and my drawing and my pictures, and she took them to his room while I stayed on the couch, straining to hear but catching only murmurs and muffled peals of laughter. His wife came out, eventually, to tell me he loved my drawing of his storefront—at first, he'd thought it was a picture and didn't recall taking it—and he'd complimented my photos, too. She went back in, then reemerged with some unpublished prints he wanted me to see, and this kept up for a while: me in the parlor, him in his room, her ferrying our art back and forth. It was kind of torturous, knowing he was right there, just past a door I couldn't open—I felt like Dorothy approaching the wizard's curtain—but in time, I'd come to appreciate how it'd gone down. I got to show him my art. I got to thank him for his. And he, in my mind, remained the wizard he was. He died not too long after that.

It was on that same trip that I met Roy DeCarava, whom I'd discovered around the same time as Van Der Zee. DeCarava took staggeringly beautiful pictures of Black folks—caught just the right details, worked magic with shadow and light, such that his images felt like paintings, or maybe movies—and he was clear, always, that he wasn't a folk artist, or a Black artist, or a street artist, but an *artist*. He was a ringleader, in fact, of the protests against *Harlem on My Mind*, his feeling being that the exhibit showed Black people only as folksy, romantic subjects while underappreciating Black artistry. DeCarava, apparently, had lived most of his life in Harlem and spent time on my block when I was a boy. I might've even walked right past him, or looked down at him from the apartment, and not known I was staring at greatness. Well, on that visit home, I was talking to my mom about him, and it turned out that she and DeCarava had gone to school together. He'd signed her *yearbook*. Nowadays, they still said hello when they passed on the street, which, she said, was a rarer and rarer occurrence. So I asked if she'd call him, see about getting us together, and a few days later, we were sitting in his home. For a while, we all talked, and I showed him my stuff, and he gave me some nice compliments, though at one point, he, Roy DeCarava—a man known for taking photos cloaked in shadows as black and deep as the bottom of the sea—grinned and said, "Richard, these are pretty dark." Not long after that, he and my mom began reminiscing about their youth. And I sat back, half-listening, but mostly just staring at the walls around me. They were covered, floor to ceiling, in massive framed photographs, some of my favorite pictures. Pictures of Black folks, by Black folks. For the next hour, an hour that felt much, much longer, I just sat there, silent, surrounded by greatness. I dreamt of someday having a room like this. And a body of work to fill it with. And a door open to amateurs toting prints they hoped I'd like.

16
Sidebar

One Thursday night, sometime in 1981, I walked into Martin Luther King Jr. School, bound for the gym where, I'd been told, the Black United Front held weekly meetings. By this point, half of the pictures I took for the *Observer* were related to issues the Front was working on, and most of my friends from the BEC were involved, and because I respected those friends' opinions—and also, maybe, because down deep, I was still that boy sitting at a window, wanting nothing more than to not be left out—I'd stopped resisting. I'd said I'd come. In the gym I found a handful of people in folding chairs, clustered at center court. It was mostly my friends—Ronnie, Avel, Joyce, Charles, Ed—but there were others, too, like the Reverend John Jackson, a preacher I'd first met during a show with P. C. and Jimmy; he was now the Front's co-chair. After saying my hellos, I began fiddling with my camera, adjusting for the light, taking test shots. As the others began to speak about schools and precincts, phone trees and teach-ins, who to target and how, I kept fiddling, not so much because I was getting good pictures but because I felt awkward, over my head, and I needed something to do with my eyes and hands. I'd be lying if I said I recalled what exactly I heard that night. But I can tell you this: I was nodding along. I was impressed. And so I came back the next week, and the next, and the next.

Often, it was that same group—my friends, Reverend Jackson, me—but if something big was going on, the crowd could swell to the dozens. This, I'd learn, was one of the Front's special strengths. They had deep connections—had, as Avel once put it, tentacles reaching into every group in town—so at any given time, they were likely working with the NAACP, the ACLU, the Urban League, the PTA, five neighborhood associations, and ten churches, all the while getting intel on the goings-on in city hall. Whether it was housing code or curriculum bias, city elections or tri-county transit, public art or police violence, if it was happening and it affected Black folks, the Front addressed it on Thursdays.

When I first started attending, what we talked about most of all was cops. This was a time when the police union, the Portland Police Association, was extremely powerful. Their president, Stan Peters, was all over the press day after day, defending cops and inverting things, such that, if you asked questions about a cop hitting a civilian for no good reason, he'd bite back and criticize *you* for insensitivity. He was tireless. Under his watch, the PPA began a "Blue Liberation" campaign, suing civilians who'd (supposedly) assaulted them during arrest. They started meddling in government, too, endorsing candidates, and even sued the *Oregonian* after the paper published an exposé on a notoriously racist cop. As you might guess, Black folks were angry about all of this—about cops gaining more power—and the Front seized on that anger. They held marches and press conferences and phone banks—I'm sure I've got a photo of each in a box in my basement—and even filed a complaint with the UN Commission on Human Rights, which went about as far as you'd guess it did. Through all of this, I stood by and I listened. I'd never been one to sit quietly in the corner just taking it in, but now, that's exactly what I did. I took my pictures, or hid behind my camera, pretending to, and I listened to the others talk about media strategy, union politics, the history of policing in Portland, and other things that, despite my forays into activism—not to mention four decades of dealing with police—were new to me.

Another thing that was new to me: weaponizing dead opossums. I'll never forget waking up on that winter morning to hear that two white cops, in the deep of night, had dropped four dead opossums on the doorstep of a Black-owned burger joint in the heart of the community. I myself had never been to the Burger Barn, but still, I was furious about the opossums. What got me and everyone I knew was the *trouble* the cops had gone to. This wasn't some in-the-heat-of-the-moment deal. Wasn't a cop, drunk on adrenaline, firing a shot he'd later regret. This was so stark, so obvious. This was a couple of uniformed men collecting carcasses and dumping them at the feet of the Black community.

In the weeks to come, there were so many marches, and I was at every one, taking pictures and chanting along. The Front put tons of pressure on Charles Jordan, the city's first Black commissioner, who'd just been elected and, somehow, given control of the police bureau. In no small part because of the Front's work, Jordan eventually fired those men. Firing cops, then like now, was a rare thing. So we celebrated. But soon, the PPA was holding "Cops Have Rights, Too" parades and applying pressure, legal and otherwise, to get Jordan off the bureau and the cops reinstated, and by the end of the month, they'd won. The cops got their jobs back, with back pay. Jordan got replaced by a guy best known for trashing affirmative action and surveilling the Black Panthers. And the rest of us got to sit with that particular sourness that comes just after you think you've bitten into something sweet.

In those days I still saw myself as a photographer, first and last, and so my activism—if you'd even call it that—was just a sidebar, just a thing I'd happen into here and there while getting my pictures. Sure, I'd go to meetings and marches. I'd feel what I felt while I was there. But inevitably, I'd slip away to go shoot a piano recital or a library opening or the polar bear exhibit at the zoo. And I don't think I understood—not quite, not yet—what a gift it was to be able to do that, to escape.

My favorite escape was probably music photography. I'd spent a lifetime mastering the art of sneaking into front rows and green rooms, but now I could just flash my press pass and there I'd be, rubbing shoulders with Dexter Gordon, Sonny Stitt, Dizzy Gillespie. I loved how it felt, standing in the dark, inching closer to the stage, looking for the image that'd say what words couldn't—fingers grazing a temple, a bead of sweat sliding down a cheek, a whispered exchange between backup singers—and then freezing it, forever. Didn't matter how much I'd already done in a given day. If someone good was playing the Schnitzer or the Starry Night, I'd be there. And sometimes, if a true great was coming to town, I'd show up at the airport like it was my job, and I'd chauffeur them around Portland. I'd take them to the BEC. Or on a drive around the neighborhood. One of my favorite pictures I ever took is of Elizabeth Cotten playing "Freight Train" in a rocking chair in front of a fireplace in a friend's home.

I kept taking classes, too, whenever I could. There was a couple, Phoebe and Ralph Friedman, who'd published a series of books called *Oregon for the Curious*—Ralph wrote, Phoebe shot—and Phoebe often gave workshops. Her thing was, you figure out what you want to shoot before you leave home, and then you go get it. Like every photographer I knew, Phoebe worshipped Ansel Adams, and she said I ought to study him, so I did. I studied his photos and I picked up his books—the ones not written in indecipherable photographer-ese—and I even enrolled in a workshop based on his teachings.

What I remember from that workshop, mainly, is how all of the teachers kept talking about "previsualization." You dream up your desired image, they'd say, and then, working with the limits of your equipment, you create it. It'd be years before I understood how to apply that advice to my work—how to use pictures to tell stories I wanted to tell—but even then I knew, vaguely, that it was useful. I remember, too, that I was one of two Black people at that workshop. On the last day, there was a panel featuring the art director for *Life* magazine, John Loengard, who went on and on about how crucial *Life* was to the history of photography. After keeping as quiet as I could, I cut in and said that, if you asked me, *Ebony* was more important. Loengard, I think, laughed and moved on. But later, I went to get a book signed by Eugene Richards, and he wrote: "To Richard, who thinks *Ebony* is better than *Life*."

When I wasn't taking pictures or studying pictures or running around with the Front, I was probably at the BEC. I'd never forgotten about men like Mr. Gill—men who exuded total composure, who asked what you were about and expected a good answer—and so now, at the BEC, I made an effort to be that same sort of positive presence. I started a stamp club and encouraged the children to collect stamps that told stories they wanted to hear; I built an abacus out of wood and plastic tubing in hopes of making math more tactile and fun than it'd been for me; I helped start a garden and managed to get folks from the SCS to donate soil and seed and give the youngsters some pointers; and above all I made sure to do what'd been done for me in Harlem: I asked what those children wanted to do and be. The answers were what you'd expect—football player, basketball player, astronaut—but that didn't matter. What mattered was that they had an answer. What mattered was that someone asked.

The youngsters at the BEC had it way better than the Black youth who went to Portland Public Schools, which, I'd learned, was one of the most racist institutions in a city teeming with them. Back in 1980—back when I was still just a photographer who showed up, went *click*, and moved on—PPS, as part of its molasses-slow approach to integration, began shuttering "low-performing" schools, sprinkling Black kids all around the district while letting white kids stay where they were. The official term was "forced bussing." But Ronnie said it better when, in a hundred interviews, he dubbed it "the most racist form of integration I've ever seen." That whole year, he and the Front did a ton of organizing, built a huge coalition. They told PPS that, barring major reforms, every Black child would boycott the coming year, and stay out of schools until October, when the state did head counts that determined district funding. Again, I wasn't in the room when any of that was being planned. I just read about it in Ms. Bogle's stories, and I took pictures that sat beside the stories, and I heard about it, everywhere, every day. I talked about it, too, with friends: I talked about how much I regretted not graduating, and how awful it was that PPS was pushing our Black youth toward the same fate. I didn't get involved, though. I was still of the mind that being retired meant being uncommitted. So I mostly just took my pictures. And when I thought I'd gotten a good one, I'd head back home, disappear into my darkroom, and develop.

Just before the year began, PPS agreed to stop forced bussing. They even promised to open a school in the community and name it after Harriet Tubman. And man, in the weeks to come, there were *so* many celebrations. I remember standing with my friends, laughing, just feeling stunned that the Front had *won*. More every day, I was seeing how different Portland was from New York, and I was starting to appreciate it, too. No, it didn't have the jazz clubs or subways, the hum or the history, but it was small enough that when you said something, folks had to listen.

Which isn't to say that that change came easily. It didn't, not at all. I still remember the day, not so long after the Front's victory, when PPS announced out of the blue that they wouldn't be opening Tubman School after all. And, man—it was like a bomb had gone off in the Black community. Given what I know of organizing now, I doubt what I remember, which is that *everyone* got out in the streets—instantly—and stayed there. I remember a storm of Front-led meetings and marches, teach-ins and grandstands. I remember being at every one, voice hoarse, camera in hand.

Before long, the Front was filling every school board meeting with sign-toting children, who made enough noise to shut down a few sessions, and in those meetings, I'd always be off to the side, holding those children in my frame, their pinched faces and balled fists in stark black and white. I kept getting good pictures—took one for the *Observer* of Ronnie standing on a desk, whipping a crowd into a frenzy while, below, a white board member frowns at his feet—and more and more often, I found myself dropping the camera and just staring at those children, who were being held back for reasons beyond their control. I don't recall thinking consciously about all the times I'd been held back. But I must've felt it in my marrow. Because somewhere in there, a switch flicked on, or off.

I'm not sure how to explain this next part. Don't know how to convey the meaning of a moment I barely remember. So I'll just say what Ronnie Herndon says whenever folks ask him how I came to be who I am. And what he says is: there was this one night when the city had organized yet another community meeting about schools, and at that meeting, as ever, he and other Front members were talking about racist bussing and racist curriculum, and white folks were saying the things white folks too often say, and I was off in the wings, crouched behind my camera, capturing it all. If things had stayed like that, it would've been just another night. But at some point, someone in the room said something particularly ignorant, and before Ronnie could reply, someone else spoke up, and that someone was me. I'd dropped my camera to my chest and was standing tall, arms crossed, my words coming out fast and sharp as air from a punctured balloon. Ronnie knew me well by that point, had a sense for what I was all about, but he'd never seen me speak in public on anything political. Not until that night, he hadn't. That night, though, I started talking. And as Ronnie says, once I started, I never shut up.

The Precinct

September 2017

I'm on my way home from the Elks Club when I pass the North Precinct and see a handful of cops on the steps. They're smoking cigarettes, sipping coffee, yawning. Must be shift change. I whip a right at the light and park my car in the back lot.

I've been trying to catch this one officer for a while, ever since I read a news story about a police stop involving a guy who'd solicited a prostitute and who had a gun. They made a clean arrest, no shots fired, but that wasn't what struck me. What struck me was that this officer in the story used a phrase I'd only ever heard used at the Academy. Now, I can't even recall what it was, but I bet the officer will, and I'd like to compliment him, which I'll do if I can ever get a hold of him. I've called. Left messages. Even stopped here at the precinct awhile ago, but the receptionist was on the phone and basically ignored me. Eventually, the officer turned up and I tried to grab him, but he said he was busy and he'd get with me in a second. Ten minutes later, he hadn't. So I left. Maybe I should've given up then. I did, after all, quit working with Portland Police a decade ago because of brush-offs like this. But I guess I was born cursed with too much persistence. Because here I am, walking up the steps.

A half-dozen cops are outside. I vaguely recognize a few—from the Academy, probably—and I definitely know the sole Black cop, whose name escapes me, but whose folks I've known since before he was born. He's staring at me. Staring like I might be wearing a bomb. They all are.

I approach the Black cop, and I ask if he'd let the officer in question know that Richard Brown is here. He looks me up and down, then goes in, the rest trailing him. Soon they're back, and the Black cop has his thumbs hooked in his vest. Which I don't like. I've got no patience for cops who thumb their vests or wear their hats backwards or cock their guns to the side, my feeling being: this isn't *Bad Boys*. So I'm peeved. And now this guy, who knows me, who's seen me at the Academy and in the community for *years*—now he says, "Some people just don't understand the work we do."

I don't even know what to say to that.

The other guys, I notice, are hanging back, giving us space. My guess is, they had a huddle and decided the Black cop should deal with the Black geezer. Now we're standing face to face. He's still got his thumbs in his vest, and I've got half a mind to slap him upside the head, but before I get the chance, the officer I'm looking for walks outside. So I step away from the group, toward the officer, and as I do, the others follow me, like they think I might mug him or, worse, call him a mean name. The officer looks tense, too. Which is baffling. All of this: baffling. For years—for *decades*—I was at the precinct constantly, and many cops had my beeper number, and a crime couldn't get committed in Albina without me getting a call. And anyone who knows me can tell you: since then, nothing about me has changed. I'm still stubborn, still a pain in the ass, but I listen, and I am *steady*. I am doing the same things I've been doing for years. Doing things that, for a time, were valued, by at least some police.

In the most level tone I can manage, I say what I came to say, about what I read in that article and about why I liked it. The officer doesn't seem to know what I'm talking about and apparently neither do I—I still can't recall the quote—so I just compliment him, and he thanks me, and it feels terrible. It's like we're acting. Or at least like he is. Like he's reading lines from a script he himself would never write. So, finally, I wish him a good night. I nod at the peanut gallery. I walk to my car.

From the precinct to my house, it's twelve blocks. I'm not ready to go home yet, so I turn onto a side road and drive through the neighborhood. My hands aren't shaking, but the way my heart's going, I know they soon will be. I turn on the radio, flip through stations. Nothing sounds good. And anyway, all I can hear is what that youngster said, playing on loop.

I take a right, a left, a right. I pass by a house that used to belong to Mrs. Smith, decades ago, and that now has a moped out front and Tibetan prayer flags lining the porch. Two blocks farther, on a lot that once held a real nasty dope house, there's a brand-new pre-fab-looking duplex. I'm feeling old. Feeling like I've driven the same streets of the same city for so long. And for what? For some youngster with a badge to tell me what he thinks I don't understand?

I turn the radio off, take a hand from the wheel, and massage my temples. I want that cop to come and see the talk I give at Academy graduations to young cops and their young spouses, a talk during which I lay out how hard it is to be a cop, and to be a cop's family, then list off everything they can and must do to stay healthy, married, alive. I want him to watch that and tell me I don't understand.

My headache's getting worse. Because most of those guys, I'm remembering, came through the Academy. They *have* seen me give that talk. And still: "Some people just don't understand."

Alberta's alive tonight. Time was, if you drove this street at ten-thirty on a Tuesday, it'd be dope pushers and dope users and not much else. Now, though, the curbs are lined with cars, sidewalks full of people. I drive slowly, following the numbers as they tick up, 8th to 9th to 10th. I'm going the wrong way. My home a mile behind me. I told myself I'd be home early tonight—I'm trying to sleep more, live healthier—but I'm not ready, not feeling like this. It's like I've got a magnet in my chest and it's sucking in every bad thing that's ever happened to me: every cop who's brushed me off, every brother who's called me an Uncle Tom, every face of every Black child I've tried and failed to keep alive.

And now here come the waterworks. I backhand the first few tears and blink back the rest. I know I should call someone. Talk. To Ronnie, maybe, or Rich from the Academy. I've talked to them both before when I'm feeling like this—feeling alone in this work—and often, it helps. One time, years ago, after weathering some particularly blistering heat from a Black man who will only and always see me as a traitor, I tracked down Rich at the shooting range, and I started talking, and I kept talking, and before long, I was sobbing. And that felt good. Replenishing. I'd like to believe it would now, too, but the truth is: I don't know that I want to be replenished. I think maybe I just want to not be here at all. I think I've had my fill of driving alone in the dark. Think I'm done bending every which way to hold this lonely, quaking middle ground. Done getting called stray cat, blowhard, traitor, terrorist.

Which reminds me. Last Wednesday I went to the Academy, like usual, and as I was leaving, I saw they were having a thing in the Hall of Heroes. So I popped in. It turned out to be a talk about terrorism. Seemed like it'd been going for a while, and I didn't want to interrupt, so I stuck to the back wall and just listened as they went over lists of local "terrorist" groups. Three of the groups they highlighted were Black ones, and I knew, beyond a doubt, that none of them were "terrorist," just activist. Which pissed me off. I would've spoken up about it, but I didn't even get a chance, because some white guy appeared beside me and asked who I was and why I was there. I'd removed my name badge for some reason, so I explained how I was an eternal unofficial board member. But the guy looked skeptical. And I realized that he suspected me of something. Of being there to gather info, maybe. On the one hand, this was no surprise—my whole life, people have looked at my skin and assumed the worst—but I guess you can only be profiled and distrusted so many thousand times before it starts to hurt in a way that's beyond healing. That's how I felt, that day. It's how I feel now, too.

There's an open parking spot right in front of the club, and I take it. I kill the lights but keep the car idling. I'm not thirsty for anything, but I'm not real eager to be alone, either, so I shut off the engine, button up my coat. As I do, I tell myself: *Tomorrow.* I don't really know what I mean by that. Don't know what I'm going to start doing or not doing, only that it's got to wait. And for now, I just lock up my car doors. I paste on what feels like a smile. And I step through the door into the club.

When brothers fight to the death, a stranger inherits their property.

—African Proverb

I often hear the criticism that, as Black men, we're not passing the torch. Many think there's some rite of passage: a secret meeting or a handshake. With the Black men I myself learned from—and there were many—it was much more about what I saw them do than what I heard them say.

PART V

BLACK MAN IN A WHITE ROOM

Portland, Oregon

1982–1990

17

Etiquette

It's a Saturday afternoon, summer of 1984, outside an auditorium in downtown Portland. Throngs of people—young, old, male, female, Black, brown, beige—stand on the sidewalk, holding signs and banners, shuffling and murmuring. They're waiting for the Reverend Jesse Jackson, who's in Portland to stump for his first presidential campaign, and who, at long last, pulls up to the curb in a beige sedan with tinted windows. The crowd's murmurs swell to cheers. The signs and banners fly high. Photographers and reporters swarm the car When the passenger door opens and Jackson steps out, fist up, the crowd erupts and cameras flash, but the people holding those cameras, they begin to swear under their breath. Because the driver of that car? It's that guy who takes photos for the *Observer*. And he's got a camera, too. And it looks like he's already loading in a new roll of film.

I first heard that story about myself from a guy named Michael Lloyd. Fellow photographer. He'd go on, years later, to win a Pulitzer for his work with the *Oregonian*, and already he was a respected ten-year vet. Not long after that rally, he called me up and asked if I'd come to his class—he taught at Portland State—and give a talk on "etiquette." I told him I didn't know a thing about that, and he laughed and said, "Richard, if a picture can be taken, you *always* pop up. You're doing something right." I was, he added, as good as anyone at getting where I needed to get to take the pictures I wanted to take. So he asked again if I'd give a talk. And a month later, there I was, a high school dropout, presiding over a room full of college students. I told them about Erich Salomon and acting the part. Told them that good photography stemmed from good citizenship. That "right place, right time," it wasn't luck. If you can find yourself in all sorts of places, at all sorts of times, you improve your odds.

"Retire early," I told those kids. "That's the best etiquette."

I'd figured out retirement. Every morning when I woke, I'd make myself coffee, and I'd think about what I wanted to do, and then I'd do it. Time had ceased to be a concern. Besides Front meetings, I had no schedule. I went where I pleased, when I pleased. People couldn't fathom how I managed to be at a city council meeting, a Jeff High pep rally, the zoo, the carnival, a Blazers game, and Grandma Lou's birthday party all in one day. "Do you sleep?" they'd ask. And I'd say, "Like you wouldn't believe." And maybe they wouldn't, but then, most folks don't know how it feels to own your time. I never took it for granted, either. Every day, I thanked my sixteen-year-old self for his foresight. Thanked my twenty- and thirty-year-old selves, too, for sticking it out in the service. Because of those guys, at forty-five I was a seasoned retiree. Busy in the right ways. Expert at owning my time.

Mostly, I was spending that time taking pictures—along with the *Observer*, I was now placing photos in the Rainbow Coalition's weekly, the Front's monthly, and, here and there, in the *Oregonian*—but it's like Ronnie says: I'd begun to talk, too. I wasn't a full-time activist, not yet, but there'd been a shift. Take the Rainbow Coalition: had this been 1980, I'd have taken photos of Jackson, retreated to my darkroom, and that would've been it. Now, though? Now, as soon as I was done developing, I got back out there to pass out papers and register voters and sit in on meetings about how to register more. Sure, I'd already begun doing some of this stuff with the Front. But now, it felt different. Now, I was putting down the camera often enough, and for long enough, that everything else could start to click.

And the Front, by the mid-eighties, was deep into just about every fight that affected Black Portlanders. We were still putting pressure on

PPS, still pushing the city to pay us the right sort of attention, still telling police to stop brutalizing Black boys. We'd begun mentoring youngsters, teaching them to have pride and know their power and use it. We'd gotten Salem to create a new voting district so Black folks could have a voice at the state level, and had then done all sorts of backroom wrangling to get the community to back one candidate, Margaret Carter, against the white incumbent (Ms. Carter won and became the first Black woman to sit in the Oregon House). And as if that weren't enough, we'd also, circa 1984, taken a deep dive into the divestiture movement. Mostly we did so because the situation in South Africa was awful and standing by wasn't an option. But it was more than that. We lived in a state that'd written racial exclusion into its constitution, in a city that'd redlined its Black population into ghettos, under a police force that arrested us and beat us and dumped dead animals at our doors. We weren't living under apartheid. But we were Black in Oregon.

At some point we paired up with a Quaker group, the American Friends Service Committee. I think this was because Avel Gordly—who by this point was everywhere, doing everything—had been hired to lead AFSC's South Africa division. Anyway, they had a nice office, just a big step up from our grade school gym, and they were good people, too. I'd met a lot of white activists through the Rainbow Coalition, and some of those folks, no matter how liberal they claimed to be, tended to want to be in control. These Quakers, though, were different. They recognized what this was (a Black issue) and who they were (white people looking to help), and so overall we worked real well together.

Before long, we began holding regular protests at the consulate. Twice a week, we'd go down there, and we'd hoist signs, holler, just disrupt business as usual. A few cops would always come with, too. For years, the Front had just stuck to the basics with cops—we shared march routes, got rally permits—but now, in the interest of keeping our people safe, we'd decided to involve them further. Portland Police kept telling us that protesting the consulate was an arrestable offense, and while we were all fine being arrested for the cause, we knew that, when cops arrested Black folks, it rarely went well. So we began to tell the cops, before protests, what we were going to do and who was ready to be arrested. We'd meet them outside the building, and they'd ride up in the elevator with us, and they'd arrest the arrestees, and a few days later we'd do it again. I'm sure we got criticized for that—for cooperating with cops, for defanging our protests—but the way we saw it, cops weren't the target of this particular action, and they were going to be involved one way or another, so why not find a way to use them to our benefit?

That was another thing: we'd begun receiving death threats. I myself didn't—I was still mostly taking pictures, not appearing in them—but Ronnie and Reverend Jackson, the co-chairs, they were all over the press and were both getting letters and calls from angry men who sounded serious. So having a police escort at our public actions felt smart. I mean, on the one hand, I still wasn't wild about working with cops—I did not respect or trust them at all—but I had to admit that, in this case, it was working. We'd found a way to get police to do what they were always supposed to do: serve us, protect us. They'd even begun setting up nighttime surveillance squads at Ronnie's and Reverend Jackson's homes, in case they were paid visits by those serious-sounding men.

All the while, we kept protesting, getting arrested, making headlines. Ronnie and Reverend Jackson got cuffed and booked. So many people did, even Margaret Carter, just weeks after assuming her post in the House. One of the only people who didn't get arrested was me, and that was mainly because we'd decided I needed to stay behind the camera, get pictures of our people in cuffs, and get them into every paper I could. We were real choosy, on that note, about who got arrested. Our aim was to sidestep the usual critiques—about protestors being filthy, shiftless hippies—and usually, our arrestees were prominent Black citizens in business attire. Still, in an editorial, the *Oregonian* called us "thugs" and compared us to—let this sink in—Nazis. Calvin Van Pelt, the honorary consul himself, whined about how ours would be "a triumph of harassment, not of ideas." And other white folks on TV screens and answering machines said all sorts of things, things I'm happy I can't recall.

My feeling about all of it was that people could say what they wanted. Could talk till they were blue from face to feet. All of us in the Front felt that way. We'd heard everything that could be said, and none of it was changing the fact that we were getting results. After six weeks of our protests, Mr.

Van Pelt closed down the consulate and admitted publicly that we'd made his work impossible. And not long after that, Margaret Carter introduced anti-apartheid legislation to the House floor and made sure to credit the Front for inspiring her to do so. Both of those things—the consulate closure, the divestiture bill—were nationwide firsts, examples that could (and would) be followed by activists around the country. And so we did what you do when you manage to score a few points against the status quo: we threw a party. Probably threw a few of them. Which, I'd say, is one of the biggest lessons I learned in my years with the Front: I learned that, when you're a Black activist in Portland, Oregon, you don't win too often. And so when you do, you better take the time to celebrate.

You better take time to celebrate because you can guarantee that soon, too soon, something else is going to happen, something that'll put an end to your celebrations. And what happened in 1985, just a few months after we closed the consulate, was that Portland Police choked a Black man to death. Lloyd Stevenson was his name. He'd walked into a 7-11, hoping to play video games, but before he could start, a teen tried to steal something. The employees saw him do it, so they chased him outside and caught him. A scuffle ensued, and a crowd formed, and Stevenson, an off-duty security guard, stepped in to contain things. It might've ended there, if not for a white passerby, who, for some reason, started mouthing off to Stevenson. He mouthed back. Soon they were tussling, and the crowd had re-formed around them, and then two white cops pulled up. They didn't ask questions. Just jumped in and put the Black man in a sleeper hold. A minute later, Lloyd Stevenson was dead.

I knew Lloyd Stevenson. I didn't know him well, but I'd spoken with him. If memory serves, he'd even come to a few Front meetings over the years. But knowing him wasn't the point. The point was, I could put myself in his shoes, as could most everyone I knew. For the next few days, we poured into the streets and demanded those cops be fired. Our mayor at that point was Bud Clark, and he'd appointed Portland's first female police chief, Penny Harrington, who responded by putting a ban—a temporary one—on the sleeper hold. This led to a predictable uproar from the PPA, and then on the day of Stevenson's funeral, two officers, whose names don't deserve mention, printed and sold T-shirts that said: *Don't*

Choke 'Em, Smoke 'Em. On the day of the man's *funeral*, they did this. In a just world, those men would've gone to prison for felony insensitivity, but in this one, they just got fired, only to be reinstated with backpay, thanks to the PPA. And the guy who choked Stevenson? He never got disciplined at all, not even after the city held a public inquest and the (all-white) jury ruled Stevenson's death a homicide. I was one of two photographers they let into the courtroom. I was there for the whole hearing. So I was there when the cops claimed they'd done all they could to save Stevenson's life. And there when the witnesses, several of them, confirmed that the cops hadn't so much as done CPR.

Around that same time, Representative Carter's divestiture legislation, which had skipped through the House and Senate, got vetoed by Governor Vic Atiyeh. It shouldn't have been a surprise. Atiyeh was buddy-buddy with Reagan and with the brass at Nike, which was still making too much money off South African labor to do the right thing. But it hurt. We'd spent a year-plus putting our lives on the line, finding ways to work with police, and punching legislation up the government ladder, only to end up here, mourning the loss of one Black life and of a bill that might ease so many more. I think we all knew that if we kept up the pressure (we did), that bill would eventually pass (it did). And yet. Those were some hard months, the sort that made me ask questions I still can't fully answer. Questions about how change happens. And whether it's possible to work the system. And whether I'll die trying.

18

The Center of Every Story

At some point in the eighties, through someone I knew from the Rainbow Coalition, I got hooked up with a group doing solidarity work in Nicaragua. Back then, I knew just enough about Nicaragua to be mad, and I wanted to know more, so I dove in, read up, learned all about the US-backed Somoza regime and the rise of the Sandinistas and Reagan's use of dirty money to fund the Contra war against them. As time passed, I stepped up my involvement—planned teach-ins and rallies, took photos and got them in print—and I began to notice something: the speakers who came to town and the Sandinistas in the pictures we used at our events? They were all light-skinned people. That bugged me. It bugged me because, growing up, my family had gone to a Moravian church—which I'd always thought was all-Black—and I *knew* I'd heard of Moravians in Nicaragua. I'd also read about the Garifuna, a group of escaped slaves who, under British colonial rule, had dispersed along the Caribbean coast. So it bothered me that there was no mention of Black folks' presence in Nicaragua. Bothered me, too, when I brought this up to (white) activists who'd gone there and who'd said there just weren't many Black Nicaraguans. I knew they were wrong. Knew I'd be unhappy until I proved it. So, in 1986 I decided to.

I could write a whole book about that trip to Nicaragua, and maybe someday I will, but for now all I'll say is: Black people were *everywhere*.

I'd been figuring I'd have to head out to Bluefields to find Black folks to photograph, but I soon realized that I could get enough for an exhibit without even leaving my Managua hotel. I did eventually go to Bluefields, and I loved it, but the point was and is that I didn't need to go to the boonies to find us. We were everywhere.

During my month in the country, I shot rolls and rolls of film of Black kids and adults, in city traffic and dusty shacks, smiling and frowning, hoisting pots of stew and loaded guns. I documented a Nicaragua that most folks never knew existed. I took a people who'd been made invisible and I brought them into the light. Though I'd always, in a way, been doing this with my pictures, it was a whole new deal to do it overtly, to go after a particular misconception and deliberately upend it. As I flew home from Managua to Portland with a bag full of film, I thought of what the teachers had said at that Ansel Adams workshop. You figure out your desired image, they'd said. And you find a way to create it.

Upon returning, the first thing I did was prepare a show. To that point, the only shows I'd held were those church-lobby affairs with P .C. and Jimmy, and it'd been years; I'd gotten too busy with the *Observer*, the Front, my life. Now, though, I pulled together my favorite shots, and I had prints made, and I started making calls. Had I tried to set up a show like this back in, say, 1977, it would've gone nowhere. But I'd spent a decade carrying my camera into every room in the city, taking pictures, and talking with the people who appeared in them, and so my pictures had gotten better, as had my reputation. Wasn't long before I was showing my work in galleries all over town. I got some good press, too, and when reporters asked why I'd taken these particular photos, what I said was, in my years as an activist— it had, now, been years—I'd come to see how the actions and presence of Black people were minimized, if not outright ignored. I told them it wasn't hard to find Black people doing good work, wherever, and that you just needed to know—to *want* to know—where to look. I told them, in more or less words, that there was something broken in the way we told stories about Black people. And I told them—or at least myself—that I, however I could, was going to try to fix it.

During my time in Nicaragua, gangs had been trickling into Portland from California, seeking new markets for dope—and in Albina, they'd found one. Our neighborhood was hurting. Housing was in shambles, thanks to decades of neglect from city officials and absentee landlords, and so many of our men and women were out of work, suffering. When folks are living like that, what they think of, mostly, is escape. And gangs offered it, in the form of a rock in a pipe. The gangs appeared gradually, but our community was small, so we noticed when strangers appeared on corners, wearing colors, dealing in broad daylight. We noticed, too, when boys we'd known since they were babies started using, carrying, selling. It was awful, especially because the police, if we went to them, mostly ignored us. Before long, shootings and muggings were a daily thing, and good people were getting caught up in it, people like Marie Smith. Ms. Smith was a teacher, a grandmother, an activist; if you knew her, just hearing her name would make you smile. Well, one day on her way home from church, some guys mugged her. They ripped away her purse, knocked her over, and then just left her lying on the sidewalk. Ms. Smith got pretty hurt. And she never was the same after that.

I can't speak for others, but for me, Ms. Smith's mugging was devastating. Because this time it wasn't just the cops who'd hurt us. Yes, they'd ignored us, left us to fend for ourselves, and that was abominable, and they needed to hear about it. But also these Black youth, for a few dollars, had visited harm upon a woman who could've been their grandmother. I couldn't fathom how they'd done that. I'd always had it drilled into me that you respected your elders. And I'd had *so many* elders who'd made it a point to be in my life. Here in Portland, that didn't seem to be the case. Most adults, if they saw a youngster on the sidewalk, they'd cross the street. They were scared. Which, to me, was a problem. We elders needed to make our presence felt in those young lives. We needed to speak up, tell different stories, better stories, about Blackness. And we weren't doing that. *I* wasn't. Sure, I'd been volunteering at the BEC and asking children questions whenever I took their photograph for this or that *Observer* story. But now, in the wake of the assault on Ms. Smith, all of that felt insufficient.

What I decided to do, for starters, was a photo exhibit. My Nicaragua show was doing well, so I figured, why not do one on Black elders? I spent a month getting photos of older folks, some of whom I knew, most of whom I didn't, and though it wasn't the easiest endeavor—one lady at the

Loaves and Fishes kept brushing me off, and when she finally did agree to a picture, it took me forever to get her to smile, because she thought I'd make fun of her for having just one tooth—eventually I pulled together a collection. And that was just the start. The point was to have an event at the YWCA that brought generations together and inspired youngsters to be curious about their elders. *Keepers of Our Story,* I called it. I invited all the folks I'd photographed, along with other elders, and I enlisted local youth to be hosts, serve tea and coffee and cookies. The hope was that the children, as they served their elders, would get to asking them questions and talking, and that'd be the start of something bigger, something that far outlasted the event. In the moment, it seemed like such a good idea. So it hurt, more than it maybe should've, when the youngsters just quietly passed out the refreshments, then left.

Though that event didn't pan out as hoped, it must've made an impression, because before long, I started getting asked to speak at schools. I even began teaching a little class at Jefferson—then and now, the Black school—for youth interested in photography. I showed them the pictures I'd taken for *Keepers*, and I shared stories I'd gathered, then told the youngsters it was their turn. I gave each one a (grant-funded) camera and tape recorder, and I showed them some tricks, then told them to find an older family member, take their picture, ask questions, and record the whole thing. The idea was that the next week, we'd all look at the pictures and listen to the tapes. Some of the youth didn't do it, but most did. This one boy had a long talk with his great aunt, whom he'd lived with for years but never really known. Just a week later, she died. And though that was sad, it was sweet, too: the boy had learned who his aunt really was, and his aunt, in her final days, had gotten to be heard.

In no small part because of that work, I'd been making a big effort to stay in touch with my own folks. I called my mother often, and man, we had so much to talk about: she was still volunteering with seniors, so we'd swap stories, and she was just so proud of me for the pictures I was taking and the work I was doing. She'd come out to Portland once a year—spent her visits assembling and tending a jungle of plants in my sunroom—and my father would fly out, too; we'd play pool, see music, catch fish, tell lies. Early in his first visit, we were out driving and he asked, "So, where's the ghetto?" and I said, "You're looking at it." And he just laughed and laughed, because out the window, it was bungalows and Douglas fir and gardens full of roses. For a moment I saw this city that was now my home through his eyes—eyes that'd seen a Jim Crow childhood, seen decades of body-breaking labor, seen a Harlem I'd never seen because he'd worked hard not to let me. I wanted to thank him, hug him, tell him how much I loved and appreciated and forgave him. But I didn't yet know how to talk like that. Didn't know, either, that in a few years, he'd be gone. So I just looked, as he looked, at a side of the city I too often forgot to see, and I smiled, as he smiled, and we drove on home.

Not long after that visit, we in the Front began ramping up for another PPS boycott. It was the same old story—Black youth getting stuck with bad facilities and worse teachers and a curriculum that made it seem like white people were the only ones who'd ever done anything—so we launched a campaign to change things. First, we recruited a slew of Black academics, and we asked them to come up with a new curriculum, one that upended history and literature and math and put Black people at the center of every story. We held a walkout, too, to try to get the district to listen, again. And to offset what youngsters were missing during that walkout—and just generally, in their classrooms' day-to-day—we started running our own Saturday Schools: there was one at a church in Northeast, another at the BEC, and a third in a housing project called Columbia Villa. I oversaw the one at the Villa. Mostly, I just opened the room, made sure supplies were there, got the teachers what they needed. Sometimes, though, I'd drive around and pick up children whose families couldn't drive them. And as much as people talk about youth not wanting to learn, I'd often come to a house, and these little children would be so excited that they'd have dressed themselves. Their socks would be mismatched. Shoes on the wrong feet. But they'd see me, and they'd come running.

That campaign went on and on. We held so many protests, sat in on so many board meetings. We took the advice of those Black academics, and we came up with a twelve-point plan for how to make the schools more equitable. That plan was recognized by experts around the world as a real fix to our broken education system, but we had to fight to get the board just to read the thing—and even then they mostly ignored it. One local education "expert," after reading our report, concluded that the *real* reason Black kids were struggling was because lots of them were crack babies. The rest of the PPS officials weren't so explicitly racist, but they were no better. Sure, they mostly said the right things, and they made small reforms, but they also took that Black-centered curriculum—which had garnered *international* acclaim—and they stuck it on a shelf where I'd guess it still sits.

The gang situation, meanwhile, was only getting worse. Every night, it seemed, their presence was just bigger, more in-your-face. More open-air drug deals. More dope houses. More gunshots. More good folk getting wrapped up in all of it. Way too often, I'd see youngsters I knew—just children—hanging out in the street, strutting, clad in gang colors. I'd stop and ask what that was all about, and they'd just say their brother was a Blood, their cousin was a Crip. And so now they were, too.

I ran into those older brothers and cousins. All the time, I did. One afternoon mid-week, I was getting some work done on my car, and a bunch of guys came into the shop, all of them covered in jewelry, oozing money. I knew these boys, in the way I knew most everyone, and I'm sure they knew me, who I was, what I was up to in the community. Still, they just stood beside me, rattling on about things they knew I shouldn't hear. At some point, I turned and said, "Hey, when are y'all gonna stop this?" They all just shrugged, but I kept on. I asked how it felt, knowing the impact they were having on the community. I asked if they knew that the path they were on lead to jail or death. I asked, and I asked, and they all shrugged, until finally, one said, "I tried to stop, Mr. Brown. I just can't."

It was clear that something needed to be done and that the cops weren't going to do much more than toss kids in jail, so a bunch of folks—Avel, Ronnie, Lolenzo Poe, and many others—began talking about how we in the community could intervene. I wasn't around for most of those discussions, but I know what came of them: the county agreed to open up a residential facility for gang-affected youth. It was called the House of Umoja, inspired by an organization out in Philadelphia. The central idea was to broaden the worlds of gang-affected youth. To surround them with all sorts of good people—good *elders*—who'd come to care about them, so that, when they got out, they'd have several landing places, just a whole web of people ready to catch them before the gangs could, again.

Since I, back in Harlem, had seen gangs, and seen friends get lost to them, I was asked to come in and talk from time to time. So I did. I talked to those youngsters about how much they had in front of them, about how important it was to dream big, to believe in themselves. And I just goofed around with them, too. We'd play games, tell stories, take pictures, whatever. I even started a model-car club with my friend Bob Robinson, which met on Fridays and whenever else they wanted it to. On those days, as I sat cross-legged on the floor, fitting tiny parts to tiny cars with boys who, not long before, had been out on the street, driving big cars they'd paid for by selling drugs to men who could've been their fathers—on those days, I felt probably as good I ever had. Eventually, though, it'd be time to leave. So I'd say my goodbyes, pull on my coat, walk out of the building. And I wouldn't make it ten steps before I'd see some other youngsters who weren't inside, not yet, but who soon enough probably would be.

Through all of this, I was still taking all sorts of pictures, still mostly for the *Observer*. Ms. Bogle had by now retired, and I'd begun working pretty closely with a journalist named LaNita Duke. LaNita was a great reporter and just all sorts of fiery—the kind of person who, if you said a thing she disagreed with, would let you know and wouldn't let you forget. So we had that in common. The two of us were a good team, good enough that once or twice, the *Oregonian* hired us together to do stories about the Black community. Once they sent us to do a piece on the break-dancing scene at Ockley Green Middle School. So we went, and we watched, and we decided we weren't doing that story. Neither of us had a problem with the break-dancing itself. Not at all. Our problem was that Black youth only got press when they were getting arrested or doing something impressive with their bodies. Neither of us wanted to do another story like that, so instead we turned in a piece on this new peer-to-peer tutoring program. It was a good piece, focused on some youngsters who deserved to get highlighted for what they were up to. Still, our editor at the *Oregonian* wanted his break-dancing story. So he found someone else to shoot and report it, then used my and LaNita's story as a sidebar.

Because of situations like that one—and because the more time I spent with gang-affected youth, the more strongly I felt that we in the Black community needed better images of ourselves—I began to turn my attention even more toward my own photography. The Nicaragua and *Keepers* shows were still doing well, finding new homes and new audiences, generating the sorts of conversations I'd hoped they would, so I decided I'd do some more installations in the same vein: more themed works that showcased a certain subset of Black folks, that pushed back against the usual depictions. And there were two I knew I wanted to do right away: one on Black men and another on Black youth.

I'm not going to write about those pictures here. For starters, I'm no art critic, and anyway, I've never been big on talking about my own pictures. I'd rather you just looked and let them do the talking. One thing I will say: in my eyes, those collections were two sides of the same coin. In one, I posed a variety of Black men—butchers, poets, professors, fathers—just living their lives; and in the other, I got children from the community to dress up as who and what they wanted to be when they grew up: teachers, firefighters, nurses, police officers, everything. I wanted to show what Black excellence looked like, and I wanted to show children imagining how it might look, someday, for them.

Those shows both had a real impact. The one on Black men, it made the gallery rounds—a few of the photos even ended up in a group show at the Portland Art Museum—and the youth collection got put up in the Avel Gordly Head Start building, where it remains to this day. I was so proud of those shows. *So* proud. I felt I'd figured out what I wanted to say with my pictures. Felt I'd stumbled upon something powerful, really and truly found my voice. All these years later, I still think that. All the time, I do. And I wonder what else that voice might've said, if I hadn't stopped letting myself use it.

19

Just About Everything

At some point, thanks to the *Keepers* exhibit, and probably due to my having been nominated by someone to whom I still owe a thank-you, I got recognized by the Smithsonian as a Community Scholar, which meant getting flown in for their Folklife Summer Institute. That institute was two weeks of talks, tours, and classes, and there were two dozen of us scholars from all over the country, working in all mediums, from quilting to weaving to drumming to painting. Over those weeks, I got to meet so many brilliant artists, go places I'd have never gone on my own, learn about recording and preserving and getting my own art funded. And though I was—and remain—so grateful for all of that, what I remember most of all is that the whole experience, like so many others, was just devoid of Black folk.

Our absence really showed. One day, some of the staff tried to take us to the Anacostia, a community museum located in that storied Black neighborhood, and we got lost. We got *lost*. Then, another day, they took us to the archives where Alan Lomax's field recordings are stored, and as we explored, our guides talked about all these Black musicians Lomax had recorded, and I kept looking around for Black folks and finding none. Finally, in some back room, I glimpsed two young brothers. Interns. So I ran over to them and started pointing and yelling, "Oh! Oh! Black people!

Black people!" I don't think the Smithsonian folks thought it was too funny, but I know those youngsters and I did.

When I got back to Portland, it was more of the same. I'd recently been asked to join the board of the Metropolitan Arts Commission, a big organization that gave big grants to local artists, and from my very first meeting, what I wanted to know was, "Why are so many of these artists white?" Luckily the MAC director, Bill Bulick, was sympathetic. He got it. And enough of the others began to that, as time passed, we were able to bring more people of color onto the board, institute basic affirmative action practices, and announce we'd be requiring arts groups to do the same or lose funding. In the wake of those reforms, many groups, all of which prided themselves on being cultural beacons, really showed their colors. After we told the director of the Youth Philharmonic that he had to diversify his office and orchestra, he told us, "Classical music isn't a part of Black people's culture." Well, I remembered, clear as day, listening to classical music with my teacher in the *fourth* grade. But I didn't try to argue with the guy. Didn't need to. I just sat back, and I folded my arms, and I told him, "Well, you find a way to change that, or you're not getting any money."

Looking back now, I can see that the MAC was sort of a training ground, a place where I'd hear things I'd be hearing for the rest of my activist life. In the years to come, I'd be told, repeatedly, by white folks who'd probably never spoken to one of us, that "Black people aren't interested in ____." I'd hear from fellow commissioners and the heads of countless arts nonprofits that of *course* everyone wanted change, but what I was asking for was too much, too fast. I'd hear, too, from other Black folks, that I was just being played, was only in the rooms I was in so artsy white people could feel good. "Richard," people would say, "do you ever *wonder* why they asked you to join?" And I would tell them, "No." I knew why I'd been invited. But that wasn't the point. The point was, I was there in the room, and I was going to make sure no one forgot it.

If there was any place whiter than the Youth Philharmonic in 1990s Portland, it was the environmental movement. Then like now, Portland was proud of its environmentalism—its bottle bill, its bike lanes, its growth boundary, its big parks full of big trees—but what no one seemed to be talking about was, that stuff all came at a cost. No one was talking about air quality in Albina, which was horrible, on account of the city having built a freeway through it. No one was talking about how Portland put all its waste dumps up in the same northern industrial fringe toward which Black folks had been getting pushed, systematically, for years. And no one was talking about the Columbia Slough, the waterway that runs between the Columbia River and Albina; for years, the city's industrial denizens had been filling the slough with chemicals, garbage, and sewage, despite the fact that poor people of color, who didn't know better or couldn't afford to care, caught and ate fish from those same waters.

There was a guy from the Willamette Riverkeepers, Don Francis, who I'd met in one or another activist circle, and who at some point asked me to come look at the slough. In a way it was still a pretty place—lined with cottonwood, full of muskrats and turtles and blue heron perched on driftwood—but there was trash everywhere, in and around the water, and no matter where you were, you could look up and see the warehouses and factories that, per Don Francis, were dumping toxic sludge into the soil that leeched into the slough. And every time we went, there were people fishing. Mostly Black folks, Vietnamese, some Ukrainians, too. The banks would be especially crowded after a big rain, when the water ran high, when it was even fuller of trash and excrement than usual. At the mouth of the slough, there was a big sewer pipe that would dump right into the Willamette on days like those, and often enough, I'd see people fishing. That was kind of horrifying, but also, it made sense. I'd fished enough to know that fish like garbage. So when the water's garbage, the fishing's good.

For years Don and others had been trying to get the city to clean up the slough. The city hadn't done a thing. So the two of us decided to bypass them. We got signs made at a local shop that warned people it wasn't safe to fish the slough, then posted them everywhere, on trees and bridge pilings, at all the hot spots. Our signs weren't up two weeks before the city yanked them down. When Don called to ask why, he was told they didn't meet code. Which was ludicrous. People were eating from Superfund waters, and the city was worried about signage code? Don was well connected, so it didn't take him long to get us a sit-down with Mike Lindbergh, the parks commissioner. When we got to his office, we were greeted by one of his young staffers. I think he'd been planning to just record our concerns and pass them on, but as soon as he saw me, he went to find Lindbergh. My best guess is that he knew giving the cold shoulder to a Black United Front member wouldn't end well. Anyway, Lindbergh did end up meeting with us, and we told him what we thought about the city and the slough. Overall, he was receptive. He agreed to put up new signs, soon, with the same language. And the only thing he added—besides a little hinge so the signs could close when the water was safe—was a city logo.

I'll say this again: in those years, I was one of the only Black folks, if not *the* only one, doing environmental work in Portland. Then like now, most Black folks were way too busy worrying about other problems—about police brutality and predatory lending and hiring discrimination and racist schools and crack epidemics and micro-aggressions and macro-aggressions and, well, you get the point—to give a second thought to the environment. It'd always been low on my list, too, but now, after fifteen years of retirement, I'd come to realize that I could always make time. It was like that exercise I'd seen as a youngster, where you fill a glass jar with rocks, then pebbles, then sand, then water. The idea was: once you've got the big things in place, you can slowly add more and more. I'm still not sure whether the environment was pebbles, sand, or water, but what I do know is, it fit in the jar. So once those signs were in place, I kept on doing the work, both with Don and on my own. He and I printed up multilingual flyers about when and where to safely fish, and we passed them out at Asian groceries, many of which bought from folks who fished the slough. Somewhere in there, I got interviewed by a paper, and from there, I got more interviews and more invitations to speak to rooms full of the sort of people most people think of when they think of Portland. And in those rooms, I pulled no punches. I said I'd seen buzzards on the banks of the slough eating trash, and I asked if we were going to wait until those buzzards were perched on the Portlandia statue before we dealt with industrial pollution. I told them, too, that I was tired of seeing news stories about how the sweet little owl's trees were getting cut down, or about how the snail darter was getting displaced from its waters. I told them how it felt, reading those headlines day after day while seeing *nothing* about the filthy river running through the Black community. I told them what it said about our city that we didn't seem to care about the overcrowding of

Blacks in jails, or the conditions of Black schools, or rampant unemployment in the community—that all we seemed to care about was, "Does my doggie have a park to play in?"

Bit by bit, I broadened my focus from polluted waterways to toxic brownfields, from solo efforts to group campaigns, from regional to national and beyond. There was, in the winter of 1992, an environmental summit at the UN—a buildup to the big one in Brazil—and some activists set up a parallel conference. It was in New York, so I went. Between visits with my folks and walks through Harlem, I attended a bunch of that conference. There were people from all over. This contingent from Chicago had been doing some mapping and surveys, and they'd found that around Cabrini Green, the infamous (and nearly all-Black) housing project, there was a circle with lethal pollution levels; they called it the Cancer Donut. And some New York activists took us on a tour that centered on a block not far from where I'd grown up. There was a big housing project full of poor folks, and across the street you had a depot where the city's diesel busses would idle for a half-hour every morning, spewing smoke at the exact time children were out on the sidewalk waiting to catch their own bus to school. And two blocks from *that,* there was a crematorium where they burned bodies at night; often people in the project would wake up to find soot coating their cars, their stoops, and their homes.

Near the end of that tour, a reporter from some major magazine— *Time* or maybe *Newsweek*—stepped onto our bus, hoping for an interview. It was mostly people of color on the bus, and almost all Americans, save for a Japanese couple—and the reporter, of course, wanted to talk to them. He wanted their thoughts on "global issues." And that just set me off. There were a million things to address right here in New York, and we were going to talk about rain forests and pandas? As the reporter tried to ask his questions, I kept interrupting. I said, hey, if you want to talk about the environment, can we talk about Harlem kids breathing bus fumes? Can we talk about folks who wake up with the ashes of dead people on their cars? And those Japanese people, to their eternal credit, they got it. They got how problematic it was that this reporter only seemed to care about what was happening, generally, far away. So they refused to answer his questions. And the reporter, rather than ask better ones, just left.

All the while, the UN conference was going on. Near the end, there was this wrap-up event, an informal cocktail-hour deal, and none of us activists were invited. There was, though, a woman from that conference who'd been sitting in with us as a liaison, and after we complained awhile, she said she'd give us her ticket. That was nice, but it still sucked, because now we had one ticket, and there were hundreds of us. So I went to Pronto Print and made copies on bright orange paper. And then we all marched to the UN, tickets in hand. When the guy at the door saw our little army, waving our orange slips, he whisked us through. Inside, it was just as expected: a bunch of well-off white people eating hors d'ouevres and patting themselves on the back for saving the whales. So we did what we'd decided we'd do: we ate their cheese and crackers, and we drank their wine, and then we shut the thing down. A few of us blocked the doors, and one woman from our group, an activist from Chicago, climbed up on a table with a borrowed microphone and told the room we were tired of being ignored by the movement, and we wanted equal airtime for carbon sequestration and Cabrini Green, for tropical biodiversity and toxic brownfields in Black and Brown communities. Then she dropped the mic, and we left the building, and we walked away from the party and back into the city.

And at that time of year, in *my* city, what was happening was: white folks were calling, wanting to talk about Black History Month. I was pretty well known by this point as an artist—as a Black artist in a mostly white city—so come January, people would call, wanting to "work together" in February. And I'd tell those people: "I don't exhibit in February." I just couldn't. Because Black History Month in 1990s Portland was a joke. I mean, in Harlem we'd only had Black History *Week*, but that, at least, was a celebration, the culmination of a year of learning about Black folks. Now, though? Now, you'd see Black people only on the sports pages, or on *COPS*, or in pictures beside racist articles about gangs and crack, and then, come February, you'd get four weeks of speeches, movies, and watered-down school lessons about MLK. I wasn't going to be a part of that. When people asked me to, I'd say that I was an artist 365 days a year, and that I'd be happy to work with them in May or July or October, if they were sincere about their request. And do you want to know how many of them took me up? Zero. *Nobody* ever called back, not until next January, when, like clockwork, my phone would start ringing.

I doubt whether my stance changed anything, but it definitely got me a lot of attention. Most papers in town, at some point, printed a piece with a headline like "Why This Black Man Boycotts Black History Month," including a bunch of inflammatory quotes from yours truly. The latter was kind of becoming my signature. If any reporter was doing a story about Black culture, Black crime, Black whatever, they'd call me up and ask me questions. I never had any problem answering them, but my media savvy, in those years, wasn't too sharp. I didn't grasp what they were looking for and how to control what they took. So I'd talk for twenty minutes, tell them every last thing I thought, and the next day, I'd pick up the paper, and I'd read the article, and way at the bottom, they'd have one line from me, and the essence of that line would be, "Richard Brown says it sucks."

Though it was frustrating, seeing myself reduced to that same one-liner, the thing was: in Portland in the early nineties, things *did* suck for Black people. The city was having a renaissance, getting lauded as one of the country's "most livable places," but Albina was suffering. If our men weren't in a cell, they were out of work. We feared getting harassed by white supremacists— those were salad days for skinheads—or by gangs, which were everywhere, doing what they wanted with impunity. When the cops did come into Albina, they rarely asked any questions. They'd just make their arrests, and they'd leave. If we criticized, Stan Peters would trot out the you-don't-know-what-it's-like argument and shut us down. And if we tried to work with them? Police culture, it was top-down, as militaristic as anything I'd seen in the Air Force, so they wouldn't listen to civilians, especially Black civilians, even though we were best positioned to know what was broken and how to fix it.

So another thing I started doing, somewhere in that span when I seemed to start doing just about everything, was showing up at crime scenes. I still had my scanner, the one I'd used to scoop stories in my early *Observer* days, and if I heard about a shooting, a drug bust, anything with Black folks, I'd head over. I'd maybe get a photo or two, but mostly I'd just watch as cops busted into a dope house, or talked a man off a bridge, or set a perimeter around a gunned-down body. Thanks to my work with the Front, I knew many officers, but we didn't communicate much. Even when standing side-by-side, we kept our distance. As time passed, though, I kept showing up, and didn't heckle or harass them. And they kept doing their jobs, often enough with real professionalism. And so things began to soften, to the point where we'd maybe exchange words. For a while, it wasn't more than that. Wasn't more than a few cops and a Black man standing close enough to talk. But even that was something you didn't often see.

Which is why I was blown away when the cops called that meeting, a meeting I'll never forget, over at Edna Robinson's house. This was at the end of another nasty, violent summer, a summer full of gang violence and police violence, a summer when tensions were so high you worried the whole city might just explode. Usually, what police did in times like these was arrest us, or ignore us, or some combination of the two. But this time? This time, Richard Walker, the chief of police, did something crazy: he proposed a meeting between cops and Black community leaders. And he said he'd like to hold it on our turf, in the home of Edna Robinson, a longtime neighborhood activist.

At that meeting, there were dozens of Black folks—activists and clergy, mostly—and on the police side, it was a broad slice, from beat cops up to the highest command staff, almost all of whom I at least recognized. And more than the words themselves, what I remember from that meeting is that there was no yelling. People were actually talking. A whole room full of cops and Black folks, just *talking*. I myself was actually pretty quiet. I spent the majority of that meeting lost in my head. All I could think about was how, for so long, and with very few exceptions, my experience had been that when it came to police and Black people, we stood in our corners, screaming, and after years of that, what had changed? Not much at all. Now, though, here we were, a whole bunch of us, actually communicating. And though I knew we probably wouldn't solve anything on this night, or the next one, or the next twenty afterward, that wasn't the point. The point was, in that room, or at least in my head, a light came on. And though that light would flicker and fade in the years to come, it would never quite burn out.

The Basement

October 2017

How my day's going: I'm scouring my house for this tripod I used to like, and I pop into the garage to see if I maybe left it there, and what do I find? An opossum, sitting shotgun in my Triumph.

I try to shoo him with a broom, but he hisses, like *I'm* the one trespassing. I can't blame him. I don't remember when I last came out here. My garage is worse than my basement. Just a big dark room full of who-knows-what, and in the middle of it all, my Triumph. This car, in its day, was the sharpest thing you ever saw. I recall driving it through Europe, feeling like I might be Miles Davis. But now? Now it's parked in the dark with four flats, a cloak of dust, and an opossum in the passenger seat.

For a moment, I stay where I am and stare at that opossum. He's scratching his cheek, watching me with glossy black eyes. Part of me wants to boot him out, push the Triumph out into the light and clean it up and fix it up and get it back on the road or into the hands of someone who will. But I told myself this morning, like umpteen mornings before, that today I'd focus on taking pictures. So I tell the opossum that for now, the Triumph's his. And then I flip off the light and head inside.

I walk through the kitchen and the living room and down the basement stairs, and when I reach the landing, I stop, and I survey the mess, and I remind myself: *it's getting better*. It is a dusty cavern teeming with piles of clothing and amplifiers and record crates and picture frames and overstuffed boxes, but it's getting better. I've been coming down, here and there, to pick through the piles, shelve the unshelved, take steps toward relinquishing things I haven't touched in a few dozen years. If I find myself losing hope or coming up with excuses, I make myself think of the Collyer Brothers, who lived just blocks from my childhood home; the Collyers, who'd inherited their mother's house, spent decades filling the place with junk, then booby-trapped the exterior, and retreated ever deeper inside, until, eventually, they died there. Now, as I step off the landing, I tell myself: I'm not a Collyer. Not a recluse. I know that. But I know, too, that whenever I come down here, I tend to lose track of time, of space, of myself. I bet the Collyers didn't think they were Collyers, either.

Soon I'm elbow deep in metal and cardboard, and though I'm not finding that one tripod, I am finding several more that I know will do the job just fine. I set the best one behind me, put two more on a shelf, then haul the rest to the base of the stairs, where I've begun a Goodwill pile that's more of a Goodwill mountain. I'll deal with it tomorrow, or this weekend. Not today, though. Today I'm feeling like taking pictures, and I've been trying lately to act on that feeling when it bubbles up. I've been going to the street fairs, taking shots of people, some of which I even like. I've been futzing with this digital, trying to finally figure out how it works. I've even been talking with some guys laying sewer line a few blocks over, asking them the how and why of what they do, and I'm toying with the idea of doing a photo essay about this thing we all need but prefer not to think about, even though it's happening right beneath our feet. And as I've been doing more of all that, I've done less of everything else: less nights at the club, less time poring over snippets to add to the newsletter, less time stewing in my chair at the Academy. Last week, I only went there once. This week, I doubt I'll go at all.

I head back to grab the tripod I chose. As I walk, I've got to step over and around boxes full of old photos, and I don't like that, so I decide to get them all up on a shelf. As I'm stacking, I see a box onto which some younger version of myself Sharpied the word "Harlem." I open it, and before long I'm pulling up a chair. There are a few I myself took, but mostly, it's school pictures, church pictures, and pictures taken by whatever poor man's James Van Der Zee my folks paid to snap the family in our Sunday best. Here's one of my sixth-grade class with me in the front row, scowling. And another of all of us kids over at my grandparents on Christmas. And one of my mother sitting on a stool at the candy shop. Once I've thumbed through that whole box, I dig into another. I find pictures of us kids huddled around the radio, of my dad in his best blue suit. I look in another box, then another, and soon, I'm not looking at all. I'm just sitting, hands on my knees, remembering. Remembering being cooped in that sixth-floor apartment. Remembering my visits home from Enid, when the city finally opened up to me. Remembering how I still hoped, for a long time after getting to Portland, that I might someday move back to Harlem. Remembering how long it's been since the last time I remembered all of that.

And now I'm crying. I'm crying in my basement in the middle of the day, which is exactly why I tend to avoid coming down here at all. So I close the boxes and grab my tripod and head for the stairs. At the top of the steps, I switch off the lights, close the door behind me, and step back into the bright afternoon. My plan for today is to just head outside, see what's happening on this block or the next or the next. My plan is to just photograph whatever captures my interest. As I'm gathering up my coat and my camera, my phone starts to ring. For a second I look and listen, like it's some exotic bird. And then I pluck my keys from the counter and, as the phone rings and rings, I walk out the door.

Perhaps travel cannot prevent bigotry, but by demonstrating that all people cry, laugh, eat, worry, and die, it can introduce the idea that if we try and understand each other, we may even become friends.

—Maya Angelou

Growing up in New York City, I knew travel would be part of my life. I remember the sights, sounds, music, people, smells, customs, different ways of life. I remember the feeling that the rest of the world was a drive across the Washington Bridge, or a subway ride downtown, or a bus ride uptown, or a walk across town. I remember feeling that just streets away from Harlem was the rest of the world, waiting for me.

PART VI

EIGHTEEN INCHES

Portland, Oregon

1990–2008

20

Into the Blue Cocoon

By the early nineties, plenty of Portlanders knew my name. To most, I was still the Picture Man, the Black guy who was everywhere, always, with a camera. But some knew me from the papers, too, as the "community activist" quoted at the end of so many stories about Black folks. And if not there, they'd seen me at this city meeting about the slough or at that Front-led rally about cops or housing. Point is, I'd become known. I was the Black man involved in everything. The Black man you probably wanted involved in *your* thing. And so it wasn't a big surprise when, sometime in 1990, Mayor Bud Clark called, wanting to know if I'd be interested in something called the Chief's Forum.

The forum was an idea hatched by Tom Potter, who'd taken over as police chief when Walker stepped down. Potter had been an officer since the late sixties, when, during a riot in Irving Park, he'd seen fellow cops beating innocent Black people and thought, "This isn't policing." Over the next few decades, he rose up the ranks, all the while studying—and eventually creating a plan to push the bureau toward—community policing. But when Mayor Clark asked me to represent his office at the Chief's Forum, I didn't know any of that. Didn't even know what community policing was. All I knew was, as a forum member, I'd get to help shape the mission of Portland Police. So I said, "Sign me up."

215

Potter's idea with the Forum was to give civilians a real say in policing. It was a biweekly meeting, with two dozen participants. There were heads of neighborhood associations, high-level officers, beat cops, the head of the PPA (Stan Peters, still), and several Black and Brown folks, including Avel Gordly and me. Basically, we'd all sit at a giant table, and we'd go around bringing up concerns. Potter, too, would ask questions—how to deal with dope houses, what constituted use of force, what cars cops should drive—and we'd talk until we'd found a solution we all could stomach.

Potter was always saying stuff I never thought I'd hear cops say. He felt that law enforcement was just a tool, just one part of policing, and that the job was more about handshakes than handcuffs. He said, as we in the community had been saying forever, that this we're-the-cops-and-you're-not attitude was a cancer. He called it the "blue cocoon." And he wanted to poke holes in it. He wanted a bureau full of cops who got to know civilians, who helped them solve problems, who knew the job was mainly about community, not crime. His views weren't real popular in the bureau. The guys who were comfy in that cocoon—Stan Peters chief among them—didn't like what Potter was proposing, and they often spouted off in the media about how they didn't become cops just to cuddle criminals. And Potter, hearing this, would just smile, and he'd tell them that maybe they ought to start looking for a new job.

I didn't agree with him all the time. For reasons I'll never understand, he supported giving cops AR-15s, which I'd been trained to use in the Air Force. Those guns were devastating: their bullets fragmented on impact, such that, even if you hit someone in the hip, there was a good chance they'd catch shrapnel everywhere else. "This is a city, not a jungle," I said, whenever we discussed those guns. My words, though, never stuck. I lost that battle, and the cops got their war gear, and even now, when I think about cops driving around in neighborhoods, assault weapons in their trunks, I get angry. Still, I appreciated Potter. No, he didn't do exactly what I wanted, but he asked questions. And he listened. And no matter how caustic my words were, he never hid from them in any blue cocoon.

I, too, was making an effort to listen, as much and as well as I could. I even did a thing I'd have balked at a year prior: I agreed to go on a ride-along. My first one took place on a weeknight, after sundown. The cop I was riding with was white, and he didn't seem at all fazed by my presence, and for hours, we just cruised Northeast, having conversations that kept getting cut off by the crackle of the radio. It was odd, being in that squad car: on one hand, I felt I was doing meaningful work, leveling up from my surveillance at crime scenes, but I was aware, too, that anyone who looked would just see me, riding shotgun with a cop. Well, around midnight we were at a busy corner waiting for the light to change, when the cop pointed and said, "See those guys up there? They're barracudas." I looked, and I saw a white Chrysler with two white men inside. I didn't know what he meant by barracudas, and I wasn't about to admit it, but he must've sensed my confusion. "That's a big fish," he added, "that eats little fish." Then the light changed, and we drove, and kept driving for hours until finally, at an hour so late it was verging on being early, a call came in. The cop, as soon as it was done, said to me, "We got your barracudas." Then he flipped on his lights and we sped over to some side street, and sure enough, there was the Chrysler, now flanked by two squad cars. The cop parked and got out, and I followed. The white guys were cuffed, in custody, but there was now another guy in the car's backseat. He was Black. Young, too, and drunk. And up front, just out of his sight, was a huge revolver. As the cops did their paperwork, I hung to the side, letting this all sink in. I had to admit it: if these cops hadn't stopped that Chrysler, this Black man probably wouldn't have lived to see dawn. After a few minutes, they let him out of the car, told him he was free to go. And he started stumbling away. I called out, "Hey, man!" And when he stopped and turned to take me in, I asked, "Are you gonna thank these cops?" He gave me a cockeyed look, a look that said he was thinking what I was thinking: who is this brother asking me to *thank* police? I held his gaze, though, and asked him to come to the car. And once he did, I showed him the gun. I'm not sure what I was expecting, but he just snorted, then walked away. Which made me angry. For a moment longer, I stood there, looking at that gun, thinking about who I was angry with and who I wasn't. Then I climbed back into the squad car.

I didn't know it then, but that ride-along would be the first of hundreds. More than I can begin to recall. And though there were some ugly incidents—once at a dope house raid, I saw a cop jabbing a woman with his nightstick and told the officer-in-command, who sent him home— I often found cops to be professional. One night I accompanied a drug team on eight search warrants, and though I'd heard many stories about busts like these—stories about cops roughing up suspects, planting evidence and weapons—on this eight-warrant night, there was none of that. Each officer had a role and stuck to it. I never once saw any of them alone with a suspect, the dope, or the money. Later I told them that if they were putting on a show for me, they all deserved Oscars for their performances. I told them, I *don't* want to say this, but I'm impressed.

I'll never know for sure whether they were acting. Maybe it doesn't matter. Maybe my mere presence held cops to a standard to which they might not hold themselves. I can't prove it, but I bet many things were and weren't done just because officers knew I was steps behind, watching. I *hope* that's the case, at least. Because it wasn't easy being there, being the Black man standing to the side, arms crossed, watching cops catch and cuff other, younger Black men. Night after night I'd see those men watching me with eyes ablaze, and I'd know they thought I was a rat. Being seen like that, regardless of my motives, was painful. I needed to believe it was worthwhile.

So I kept at it. I kept at it because every night I learned something about police that I could share with Black folks. And because, as time passed, I began to realize something. All across the city, there were still *many* Black activists out there criticizing cops. I knew that'd always be the case. And that I, always, would be critical, too. But now, given my exposure, I realized that I could *also* be a Black man who, from time to time, told cops what they were doing right.

Before long I was doing so at every Chief's Forum. Even at meetings when I was blowing up in anger—not a rare thing—I'd make sure to also tell a positive story about police. It'd maybe take me a whole two weeks, but I'd always find something to mention. It didn't have to be a big deal. The one I always think of is when I was riding with a white cop one day, and as we were waiting at a stoplight, I saw a little Black boy waving at us from a car to our left. Just before the light changed, the cop saw him, too. And then he dropped his window and waved, and that boy smiled so big. A few days later, I brought it up at the forum. I said that that wave was just a simple thing. Was barely anything at all. But over the years, I'd seen too many cops, all caught up in their screens or their heads, miss moments like that. And moments like that, they were big. They were the building blocks of everything else.

Those conversations, though, came at no small personal cost. One of the biggest rules in the Black community, since forever, was that you don't talk to cops, period. So when word got around that I was doing what I was doing, people started talking—to my face and behind my back—about how I'd become an informant. And that hurt. Here I was, giving boatloads of my time, having (mostly) patient conversations with (mostly) white men in badges, all in the name of trying to make life safer and easier for Black folks. And Black folks, in turn, were gonna call me an informant?

The first time I recall it happening, I'd just come off witnessing a search warrant at a house near Killingsworth. As I was leaving, I heard a voice say, "I *knew* he was a cop." I turned to find a group of people staring at me from a raised porch. I walked over and I asked what they thought they knew about me, and none of them said a word, so I told them exactly what I was doing with police, and why. Still they said nothing. So I walked away. In the months to come, though, I kept hearing stuff, and the theme was: this guy, he's only involved in the ways he is so he can keep tabs on us. My activism, my photography, my work in the schools and at Head Start and House of Umoja—all of that was just surveillance. Even the youth got in on it. We'd be building model cars, or watching a movie, and a boy would say, "You a *cop*." I'd ask where he'd heard that, and he'd shrug. At first, I tried changing minds, which I ought to have known wouldn't work. When I was little, the best way to make me believe a thing was to tell me I shouldn't. So I just started saying, "Look, I'm no cop. But, if you think I am, I guess you shouldn't do anything around me that you don't want cops to know about." Then they'd say, "Mr. Brown, you crazy." But they'd soften. And the more I played along, the less they brought it up.

That, of course, didn't work with adults. With adults, I had to address things head-on. And one way I did that—beyond one-on-ones in barbershops and in bars and on corners—was to ask Potter to televise the Chief's Forum. How I sold it was, if Potter wanted policing to be transparent, he ought to broadcast our meetings on public-access TV. I was sincere in that point, but I had selfish motives, too: I hoped that folks would tune in and see that I wasn't kissing ass. Potter liked the idea, so before long, there we were, on TV. And now, whenever I'd take issue with something—like, for example, when cops talked about gang-affected youth like they were evil robots—I'd know I was doing double-duty: I was making my point to others on the forum, who needed to hear what I had to say, and to Black folks, who needed to hear me saying it. And they did. After every blowup, I'd get a call from someone Black who'd been watching, and they'd say, "You keep giving them hell, Richard."

In those days, I was getting all sorts of calls, many of them from folks who'd had a bad run-in with cops and wanted me to raise a stink on their behalf. Sometimes I would. But more often I'd try to explain why the cops did what they did. I'd begun to grasp some of what went on in cops' heads, and knowing that felt important, so when Black folks called, angry about getting cuffed too tight, or about how their son got stopped and slammed on a hood for no reason, I'd say I was sorry to hear that, and then I'd say, "Here's what to expect *now*." I'd say that, given certain stimuli, cops are going to act in certain ways, so if you're wanting to raise hell, you should know this is what'll happen. My goal, always, was to help others see what they were up against. But most didn't see it that way. They'd hang up. They'd tell others, "Richard Brown supports cops." And they wouldn't call again.

Like I said, words like that hurt. But I never really considered stopping. There was just too much to do, and I couldn't let my feelings get in the way. So I kept working with police, with gang-affected youth, and with the Front, whose focus had become housing. Albina was on the cusp of gentrification, which meant landlords were letting the place rot. Folks were living in squalor, and since they feared eviction and often didn't know their rights, they kept quiet. So we launched a campaign called "Eyesore of the Month" aimed at exposing slumlords. The first eyesore was on Alberta, a falling-down four-plex with a collapsing, doorless garage. In that garage there was a refrigerator. Just sitting there in the open. So we had a press event, and after saying our piece, we—me and Ronnie—ripped the door off of the fridge to make the point that, on top of all the rest, this was a real safety issue—a youngster climbs in there, they might not be able to climb out.

We got good press for that action, and one result was that we heard from a woman in the process of buying a home from the same owner. They had a deal that she'd put in sweat equity in lieu of payment, which could've been fine, maybe, except the agreement was she had to work on one of his *other* homes. We did some research and learned that this guy had twenty properties, and at most of them, he was screwing over poor people. We visited his house, tried to reason with him. Then we got the attorney general involved. Eventually the guy ended up turning over his buildings in exchange for no charges being pressed. And the buildings, in time, got rehabbed and turned into low-income housing.

On the steps of one of those buildings, I posed for a photo with a city commissioner; the picture landed in the *Oregonian*, and the caption mentioned "Black United Front Co-Chair Richard Brown." When I saw that, I freaked. Ronnie had been sole chair for a year or so, ever since Reverend Jackson had passed away, and we'd never talked about anyone succeeding him. So I called Ronnie. I said I wasn't sure where they'd gotten that idea, but it wasn't from me, and I kept at it, went on and on until, finally, Ronnie cut in and said, "Sounds right to me, Richard." So that's how I became co-chair.

Maybe because of that title, I began taking the lead more often. This played out around the eyesore campaign and media relations (I was now saying "I think it sucks" at least once a week), and especially around police stuff. I joined Ronnie—Avel Gordly did, too—when he sat down with Dan Noelle, a Portland Police high-up, to talk about how cops and Black leaders might work together on gangs and crime. I joined him, too, for meetups with Bob Lamb, a community policing guru from Seattle. Bob was decades deep in the work, and he would come to Portland whenever something big was going on—the first time, I think, was when skinheads killed an Ethiopian immigrant named Mulugeta Seraw as he was walking home from school. The community exploded, and the Front, in response, organized rallies and marches and demanded cops actually crack down on white nationalism. And throughout, Bob Lamb stood by us, offered support. He was a trove of wisdom when it came to working with cops, and he gave us so much good advice, all of which pointed toward: you've got to engage them. You've got to make them work with and for you.

And Portland Police, despite Potter's ongoing reforms, really weren't working for us. Folks in the community were getting so fed up with daily gunfire, with gang members loitering on their lawns, with abandoned cars, trash in the street, neglectful landlords—just everything. And when we would try to call the city for help, what we'd usually get was a busy signal, or some employee saying, "That's not my job," then hanging up. And that, as much as anything else, was what we were angry about: we were angry about not having any kind of outlet for talking about what we were angry about.

So we decided, in the end, to create one. On a Thursday night late in 1991, we called a meeting at a church on Vancouver. We invited everyone in the community, as well as every political person in the city, county, and state—the people who, supposedly, could help us with our problems. There ended up being hundreds of people there. It was me and Ronnie together at the podium, getting things started, and what we said to the political people was: you're not here to justify your actions; you're here to listen. Then we told them—and invited others to take the mic and tell them—about everything that was and wasn't happening in the community. We told them about open-air crack sales, about rampant prostitution, about crumbling infrastructure, about abandoned cars, about being afraid to walk at night, about how there was no way white people in Portland, Oregon, would ever put up with any of this—and we told them, at the end of the meeting, that we'd be holding another, the next Thursday, and on every Thursday to come, and that we expected someone there from every city bureau, every county bureau, every entity purporting to deal with the public good. I didn't know, then, that I'd end up leading those meetings. Or that we'd come to call those meetings—borrowing a phrase coined by LaNita Duke—Hope and Hard Work. I didn't know Hope and Hard Work would meet every week without fail for sixteen years. All I knew as I stood in that room beside my friends in the Front, before an audience of frustrated Black people and receptive public servants, was: this was something new.

21

Hope and Hard Work

At our first proper meeting of Hope and Hard Work, we had a huge turnout, again. Probably a hundred community members, plus resource people from all government bureaus. I was now the sole facilitator ("This is your thing," Ronnie'd said, and the rest had agreed), and my plan was just to create a space where folks could voice concerns. So after welcoming everyone, I opened up the mic. And I braced myself. It'd been an awful year in Albina. Dope was being sold on once-quiet side streets. Gunshots rang out at all hours. Weeks back, somebody had rolled up on a youngster—a boy I knew, a boy we all knew—and emptied a Glock into his body. As I stood waiting for the first hand to go up, I *knew* folks were going to unload about all of that, and that I was going to have to figure out how to answer when they said what they wanted was to stop the violence. Imagine my relief when the first lady to take the mic—and the next few people after her—said, "The real problem is the streets are dirty."

The next week, I made sure the street maintenance people were there. They said, of course, that they'd been doing their job, and others said, "Oh no you haven't," and I let that go for a bit, then said, "Okay, the streets are dirty, let's build from there." So we did. And we soon realized the problem was that the streets *were* being cleaned, but the cleaners never said when they were coming, so they'd only be able to get to the middle and would just shoot piles of stuff under parked cars. At some point I said that in New York, sweepers would post routes in advance, and if you hadn't moved your car, it'd get towed, and then the whole street would get cleaned. The sweepers tried to say this couldn't be done in Portland, but I cut them off with what'd become a Hope and Hard Work mantra. "We don't want to hear what we can't do," I said. "We want to learn how to do what we want to do." So we went from there. The city agreed to notify people. They began cleaning right to the curb. And folks were happy, so happy that the sweepers, who initially limited the practice to Northeast, made it citywide policy.

That was the very first thing we did at Hope and Hard Work.

Around this time Vera Katz got elected mayor. I'd had a good relationship with Bud Clark, but Vera and I, from day one, got along so well. She was from New York, so we had that, but also, I just loved how well she listened. Before she was even elected, she began coming to Hope and Hard Work, and while there, she did what I asked, which was: nothing. She didn't chime in, or question what folks were saying. She just sat. And so she set an example for other resource people who might've wanted to get defensive or skip the meetings but couldn't, because their boss was there, sitting quietly, nodding.

It took a bit for some of those folks to come around. Like, for instance, Halpin and McCausland, the local beat cops. Those first few months they'd come, because their commander said they had to, and they'd say what they'd been up to, and then they'd sit down and look at me in much the same way I'd looked at teachers back in junior high. And then one night, a brother came to me, and he pointed at those cops and said, "They shouldn't be here." The two of them, he said, had once come to his home after he'd called about gang members being in his yard, and one had asked, "What'd you expect, moving to this neighborhood?" Which made him mad, and me, too. So I asked him to present his concerns at the next meeting. When he did, the cops denied it. And just like with the sweepers, I let them go back and forth, then said, "Look, we can argue, or we can build from here." So we did that. We built. And though it didn't happen overnight, things started shifting. Folks became more receptive to Halpin and McCausland. And over time the two of them opened up, too, to the point where, eventually, they'd tell me that Hope and Hard Work was the most meaningful part of their job.

That, I think, was what made Hope and Hard Work different from anything else happening in Portland or most other cities: we were encouraging dialogue between Black folks and police. "This is a place," I'd say, "where no one is gonna call anyone names." That was our only rule: there'd be no screaming or insults. Just good conversation and a spirit of yes-we-can. And in that spirit, we got things done. No, we weren't solving world hunger or the crack epidemic, but we did help a lot of folks settle disputes, get their questions answered, their voices heard. We taught people, too, what it meant to organize. If anyone came with a complaint, I'd ask that they'd show up the next week with the numbers of everyone on their block, such that pretty soon every Hope and Hard Work attendee was a branch on a huge phone tree. And when, about a year in, I started producing a newsletter with stories about organizing in other cities, I'd ask those same folks to distribute through the networks they'd built.

The biggest thing we focused on, throughout, was how to keep our youth away from gangs. We talked and talked about what to do, and we came up with so many ideas, one of which was to start a billboard campaign. We chose a slogan—*Hope you have a mother who loves you, guns don't always kill*—and decided (this, I admit, was my idea) that the visual would be of a teen who'd been shot, half his face just gone. From there, we moved fast. One woman wrote a proposal and got us $1,000; I asked a company that owned billboards on MLK to donate the use of four, for four months; someone knew someone at an ad agency, and they agreed to do the art pro bono. Once we had the agency's mock-up—hand-drawn, like a comic—I showed it to some youngsters at Jefferson, hoping they'd be horrified. But they *loved* it. "Mr. Brown," some said, "can I have one for my bedroom?" So we canned that idea and tried an image of a young man in a wheelchair with his mom spooning him food. The youngsters at Jeff didn't like that one at all. So we got it on billboards, made posters, used our networks to put them up all over. As time passed, folks would ask if it was working, and I'd shrug and say, "You can't take credit for what doesn't happen." I'd tell them, too, that sometimes children I knew would see the billboard and ask me, "Mr. Brown, is he a Blood or a Crip?" And I'd just give them the same look I'd gotten from elders when I asked a foolish question. And then I'd nod, and I'd say, "Yeah."

Nights I wasn't at Hope and Hard Work or doing something related, I'd often end up on ride-alongs. I was most often going out with Harry Jackson and Derrick Foxworth, two Black officers with years of experience. Foxworth, I think, was part of the team that took me on that eight-search-warrant night; he brought me to my first murder scene, too, and my second and third, and since I often knew the folks involved, I'd act as a go-between, make sure the victim's loved ones got whatever they needed.

I'd begun to see some of the abusive behavior I'd initially been expecting, and whenever I did, I spoke up. One night near Halloween there was a fight at some club, and a bunch of police showed up, including the guy I was riding with. For a while, the cops just stood outside, openly gawking at all the women in skimpy party clothes, until eventually, one of the guys who'd been in the fight came outside. The cops told him to leave, and he began to, but then turned and said, "I need to give my keys to my friend." At that, the cops piled on him. So I went to the officer in command and I told him his guys had jumped this man for no good reason. And he just said, "I don't want to second-guess my troops out here." Which upset me even more than the pile-on had. I was coming to see that this dynamic was just central to police culture. They were so averse to second-guessing, because it might affect "morale." It often felt like working with youngsters—you'd try to give them a talking-to about messing with someone, and they'd pout and make it about how you were being so *mean* to them.

I made sure to bring that up at the Chief's Forum. Made sure to bring up air-conditioning, too. I always got *so* frustrated when I saw cops cruising town on summer days, windows up, AC blasting. My feeling was, how are you gonna police the city if you're locked in a cage? The more I rode along, the more I felt this. And I was always harping on it. When, at the Chief's Forum, we discussed Portland Police buying new cars, I said we should get ones that didn't have AC at all. When one cop asked me if I had AC in my car, I said, "Yeah, I *paid* for mine." In the end, the bureau never did anything about it, but my words did have an impact. Many higher-ups—Foxworth included—made it a point to drop their windows to set an example. And Officer Brian Dale, a Hope and Hard Work regular and just a good policeman, would always keep his windows cracked, whether it was over a hundred or below freezing, and whenever he saw me on the street, he'd holler my name and stick out an arm and wave.

A year or so after I'd joined the Chief's Forum, Potter invited me to come to this policing conference at Quantico. It was odd being there at FBI headquarters, and whenever I found myself near the J. Edgar Hoover statue, I made sure to let anyone in earshot know I was planning to tear the thing down. But I also did what I'd been invited to do: I shared stories about the work I was doing in Portland. I told a crowd full of cops about going out on search warrants, about sitting with families of murder victims, about weighing in on everything from the bureau's mission to its uniforms, and about how, if a citizen called the mayor to complain, she'd often tell them to bring it to Hope and Hard Work. After I gave that speech, a bunch of officers came up to me, and what they all said, basically, was, "Y'all don't *really* do that stuff, do you?" I told them that, yes, we did. And only upon seeing their slack-jawed, stupefied reactions did I really realize: we're doing something, in Portland, that no one else is doing, anywhere.

Soon after that, Potter retired, and Vera Katz appointed Charles Moose to take his place. Chief Moose, years later, would become known as the officer in charge during the DC sniper crisis, but then, he was just a Black officer who'd risen up the Portland Police ranks. In my opinion, he was a great chief. He was strong on community policing, and he never forgot he was Black. He spoke up about it *all* the time. One night, he was to teach a class—he was a PSU professor, too—and he was late, and one of the students called 911 to find out where he was. Well, 911 called Moose and filled him in, and when he got to the room, he told that student exactly what he thought about that 911 call. The incident got a lot of press, and it was a big story about his temper, his "intolerance." And my feeling was, no *way* would that student have called the cops—which is what he did—if his teacher had been white. Moose's temper was only an issue because he was Black. So I sympathized with him. And whether or not he ever went overboard, the point was, he spoke about what everyone else avoided. Over and over he gave Portland, Oregon, a chance to talk about race, about Black folks, about what we put up with. And if Portland, Oregon, needed anything more than that, I'm not sure what it was.

Unlike other cops, most of whom lived outside the city, Moose had a home right in the community. I respected him for that. Because it wasn't easy. There was this young guy I knew who always had his birthday party at a beach on the Columbia, and every year, it'd be drama, so Moose, in his first year, decided to put restrictions on that party. Which wasn't a popular decision. I ended up involved, given my work with gang-affected youth, and it seemed we'd found a solution, but at the last minute, the cops flipped their stance and all but shut the party down. The next day a big crowd showed up on Moose's doorstep to protest. And he didn't like that at all. So the next day he made a statement to some reporter that he regretted buying a home in the community. That led to more protests, and just a lot of nasty talk about Moose, and on the one hand, I agreed: it was a foolish thing to have said. But on the other: he didn't move. He lived under a microscope, and he didn't move.

One rainy night a year into Moose's tenure, I was out with Harry Jackson, and we got a call about a yellow sedan that'd been involved in a shooting. We headed over, and there were all these cops lined up, barking at the sedan's driver. They kept telling him to get on the ground, and he kept saying he didn't do nothing, and his kids were in the car, and he wasn't lying down in front of them. I could see those kids' tiny hands, pressed against the car's windows. Sergeant Jackson could, too. So he called off the stop. The others didn't like that, but soon they stood down and left, and Jackson tried to talk with the guy. But he was so, so upset. The cops, he said, had *terrorized* his kids. The littlest one, a two-year-old, had wet himself. Well, I felt for him. I gave him my card, told him to call if he wanted to talk. He didn't. So then I went to the precinct and told the commander, "*Someone* has to talk to him." And he nodded but didn't do anything. When I went to his boss, it was the same deal. Finally I just told Moose. He said he'd take care of it, and I can't say I believed him, but the next week after the Chief's Forum, Moose took me aside and told me he'd gone to the guy's house and talked to his mother. She was livid at first, but he kept on until finally she smiled and said, "You look bigger on TV." She ended up inviting him in for coffee, and he explained what'd gone down. Which, for me, was enough. I got it, why the guy'd been pulled over—you don't see many yellow sedans—but the cops owed that family, like many others, an explanation. And Moose, unlike most of the rest, sucked it up and gave one.

The two of us, of course, sparred sometimes. Once, at the Chief's Forum, were talking about some training, and I wanted to see it happen soon, and Moose was giving us the same-old about how change takes time, and so I said, "We can train monkeys to go to space, but we can't teach officers with diplomas to do a few simple things?" At that, Moose's whole demeanor changed. "Mr. Brown," he said, "my officers are *not* monkeys." I was shocked because I didn't feel I'd said that, and I didn't think anyone else had heard it that way. But I kept quiet for the rest of the meeting. Once it was over, I headed to his office to talk. His door was open, so I took off my cap and tossed it into the room ahead of me. After a brief silence, I heard laughter. "Richard," Moose said once I'd stepped inside, "I just can't be seen letting anybody talk down my officers like that." And I understood what he meant. So I picked up my hat and I took a seat and we talked about how to get moving on that training.

Meanwhile, given my increasingly visible work, I was getting interviewed constantly. I'd still spout off sometimes, give twenty-minute answers to ten-word questions, but I was coming to see how newspapers did things. I knew they'd get me to talk and talk, then take the most outrageous one-liner and toss it into the last paragraph. So I was learning to be more sparing. I practiced answers to imagined questions, such that, when my phone rang, I was ready to say what I wanted to say, something complete, something so simple and specific it couldn't be taken out of context. That was the goal, at least. It didn't always go as planned. But sometimes it did. And that's about the best you can hope for.

I was still on the other side of things, too, taking pictures for the *Observer*. And lately I'd even been taking charge of layout. That began how most things began: I volunteered to do it once, and then again, because I liked to learn new things and to be useful, and the editor was happy to take me up on my offers. He never offered to pay me, though. Many nights I found myself there till near-morning, doing all the things that needed to get done, and for all of that labor, plus the pictures of mine that'd ended up running, I'd make five or ten dollars. On one hand, that was fine. I was retired, and I wasn't doing this for the money. But on the other? I felt pretty underappreciated. Pretty used.

Partly because of that, and also because I've never been one to keep quiet about what rubs me wrong, I at some point ended up having a talk with a guy who did the paper's ads. I was at the office alone when this guy called, looking for our editor. He was out, I said, but as long as we were on the line, I had a question. I'd noticed our paper only ran ads for cigarettes and liquor, and I wondered: could we get some milk ads or yogurt ads? Black folks, I said, do more than smoke and drink. The guy said he knew that, and then he told me about tiers and circulation, about what our paper could afford. I had some thoughts about all of that. But when we finally got off the phone, I felt we parted cordially.

The next day I got a call from the editor. He was not pleased. "You don't need to be talking to anybody who calls," he told me. "Those ads are not your concern." I kept my calm, tried to make the same points I'd made to the advertiser about the message we were sending to readers. I doubt he heard a word, though. I don't think he'd ever cared for me, and now he had an opening to say so. His feeling was: I should take my pictures, do my job, and leave the rest to him. My feeling was: you're paying me five bucks every few days to do hours of work that needs to be done for this paper to exist, and you expect me to keep my mouth shut, too? So we went back and forth on all of that for weeks and weeks.

And then I got fired. After fifteen years and so, so many photos and hours of free labor, I got fired. The editor asked for my keys, and he told me not to come back, and he promised he'd gather up my boxes and boxes of pictures and send them to me. But then he didn't. He just ignored my calls for a year until, finally, I had to take the *Observer* to small claims court. I had to *sue* them just to get back my own pictures. When I finally got those boxes back, I couldn't help but think of where this had all started, with Ms. Bogle, and where it'd ended up. And that got me pretty sad. So I took the boxes down to my basement. I stuck them up on some shelves. And I walked away and locked the door behind me.

22

Block After Block

By the fourth year of Hope and Hard Work, we'd picked all the lowest-hanging fruit—got the streets swept, abandoned cars towed, slumlords exposed—and our conversations, at last, had landed where I'd known they would: on stopping the violence. Night after night, young men in gang colors were out on the corners, selling and shooting. Folks were terrified. A woman I knew, on whose lawn gang members liked to loiter, came to me crying because one day she'd woken up to find her basset hound sick, spitting blood, on account of someone having fed it broken glass. Another woman had to leave Hope and Hard Work an hour early every week to avoid being on the street near dark. The situation was untenable. We needed help. But when we asked the police, they'd say they didn't have the capacity. They'd say so even though we all knew that if a doctor in the West Hills called with the same complaints, the cops would be there in ten minutes. I made sure to raise hell about that, wherever I could, and that felt good but changed nothing. So some of us from the Front got to talking about what else we could do, and in the end, we decided we'd organize a neighborhood foot patrol.

I myself had never done a foot patrol, but I knew about them. I'd heard things at the Chief's Forum and during my talks with Bob Lamb, and I'd read, too, about this group, the Guardian Angels, that'd done patrols in

Portland neighborhoods. As I heard it, most patrols tried to cover lots of ground, usually just on weekends, for a few hours. That seemed like a watered-down approach. If you were just passing through, here and there, the gangs could learn your patterns; the guy on the corner could leave when he saw you coming, wait you out and come back once you'd passed by. And so we decided we'd pick the worst street in Portland. And we'd clog it, night after night after night.

We went to the North Precinct and asked to see some records, and we determined that the most violent spot in Albina was Beech Street, on the six blocks between Williams and Mississippi. We did a door-to-door survey, asking among other things if people would like to be part of a foot patrol. A lot of people said yes, they would, and soon I had this big vision: it'd start with us, patrolling Beech, and then some churches would organize patrols, and before long, folks all over would be out there, until the city was so saturated with good people that there wouldn't be space for those who wanted to do bad.

The plan was, we'd have a crew on Beech every night from six to eleven; I pledged to be there all night, every night. We wanted to make sure volunteers felt safe, so we held a training during which cops, EMTs, and lawyers—Hope and Hard Work regulars—gave us tips and resources. We got McDonald's to donate yellow rain slickers to keep us visible. A neighbor donated writing pads so we could make notes. A phone company gave us a few cellulars, a box store provided flashlights, the precinct stocked us with batteries, and neighbors on the block who couldn't walk but wanted to support offered to keep us fed and watered and caffeinated. Once we'd organized all of that, we made some final calls and final preparations, assembled the biggest group we could, and then we got out there and walked.

At our first patrol in July of 1994, we had twenty people, mostly Front members and Hope and Hard Work regulars. And man, did we get a lot of press. Journalists from most every paper came to take pictures as we walked, waving to residents, some of whom left their porches and joined us. It felt festive, lively, like the beginning of something that wasn't ending anytime soon. So we got back out there the next night, and the next and the next and the next. Sometimes, a plainclothes cop would join in, but usually it was just us civilians, five or fifteen of us, walking Beech back and forth, back and forth. Mostly, nothing happened. We'd see young men sitting on porches or rolling by in their cars, and they'd sometimes heckle us, but mostly they'd just sit and watch, try and figure us out. Once a night, at my request, beat cops would come through, and when they stopped, I'd talk to them through the window. Usually we didn't speak about anything of substance. But we always had our talks in plain sight of the young men up on those porches, the idea being, if they were doing something wrong, they'd think we were talking about it, and they'd stop.

From day one my biggest concern was for the group's safety. So I took steps to ensure that mine was the face that stood out. When cops came by, I talked to them. And if someone started calling us names, I confronted them. I took the lead because it felt right—if I was asking folks to be out there, I ought to be the one to answer—but it's not like my fellow patrollers were a bunch of frightened bunnies. Not at all. Night after night they stepped up. Once, early on, a group of us was out walking and some guy, who probably wanted to see if a cop was among us, called out, "Oh, officer." Well, every person, with no prompting, spun and faced him, as if to say, "We all might be." Another time we all heard gunshots just blocks away. I figured the others were going to run for cover, hide in bushes, so I was shocked when, without a word, every person started walking toward the gunfire.

I'd hoped, initially, that it'd be neighborhood residents on the patrol. But when I tried to coax people off their porches, they'd say, "I have to live here when y'all leave." There wasn't a lot I could say back. And so, though we sometimes had folks from the block, it was often a bunch of people from far afield. There were two women who'd come from Hillsboro, a suburb on Portland's western fringe. There was a guy who lived on the other side of the river. And an old couple from East County, and someone from Salem. Many of these people were white. If you'd have asked me ten years earlier if I thought I'd ever patrol my own Black neighborhood with white people from elsewhere, I'd have asked if you were high. Now, though? I just appreciated the help. And I appreciated these white folks, all of whom understood their role, which was to keep their egos in check and walk beside us.

Night after night we'd be out there. Even when the streets were empty, and it was raining so hard we could barely see our feet, we'd walk. In autumn, we'd clear storm drains. Come December, we'd help hang lights and shovel snow from the paths in front of seniors' homes. Once we even lugged a piano into someone's house. We'd just keep an eye out, too: at one house, there was a boy who had mental problems, and we'd pop in, do a welfare check, make sure he and his family were okay. As time passed, people on the block came to appreciate us. One lady, the one whose hound had eaten glass, liked to bake us cookies. A man who owned a grocery on the block would let us use his bathroom. Even the guys on the corners got a kick out of us, I think. One night a bunch of us were out in our yellow slickers, and a car pulled up beside us and the driver said, "Y'all look like a school bus."

Finally, after about six months, I checked in with North Precinct, and I learned what I'd already begun to assume: crime on Beech Street was way down. As soon as we got that news, we did what we always did when we had anything like success. We had a potluck. Sat down and shared a meal and talked about how great it was that those guys who'd been on the corner weren't anymore. Because that was real. No, we hadn't *stopped* anything. But that'd never been our goal. From day one, I'd said we'd never get drugs or gangs out of Portland. What we could do? We could push them off Beech. And if they moved a block north? Then people there would want to know how they could do what we'd done. And so it would go, block after block, until, eventually, the gangs would have to sell dope from a barge in the Willamette. I said all of that at our potluck, at the Forum, anywhere else I could. I told everyone I spoke to about our patrol and how it was changing Beech, just like it could change their street. And then, every night, whether or not I felt like it, I got back out there, and I walked.

That's just how I spent my evenings, though. There were nineteen more hours, every day, and while I'd guess I spent a few sleeping, what I did, mostly, was what I'd been doing for years: more and more. On top of the Chief's Forum and Hope and Hard Work and ride-alongs and various visioning committees and meetings of the MAC and the Citizens Crime Commission and the boards of House of Umoja and Albina Head Start, I'd also begun going to Narcotics Anonymous. A guy I knew asked me to come support him, so I did, and then I just kept on going. In the meetings, I'd sit and listen. Afterward I'd hang around and listen more. And often, a guy would be telling me some self-destructive thing he wanted to do, and suddenly, he'd hear himself. "Mr. Brown," he'd say, "I know I need to stop." So then I'd speak up. Thanks to Hope and Hard Work, I had a sense for the resources out there, and I'd share all I could about jobs, housing, whatever. I'd help folks redirect their energy, too. I'd now amassed many cameras, so if someone showed interest, I'd give them one and teach them the basics. There was one guy who got real into it, and I taught him all I could, gave him equipment, too, and for a while there, he was the go-to guy for all sorts of events, especially in the recovery community.

I was at Umoja pretty much daily, too. I'd occasionally give a youngster an earful—about what I'd seen and what was in store for him if he chose to keep up that gang life—but mostly I just tried to show those boys that I cared, that a community did. We'd gotten hold of a projector, and on Saturdays, we'd make popcorn, and we'd let the boys invite their people in, and all day long we'd watch movies and goof around. The hope was still that, if we kept this up, the youth would get to know all sorts of adults, get to know them well enough that once they got out they'd have a real community. With the same goal, I started an oral history program. I'd have the grandparent of one of the youngsters come in, and they'd talk about what it'd been like for them to grow up Black in such-and-such a place at such-and-such a time, and then I'd get the youth to take their picture, maybe even goad them into asking a question or two. I tried to get them to write about what they'd learned, which rarely went over well, and to make up family trees, which sometimes did. I asked them what advice they thought they'd give youngsters once they themselves had become grandparents. Really, I just did whatever I could to give the impression that their lives and stories mattered, and would continue to, for years.

And yet. So many of them would leave the House of Umoja, and they'd go back to slinging dope and holding turf, and soon I'd be standing beside a sobbing mother at another funeral. *So* many funerals. The loss of life, in those years, was incessant. Boys with whom I'd built tiny sports cars, or watched *The Nutty Professor,* or talked with about what couldn't get talked about elsewhere—those boys would leave Umoja, and they'd get shot, often by another child I'd known and tried to get through to. Every time I went to one of those funerals, I'd find myself traveling back to my youth, to the boys I'd grown up with, boys who'd flown pigeons and played drums and talked big about all the things they were gonna do, only to end up addicted or arrested or dead. I'd wonder when and how and if any of this would ever change. And then I'd pay my respects, and I'd try to move on.

After one funeral, for a boy I'd known particularly well, I went straight to a meeting of the Citizens Crime Commission, which I'd recently joined at the request of Fred Stickel, the *Oregonian*'s publisher. The CCC was made up of mostly white businessmen who met monthly to talk about crime. Well, not five minutes after I took my seat, some of the others started talking about gang members, talking about them like they weren't even people. And I just lost it. I don't recall what, exactly, I said, because as soon as I opened my mouth, I started crying, and not just crying but bawling, which—at least at that point—wasn't a thing I did in front of other people. But I kept speaking, through hiccups and tears. I went on about respect and empathy and basic decency. And as I spoke, the other men did what men do when another man cries: sucked their cheeks, looked at their hands. Finally, after who-knows-how-long, I sputtered to a stop. I slumped in my chair. And for the rest of the meeting, I sat silent, wondering where that'd come from and how long it'd be before it came back again.

All of this made me feel even more committed to doing foot patrols— to doing whatever could be done to keep our youth away from gangs—so I was thrilled when, about a year after we'd begun on Beech, some Hope and Hard Work regulars started a patrol of their own. Theirs would be on Mississippi, which ran perpendicular to Beech. They planned to do it on weekend nights for a few hours. I had misgivings about that strategy, but I kept quiet because I was thrilled that other people, finally, were going to join us. So I told them all I could. Gave them tips on planning, recruiting, staying safe. And once they got started, I made sure that our two groups met up once or twice a night at the intersection of Mississippi and Beech to say hello, swap stories, try and keep each other's spirits high.

I hoped, for a while, that this might be just the beginning—that two patrols would become three, ten, two hundred. But that passed. Because besides those folks on Mississippi, nobody else jumped in. Sure, people would ask me if *my* crew could come walk their block. I'd say that we were busy on Beech, but I'd be happy to show them how to do it themselves. And there the conversation would end. And even on Beech, it was getting frustrating. Every night I'd approach folks on the block, and I'd ask them to help sustain a thing that—and we heard this all the time—was making their lives better. Whether it was fear, lack of time, or something else, I can't say. All I know is, people from the neighborhood rarely joined. Too often, it'd be me and three people who didn't even live in Portland.

I kept trying, though. Kept talking up the patrols to Beech residents, to Hope and Hard Workers, to church leaders. I'd organized some with clergy—thanks to Reverend John Jackson, who'd worked hard to build bridges between religious and lay activists—and I knew that, if you were organizing Black folks, you ought to at least try to go through the church. So, I tried. Tried particularly hard with Bishop Wells from Emanuel Temple, with whom I already had a good relationship. But no matter what I said, Bishop Wells would just nod and tell me, "The Lord wants me to do other things." So I'd let it go, and I'd pick it back up the next time we saw each other, and it kept on like that until finally, after some meeting, Bishop Wells came up and said, "Richard, I want you to know that last night, the Lord came to me, and he told me I needed to get more involved." Well, I was thrilled to hear that. And I told him so. And then I said it'd be great if, the next time he went to one of his preacher meetings, he could he get everyone's addresses, and also ask them to leave their windows cracked, so that I could swing by their houses some night and, in my best Lord voice, tell them all the things I thought they needed to do.

Eventually I went to one of those meetings, and I talked about our patrol on Beech. I talked about how simple it was, and how much more effective it'd be if it was happening everywhere at once. In my mind, all I was doing was *proposing* that those clergymen consider patrolling the block around their church. But those preachers didn't hear it that way. One of them stood up and asked, "Who are *you* to tell me what I need to do?" I tried to say I wasn't telling them they *needed* to do anything, but by then, it was too late. I'd lost them. So I left. And for a long time after that, I left the church alone.

One night around that same time, a white woman I didn't recognize came out for the patrol. An hour in, while the group was taking a bathroom break, this woman broke off and stepped onto the porch of a nearby house and started talking with the folks who lived there. It felt odd, so I stepped close. And though I didn't catch it all, I heard enough to know that she was shopping houses. Trying to get a sense for who might be selling. At that point, gentrification hadn't begun in earnest, but there'd been whispers, and I knew a vulture when I saw one. So I asked her to leave. Told her this wasn't the place for that and she knew it. That felt good, for a minute. But once the adrenaline had burned off, I just felt pretty tired.

Every day, someone would ask how I kept doing the patrol without a break, without burning out. And I'd tell them it was easy: I only did things for as long as I wanted to. As long as I was feeling useful and hopeful, I'd keep going, but as soon as something started to feel like a battle I knew I wasn't going to win? I'd stop, and I'd move on. With the patrol, I did it because it had to be done, and because I had the time, and because, for a while, I believed it might become something more. But it didn't. It didn't, and at some point, I just began to feel like we'd done all we could do on that street—crime was down, neighbors were happy—and the patrols weren't catching on elsewhere and probably wouldn't. So after fifteen months of walking those blocks—after two-thousand-plus hours on Beech, plus many, many more spent organizing, recruiting, ruminating—I did the only thing left to do: I stopped.

23
Tug of War

In the mid-nineties, five years into Hope and Hard Work, Vera Katz launched a citywide program called Neighbor Safe. The idea was, crime feeds on isolation, so let's get folks out of their silos and into each other's lives. The program began with mailers, billboards, and TV spots, all trumpeting the idea that neighborliness is kryptonite to crime, then continued with a slew of meetings, one in every precinct, where residents could air concerns to Mayor Katz and Chief Moose. The whole thing went over well. Got lauded by citizens and policing gurus in Portland and beyond. And though I don't remember if it was ever publicly acknowledged, I do know—because Vera told me, many times—that there never would've been a Neighbor Safe if there hadn't first been a Hope and Hard Work.

If I had to pinpoint a time when I felt most hopeful about my work with Portland Police, I'd probably say it was in those years, when some of Potter's reforms had taken root, when community policing was more than a buzzword. Every officer was told to adopt it as a core philosophy—told to get to know folks in their precinct, to *listen* to them, to work with them on long-term problems rather than just responding to the radio—and though plenty of them still thought it was some bleeding-heart nonsense, the bureau was overall getting praised for its culture shift. At the national conferences, which I'd begun following, the talk was often about Portland.

And when the White House created a program, COPS, that granted money to cities that prioritized community policing, not only did Portland get a good bit of money, Chief Potter and Chief Moose were both finalists to direct the whole thing.

I, too, had begun to get some recognition from all corners of the city. I was given a Spirit of Portland award for my work on Beech Street; I was deemed a "Good Guy" by the Oregon Women's Political Caucus; the Crime Commission gave me a "Distinguished Service Award"; I got Citizen of the Year honors from Portland's biggest Black fraternity, and from the Albina Ministerial Alliance, too. And though all of that felt good—felt good to know that I, high school dropout, had become a person other people looked up to—what mattered most, in those years, was the recognition I was getting from cops. And I'm not just talking Moose and Foxworth. Not just Black police. No, I mean the white rank-and-file: the sorts of cops I'd never have imagined knowing or liking. Not all of them liked me, of course, but the ones who did—the ones I'd ridden with, or met at Hope and Hard Work, or chatted up on the street—the way they often put it was: "He actually tries to learn about what we do."

Officer Steve Collins put it that way. Collins, he'd come onto the force in the early nineties, hoping what many cops hope: that he'd be a resource, a peacekeeper, an old-fashioned beat cop who'd help folks deal with day-to-day issues. But what he found—and remember, this was at the *height* of community policing—was that he was just a utility guy; he spent his days chasing the radio, driving circles around his district, which was ten miles wide. "We're just putting out fires," he once told me after a Hope and Hard Work meeting, "and we can't stay long enough to even do that, so they smolder, and then they start up again." He'd come to that meeting at the recommendation of his friends, Halpin and McCausland, and before long, he became a regular. He loved sitting with folks in the community, hearing what they needed help with and doing what he could to empty out the rumor mill. If he ever heard a complaint about an incident with a particular cop, he'd go pull reports, and he'd find the cop in question and bring him to the next meeting. The cop and the civilian, they'd sit and talk, tease out all the details, come to an understanding. Understanding, he said, was where it all began. I tended to agree.

With this in mind, I'd dropped any knee-jerk resistance and committed myself to learning. I'd signed on for Portland Police's inaugural Citizens' Academy—where I got clear on the hows, whens, and whys of day-to-day policework—and did the FBI's academy, too. I kept going on ride-alongs, kept sitting in at the Chief's Forum. Part of it was, I knew I'd be better heard by cops if they saw me trying to empathize. Part was, I was eager to gather more info I could share with other Black folks. Mostly, though, I was just the type who, when something was broken, I wanted to pick it apart, try to fix it.

I wonder whether anyone around me ever grasped how vulnerable I was making myself. I never spoke about it, so I can't say, but I myself was always aware of how I might be seen by young Black men who got busted on my watch. One night I was with a team serving a search warrant at a dope house. The place had a big steel gate at the door, and the cops ended up running a cable from their truck and ripping the gate and door off the house. Inside, a half-dozen Black men sat with a stash of dope and weapons. Usually, given my work in the community, I'd know at least one person in every room, and they'd know me. But these men? Strangers. Fresh from California, no doubt. I didn't want this to be the first time they saw my face. So for the rest of the night, I stuck to the shadows. Several years later, though, at an NA meeting, I'd end up seeing one of the guys from that house. After avoiding him for weeks—still, years on, I was cautious—I'd ask if he remembered me, and he'd tell me that, yeah, he did, but he'd always just figured I was there to keep an eye on the cops. It'd feel good, so good, to hear that—to learn that I'd been seen for exactly who I was—but like I said: that wasn't until several years afterward. And so on that night at the dope house, and many others like it, I felt like I'd felt in Saigon, when I'd slept with my rifle tucked beneath my bunk.

Because, in those years, it was guns, guns, guns. So many kids were carrying. And I'm not talking pistols. I mean *guns*. Guys in gangs treated their weaponry like their cars, like status symbols. If you didn't have something flashy, something that looked like it belonged in a war zone, you weren't respected or safe. And it wasn't just about *having* the weapons. You had to fire them. At people. And that senseless violence made me so angry. I wanted, badly, to stop it. Still, I'd bristle if cops brought it up. Because who were they to talk, these men who rolled up to traffic stops with AR-15s? That was maybe the hardest thing about those years: the balancing act. In theory, I had a simple mission—to make life better for Black people—but in practice, it was nonstop tug-of-war. Trying to stop Black-on-Black violence while combating white Portland's view of it; trying to empathize with cops while never giving them a pass for their behavior; trying to look just angry enough to let Black folks know I had their backs but not so angry that police would stop listening; trying and trying, but hearing from police that I was asking for too much, and from Black folks that I was giving too much away.

I don't know that I ever escaped that tension, but to the extent I did, it was because I made sure I never let a day go by without doing something, or several somethings, with and for Black people. I'd swing through the Albina Head Start, of which Ronnie Herndon was director, to play games with youth or chat with staff. I'd accompany a friend to an NA meeting or parole hearing. I'd sit in the stands at a Jeff High football game, or meet with a youngster to show him how to take pictures, or show up at an event, like I used to, and snap a few of my own. And no matter how busy I was, if I got asked to help with something, anything, I'd try to find a way to say yes.

That's how I got started with Community Court. It was a new program where folks charged with lesser crimes—shoplifting, public intoxication, soliciting prostitution—could get service hours rather than time in a cell. Community Court was held at the King School facility, which meant it was easy to get to, and also, it was embarrassing because you saw people you knew. The DA, at some point, asked me to get involved for that reason: he wanted me to be the elder who sat and watched and helped folks feel a shame that'd compel them to think twice about reoffending. So week after week, I did. I liked watching Judge Roosevelt Robinson, who was fair and creative; often, as part of his sentencing, he'd ask defendants questions about Black history and make them come back with answers. And just like with Hope and Hard Work, you had resource people there, ready to help folks find housing, benefits, whatever. Attendance was high because defendants could arrive on foot rather than bus all the way to the county courthouse and because we treated people like people. One guy, who'd gotten arrested for being publicly drunk, said at his hearing that it was because his cat had died, and that that cat had been like a son. So I hopped up, asked the judge to hold on, then ran to the Humane Society, where I got them to give me a cat for free. That guy, that day, went home with service hours and a new son.

Somewhere in there, Judge Robinson and I both sat in on a session of Multnomah County's African American Program, a weekly group for newly paroled Black men. There was a funding issue, and the folks behind the program wanted me and the judge to see it and vouch for it, which we did, but that was just the beginning. I liked it so much I came back the next week, and kept coming, and soon I was a regular at this thing I'd come to call "the group." Some parole officers, tired of seeing Black men reoffend and recycle back to prison, had started the program. It began in prison with men sitting down weekly to talk about what they'd done and how they hoped to change, and then, when they got out, they'd keep going in the group. The parole officers in charge had been working with offenders for years, and they didn't put up with excuses. They'd out and out scream at those men, get in their faces, just unload. That approach seemed to work okay, but I found it distasteful. All I wanted was to sit with these men, ask them what they weren't being asked elsewhere, and just listen, just let them talk about disappointing their kids and wives and grandmas, about how they'd stop selling if they could find a job, about how much it hurt to know they wouldn't.

And so that's what I did, for a long time. I showed up to the group week after week, between all the other things I was doing, and I sat in my chair and took folks' words in. Even when, a year or so on, I was asked to start facilitating, I mostly listened. I'd go around the circle, and I'd ask every guy, "How you doing?" And whatever the response was, I'd just make space for it. There was one youngster, though, who came for a while, who always said he was doing good, about to get rich on some or another scheme. I *knew* he wasn't good—between meetings, I'd see him running around with a bandanna on his face, acting crazy—but I didn't challenge him. He was a bright, bright boy, and I didn't want to poke holes in what he said he wanted to do. So I'd nod and I'd say, "Okay," and I'd move on. Well, then he got killed. Shot to death by another youngster. By that point, I had seen so many boys get killed, by cops or each other, but this one hurt me to my heart. I could not help but feel that, if I'd challenged him, maybe he'd have gone another way. Maybe he'd still be alive. But now, all I could do was wonder and mourn and swear that I would *never* let that happen again. From then on, I decided, I was going to make you tell me what made you okay. From then on, if you were doing something you shouldn't do, I was going to tell you, whether or not it'd make you hate me.

Around that same time, Chief Moose stepped down, and Mayor Katz asked me help choose his replacement. So I sat in with a couple dozen others—cops, political types, and quite a few civilians—to review resumes and sit in on interviews, and before long it was down to two guys: Mark Kroeker, who'd been second-in-command in LA during the Rodney King riots, and a Black officer from DC. I liked the Black officer. I especially liked when, just before his presentation—a real sharp presentation—he paused and said, "It's kind of scary, talking in front of a bunch of citizens like this." That meant a lot to me. It showed me he could be vulnerable. Told me about the posture he'd assume when he was chief. So then Kroeker came in and did his thing, and before long, I'd decided that the guy from DC was just way better. I figured everyone else would agree. But a second after Kroeker walked out of the room, this guy I sat with on the Crime Commission, an old FBI guy, he said, "We don't want someone who's afraid to talk to citizens." And everybody jumped on that train. And by the time I said my piece, about what I'd liked, it was too late. A few days later, we had Chief Kroeker.

I won't lie: I was pretty unhappy about Kroeker. Weeks earlier when I'd learned he was on our list, I'd gotten in touch with some LA folks I knew through the Black United Front, and I asked them to ask around. I'd learned that when Daryl Gates—the guy in charge during the riots—retired, Kroeker got beat out for his job by a Black man from Maryland, and he was real bitter about losing to a Black guy. So that pissed me off. But now, that was irrelevant. Now, he was chief. And I'd long ago come to terms with the idea that, if I was going to work with cops, I had to be able to work with whoever, on whatever. And so I just told myself to have a good attitude.

For the first year, we got along well enough. Sure, we disagreed, but I did find him to be smart and respectful. He asked questions. He listened. He even came, with his wife, to a Hope and Hard Work potluck. So I tried to be patient. I even went to bat for him a few times. When the rank-and-file were clamoring to get switched to a four-day workweek, and he was weighing whether pleasing them would be worth the flak he knew he'd get, I said he should do it. I told him that happier cops were better cops. "I'll back you up if you do it," I told him. And so he did, and I did.

By the end of year one, though, he'd done little to back up his talk about amping up community policing and clamping down on racial profiling. What he'd done, mainly, was move the bureau slowly toward the quasi-military outfit he'd run in LA. He fought for bigger, deadlier guns. He got funding for a giant mobile command unit—a police RV—that was so unnecessary, especially since we already had one and it rarely got used. And above all, he showed himself to be a real circle-the-wagons type of leader. He was always talking about how great his officers were, just *great*. One day at the Chief's Forum, he was going for it with his great-great-great routine, and after a few minutes of just sitting there, fuming, I shot up and said I was tired of hearing so much about his officers being great but nothing about how they were messing up. And he didn't like that. He lashed back at me. After the meeting, I caught up with him and I said it wasn't personal—I was angry not at him but at the dynamic that kept cops from ever having to respond to criticism—but I don't think he heard what I was saying, not then, not ever.

And man, I had a hard time with his staff. I don't know whether Kroeker was directing them quietly, behind the scenes, but his staff were always trying to dial me down. They'd interrupt me during the forum, tell me I couldn't say this thing in that tone. They even tried to move me away from him. We'd always sat at the same long table, and I, for nine years, had sat right next to the chief. I don't think I'd done that on purpose; it was just the first chair you saw when you came in, and I was always early, so I took it, and kept taking it, and eventually folks knew: that's Richard's spot. Well, one morning, I walked in to find that we had nametags, and mine was at the other end of the table. So I grabbed my tag and moved it back to my seat. When his staff came in ten minutes later, they said I needed to move, said there'd been changes and the co-chairs needed to sit beside the chief.

I stayed where I was. "If they really need to sit by him," I said, "then they need to be here before me."

That was what irked me most: I'd been here before *all* of them. I'd paid my dues, learned all a civilian could learn about cops, and come to the forum week after week for a decade, because I cared, because I brought what no one else did or could. *So* many police, from Moose to Harry Jackson to Steve Collins, had told me that even though I could be a real pain sometimes, they were glad I was doing what I was doing, and they wished there were more Richards out there demanding better training, better community connections, better everything. Now, though? This chief and his staff treated me like a pest. And they treated the forum like it was a show-and-tell, just a venue for Kroeker to share his plans and get patted on the back. And man, he missed *so* many meetings. Dozens. At some point, I made a remark about it to a reporter: I said he'd missed more meetings, in his year as chief, then I had in a decade on the forum. Well, Kroeker or one of his staff saw that story. And they went to the records. And at the next meeting, one of them came to me all smug, because, lo and behold, I'd missed two more meetings than Kroeker. I'd missed two more meetings, in nine years, than he had in nine months. They thought that proved something. So did I. We just didn't agree on what.

So whenever I met with Vera Katz, I shared my doubts about Kroeker. I told her, all the time, that he reminded me of the fable about the naked emperor. "He's running around naked," I'd say. "He's touting his great cops and his great toys, but he has no idea how he's seen in the community." Usually Vera would laugh or ask me to explain, but finally one day she said, "Richard, I don't want to hear this BS anymore." She said it kindly, with a smile, but I could tell she meant it. So from then on, I laid off. I knew I had a tendency to overspeak my mind, and I respected Vera and valued our relationship. Now, though, I wonder whether I would've kept pushing if I'd known where things were headed. I wonder what I'd have done if I'd known those years with Kroeker were no blip, no anomaly. If I'd known they were the beginning of the ending of a story I'd spent decades learning to tell.

24

One Last Thursday

One day near the turn of the millennium, just after speaking at a policing conference—I'd been getting asked more and more to talk about what I knew and how I'd come to know it—I was approached about taking my show on the road with the Western States Policing Center. I'd heard about Western States, here and there, and now I learned they were a federally funded program that sent teams around the West to help cities take steps toward community policing. That sounded like the exact thing I hadn't known I wanted to do, so I told them to sign me up. In the coming months, I met the team, studied up, memorized their curriculum, and before long, I was a certified instructor, flying to Hawaii and Alaska, talking about Albina.

The trainings lasted four days, and the only stipulations were that we had to be invited by police, and they had to agree to bring civilians along with them. I'd always add another request: I'd ask that the mayor or someone from their office attend, because, as I'd learned, when the mayor was bought in, everyone else was, too. That was one spin I put on those trainings. Another was, I tended to go off the curriculum. Not out of any bad feeling. I just knew what I wanted to say, and what I wanted to say came not from a PowerPoint but from my own experience. So I did what I'd always done: I improvised.

My presentations varied, depending on whom I was talking to. If I was with police, I made it clear that I understood their job, or at least I tried to. I'd tell them what I'd seen and learned on ride-alongs. And then I'd talk about cities that didn't do community policing. In those cities, I said, everyone got isolated. Civilians *and* cops did. We all knew, I said, that police tended toward family problems, addiction, depression, and suicide, and my message about that was, if you're siloed from your community and they hate you for it, how do you think *you'll* end up? Then I'd ask them if they felt like their bureau had enough people to get the job done. And they'd invariably say that no, it didn't. And so I'd deliver the punchline: sounds like you *need* civilians to help you.

With civilians, I'd share what I knew about being an engaged citizen, and how I knew it, and once we had rapport, we'd dive in and talk about what wasn't working in their city. There'd always be a hot spot—drug-selling, prostitution, profiling—and once we'd located it, we'd problem-solve. I loved that part. Because the solutions, like the problems, were often the same. There was always a precedent. I'd tell folks how we'd faced similar problems in Portland. I'd tell them about Hope and Hard Work, about foot patrols, phone trees, goals, and celebrations. But I'd never say, "This is how you're going to solve it." Because my thing was, there is no best way. There's only what works for you.

It was such a boost, doing those trainings, being surrounded by so much fresh energy. Like in Vegas, there was a group working hard against drug dealing, and they'd decided to run a foot patrol, and one night they planned one where, supposedly, there'd be two hundred marchers. I arrived early, and I stood with a handful of people, checking my watch, thinking, *Yeah, right.* But at five to the hour, I heard chatter. Then more. And then *so* many people rounded the corner, banging drums and chanting. That whole night, I just got to be part of it. Got to walk block to block with those folks, go right up to dope houses and raise Cain on the steps. A small part of me was maybe hurting, wishing we'd gotten the patrols to stick a little more in my city, but mostly I was just happy to be here, in this one.

The spot I loved best was Gallup, New Mexico, a town on the edge of the Navajo Nation. We went three times to help folks with all sorts of problems, the biggest being that some of the Navajo police were pretty abusive.

One in particular had refused to even entertain the idea of community policing. When you've got a cop like that, I said, you've got to get the ear of someone above him. So the citizens of Gallup did. They talked to their chief, and he made the guy come to our training, and the group harangued him until, at last, he apologized and promised to do better. So then we had a celebration, and I had a hard time wanting to leave. I just liked those folks. And the feeling was mutual. They kept telling me I ought to move to Gallup. Even joked about burning down my house so I'd have to.

Especially given what was happening back home—at the Kroeker-led Chief's Forum, on the streets, in ever smaller meetings of Hope and Hard Work—doing those trainings felt like a breath of fresh air. And I was just good at them, too. Good enough that, after our workshops, folks would often call me, specifically, to get advice about this or that problem, catch up on what had and hadn't worked. Good enough that, at the end of my third season, I'd gotten a plaque that said *Trainer of the Year.*

But you know what they say about good things. And you know what happened on September 11, 2001, and what happened afterward. In the world of community policing, the focus shifted—a lot. Western States got its money from the government, and since the government was suddenly all about terrorism, now our trainings had to be, too. I hung on for a little while. Learned the new language and procedures. But my heart wasn't in it. Having to put such a specific focus on one thing—particularly a murky thing like "terror"—undermined the openness and flexibility that, for me, was central to community policing. And so I stepped down from my trainer role. I stepped back from Gallup and Vegas and the rest. I turned, for the umpteenth and final time, toward Portland.

And in Portland, it was just more of what it'd always been. Police shot an unarmed Black woman named Kendra James, then left her lying in the street for an hour, cuffed up and bleeding out, until she died—and though Kroeker, to his credit, did fire the involved officers, it wasn't long before the union got them reinstated. Meanwhile, gentrification had hit the point of no return: so many Black folks were giving up their homes, moving east, past 82nd, out to The Numbers, and Black-owned barber shops and record stores were getting replaced by bars and coffee shops full of bicycle-loving white folks who didn't seem to have a speck of awareness of what'd been there just months before. Top to bottom in Portland, it felt like white folks didn't know, or care, that Black folks existed.

The meth epidemic, in those years, was at its height. And though I had plenty of sympathy for the people who got caught up in it, I was angry, too, at the city, the media, and everyone else who was suddenly wringing their hands over meth after years of ignoring the crack epidemic in Black communities. White folks on meth, I noticed, were "victims" of an epidemic. But Black folks? We were just crack addicts, with crack babies. At some point, I found myself at a meeting about what Portland as a city needed to do to deal with meth, and after an hour of listening and fuming, I got up and snatched the mic from whoever was talking and said I didn't want to hear another word about meth unless we were gonna talk about crack, too. And then I gave the mic back and walked out of that room.

That same year Chief Kroeker stepped down, and he was replaced by Derrick Foxworth, the same Foxworth who'd taken me on so many ride-alongs, who'd always seen the value of engaging a civilian like me. On one level, this was a relief—my relationship with Kroeker and his staff had gotten ugly—but things just felt different. Maybe it was that, under Kroeker, the bureau had just shifted too far from community policing. Maybe it was that Foxworth just wasn't able to wrest it back. I can't pin it down, exactly, except to say that, though I was still sitting on the Chief's Forum, still doing ride-alongs and showing up at crime scenes and trying to solve problems with cops who came to Hope and Hard Work—still doing all the things I'd been doing, happily, for years—I just felt like my volume was getting turned down, click by click, day after day. And though I responded to that, of course, by trying to turn it up, all that did was put people off and leave me feeling tired and hoarse.

I still did have other things to fall back on. I'd now been running the group for years, and I was getting a better sense of what questions to ask and what silences to respect, and hearing hopeful stories from men who'd avoided relapsing or reoffending and had landed good work. I still spent time at Albina Head Start and in the schools, and I'd started a new model-car-building club with my friends Bob Robinson and Mike Bell at the Blazers Boys and Girls Club. We got a toy shop to donate cars and a body shop to build a paint booth, and we made a compressor out of fire extinguishers and refrigerator parts; and though the youngsters mostly just wanted to do the little snap kits, and I wished, sometimes, that they'd opt for something more intricate, mostly I just felt good, seeing them feel good.

And yet. My overall feeling, in those years, was that things were beginning to wilt. I'd termed out of the MAC. I'd drifted from my environmental work. I'd up and quit the House of Umoja, based on some management decisions I don't even want to begin to get into. It'd been years since I'd taken a picture worth holding onto, and that was really getting to me, especially because most folks, when they saw me on the street, would still ask about my pictures in such a way that I knew they defined me by what I'd done rather than what I was doing. And what, really, was I doing? I wondered that, every day. I wondered what, exactly, all my work had amounted to. And I wondered, for the first time in a long time, whether this was really what I wanted to be doing with what time I still had.

Even Hope and Hard Work was floundering. At its height, we'd have a full room, have so many things to talk about that we could've met for twelve hours and barely made a dent. Now, though? It'd often just be me, a few neighborhood folks, and some bureau reps who looked like they'd rather be anywhere else. In a way, this was good: gang activity had gone down, so folks had less to complain about. But that wasn't the whole of it. The neighborhood was changing, too. Suddenly you had all of these white people with no roots in Albina, no sense of history or responsibility. To them, this was just a nice, safe neighborhood. I don't know if they even read the handbills we left in their mailboxes. I just know that every Thursday, for months, it was the same small crew of us old-timers. And so, after sixteen years, and countless tiny victories that added up to something far too big to see, I called Hope and Hard Work to a close. There was no press release, no event. We just met for one last Thursday. And then we didn't meet again.

Around that same time, Chief Foxworth stepped down and in came Rosie Sizer. I'd known Sizer for years, and I thought we'd always had a good relationship, and so I was a little shocked when, in her first year as chief, she set about to snuffing out any trace of community policing. After a decade-plus of getting weekly (and, at some points, daily) calls from cops who wanted me to come out and support folks at this or that crime scene, suddenly my phone stopped ringing. And at the Chief's Forum, I'd often get told I was being "disrespectful," though I was just saying the same things I'd always said. Overall, I got the feeling that Rosie Sizer and her team felt that people like me had too much to say. It wasn't enough to just dial down our volume anymore. We needed to be turned off.

And so it was no real surprise when Chief Sizer, less than a year into her term, announced she'd be shutting down the Chief's Forum. The forum had done all it needed to do, she said. Said it like she thought community policing was some extra-credit project, and we'd completed it. And then she threw a party at city hall to "celebrate" the civilians who'd been on the forum. She stood up, and she thanked us, and she gave us each an honorary mug. Just a little blue mug with a city logo. As I stood there holding my mug, I felt like I'd had my heart ripped right out. So I left. I took my honorary mug, and I went home, and I stuffed the thing on some basement shelf. I assume it's still down there.

I kept busy for the rest of that day. Swung by Albina Head Start, headed to an NA meeting. I did the things that I knew would make me feel good, that'd keep me from feeling how I knew I'd feel if I had to slow down and sit with my thoughts. And the next morning, I woke up and I told myself, I'm done with Portland Police. I told myself that I'd just happened into this work, and now, I'd happen right out of it. It was time for me to do something else, something I'd had to leave aside, something like fishing, or photography, which I hadn't done in so long I questioned whether I still knew how.

All these years later, I often wonder whether I really could've let myself do all of that. I wonder if, had I been faced with a few quiet months and a chance to settle into them, I'd have started behaving—at last—like I was really, actually retired. My guess is: probably not. I just don't think I've ever been built that way. And anyway, I'm not sure what use it is, wondering. Because here's what happened. One day not long at all after I'd walked away from Portland Police, I got a phone call from my good friend Avel Gordly, who was now a state senator and knew I knew as much about police as anyone in the state, and also knew I'd suddenly stumbled into a whole lot of free time. And what Avel wanted to know was, would I be interested in serving on the board of an Academy down in Salem?

The Presentation

October 2018

Today's Friday. Graduation day at the Academy. I walk from my parked car toward the sun-bleached building, yawning out of my freeway coma, silently rehearsing my lines. For years now, at graduation, I've been giving a talk for the families of officers-in-training—husbands, wives, fiancés—and what I tell these people is that they, the civilians who love cops, have a job to do. I tell them they need to help their officers hold onto their humanity because police work, every day, threatens to steal it away. I tell them that the divorce rate for marriages involving a cop is over seventy percent. I tell them to make a list of what they enjoy doing and revisit it, often, to make sure the good stuff hasn't fallen off. I tell them all of this because isolated, depressed, angry police are much more likely to make the worst kinds of mistakes. Because these would-be cops and their loved ones are people. And because I know, probably better than they do, how much they'll sacrifice in the years to come.

I wonder who's going to give this speech when I'm gone.

As I approach the building, I can't help but see the Wall of Heroes. I feel what I always feel when I see that wall, but I keep walking because I've been trying hard to make peace with the wall and the name that shouldn't be on it. Been trying to make peace with lots of things.

I step inside, check in at the front desk, get my name badge, and say my hellos and shake hands and muster a smile I almost believe in. Before long, I'm in the Hall of Heroes, standing up from my chair and saying what I say to cops and their families, and everyone's leaning forward in their seats, listening, engaged, and I'm wishing I was engaged, too. But I'm not. I'm just tired.

When the presentation's over, I sit down and stare at the wall and think about what I've been thinking about all week: my business cards, the ones that'll just say, *Retired.* I still haven't gotten around to making them. The problem is, I keep wanting to add stuff. First it's that Maasai quote about the children. Then a picture I took in the eighties. Then this cartoon of me that an old friend did. Then I wonder if I shouldn't still make a deck with several cards, cards that speak to all the things I now seem to be. *Richard Brown, Relapsed Photographer. Richard Brown, Unlicensed Group Therapist. Richard Brown, Stray Cat.* And now, again, I'm wondering, when will I ever really be *Retired?*

The graduation wraps up, and soon I'm in the lobby holding a cup of triple-shot mocha and chatting with whoever grabs my elbow. It strikes me, today and always, how odd it is that I'm standing in a room full of cops, and that I know, or at least recognize, almost all of them. One of those cops, a guy named Miller, comes up and says hi. Miller passed through here years ago and is now chief in a Portland suburb. I like Miller a lot. He makes a good effort at community policing—has his officers keep their AC off and windows down, is thinking of starting a Chief's Forum—and he's got like a half-dozen kids, all of them cops, following in their father's footsteps. He introduces me to the youngest, who just graduated. Says a bunch of nice things about me, too. About how my presence in the room, here at the Academy, is invaluable. About how cops-in-training wouldn't learn half of what they learn if I wasn't in the back row, chiming in. I thank him, and then I start talking to another cop, a state trooper, and I can hear Miller over my shoulder, and he's still talking about me, saying things that match so completely with how I'd like to be seen that I'm wondering if he can read minds.

I'm barely listening to this trooper. I'm too lost in this buzz, a buzz that isn't so different from the one I get at the club when troubled youth turned good dads come up to thank me for helping them save their own lives. Lately, I'm of two minds about this buzz. On the one hand, it's nice to be seen for what I've done, to know that my work is working, rippling out further than I'll ever know. And yet. I don't do the work I do for some buzz. If that's all I'm getting from it anymore, maybe I ought to stop.

There's a hand on my shoulder. I spin around and see that it belongs to Rich, who's shaking my hand and asking me what's good. "I'm still here," I say, and he smiles, and I smile.

We get to catching up, and soon I'm leaning close, talking smart about the revolution, and Rich is, too. We're kidding, but also, we aren't. I'm not, at least. I've still got a flicker of hope that Rich and the rest will hold strong, keep pushing for small changes and big changes until well after I'm gone. I'm hoping, too, that Damon will soon end up on the board; hoping that Beth will keep digging into her work up in Portland; hoping that all the youngsters I've helped off crack and guns will find a child not their own and take them under wing; hoping that all the cops I've ridden with and argued with and stood up for and against will remember that some civilians *do* understand. I'm hoping that everyone who's ever known me and found inspiration in any part of my story will find a way to snatch up whatever they like and make it their own. I'm hoping that the work I've done won't die with me.

Rich has to go—it's time to teach cops to punch and get punched—and as he walks away, I see that the lobby's opening up, people clearing out. I know I ought to do the same. I ought to go on home. But that buzz is turning into something else. Something bitter. Something sour. I've got this urge to just call out, to ask these people to sit back down and hear me out a little longer. I want to tell them that I still have so much more to tell them. I want to tell every cop in this room that so much could change if they'd just slow down, just wait a little longer to draw their guns, long enough to see they might not need to draw guns at all; that they need to stop talking about "fearing for their lives" and "getting home safe," as if the people they shoot don't want that, too; that there are so many smart, patient civilians who would listen to and work with them if they'd finally just step out of their blue cocoon. And I want to talk to those civilians, too. I want to tell them that we need them—legions of them—to do this work, and that they need to be prepared to do it for years, of their own volition, with not a single backslap or attaboy; I want to tell them to please hold onto their anger, to let go of their need to blame, to become fluent in the language of where-do-we-go-from-here. I want to tell all of them—cops, civilians, everyone—that if we just stay where we've always been, standing at opposite ends of a yardstick, screaming at each other, we are never going to change anything at all. I want to tell them that the view's much better from eighteen inches, but at the moment, it's still kind of lonely.

The lobby's pretty empty, though. I guess I've lost my audience. So I wave goodbye to the receptionists, and I head for the door, still feeling the sweet and sour of that buzz, still thinking with my two minds. If you asked me right now, I'd either tell you I'll keep coming here until I can't sit up anymore or that I'm quitting tomorrow. Then I'd probably change my mind.

I'm out the door, yanking off my badge, trying to remember where I parked, when my gut tells my feet to stop. So they do, and I do, and I turn and find myself in front of the Wall of Heroes. Suddenly I'm feeling all of it: that weight, these years. Feeling like today is not just today. Like it's also last Tuesday, and the previous Friday, and a hundred-some days before that, and on every one of those days, I'm standing here. I'm jangling my keys against my leg, chewing my tongue. I'm thinking about heroes, about what matters and what's possible and who gets to decide. I'm thinking that getting a name removed from that wall is probably not possible, and that it doesn't matter, not really, since the issue with police is not bad apples but poisoned soil. And yet. I put my keys in my pocket and walk back inside.

I stop at the front desk and ask if the director's still in. He is. I put my badge back on. As I walk up the stairs and down the hall, I try to get the words right in my head, and a few steps from the door to his office, I stop. Breathe. Clench and unclench my fists. I really don't want to have this conversation. Not again. Not at all. I'm here, though, holding this badge and these words at this door. I might as well knock.

So I blink hard, breathe, and breathe again. I try to ignore what's going on in my chest. I ask myself that same tired question, the one I've been asking for so long, for too long: if I don't, who will? And then I raise myself up. I take a slow step forward. And I answer.

Afterword

I'd always figured—even after I gave up on writing a how-to and started writing a memoir—that I'd end this with a timeline, or maybe a roadmap. I still wanted something neat, something I could package up and hand you, something you could hold in your hand as you tried to trace my steps.

I'm not handing you any package.

What I'm doing, instead, is trying to trust you. I'm trusting you, like so many of my forebears trusted me, to make what you will of what and who came before. Trusting you to look at the paths I took and where they took me. Trusting you to take what you like, as you forge a path of your own.

And honestly? I myself have never been much for following checklists. I've made use of my share—in the military, especially—but even then, I just used the checklists until I understood them, and then I made changes and more changes until those checklists followed me. And these days, I mostly avoid them. Mostly, I try to approach my life like it's a math equation. I set my sights on whatever I think the answer is, and then I try to find a way to get there. Because there's never only one right way. There's just the answer. And you solve for it, however you best can.

Which brings me back to trust. I assume that most all of you reading this are younger than me. You're this book's audience. You are why it exists. Everything I have ever done, I've done because I want this world to feel a little bit better for you who come next. And though we seem, at the moment, to be headed in that direction—toward a better world for young

Black people—that'll only stay true as long as legions of you are working hard, day after day, in every way you know how.

So once you've turned this final page, once you've shut this book and placed it back on a shelf, I hope that you will remember, if you remember nothing else, to ask yourself and your community and those who claim to be your leaders this question, as loudly and as often as you can:

And how are the children?